Hélène Smit
DEPTH LEADERSHIP

Hélène Smit

DEPTH LEADERSHIP

UNLOCKING UNCONSCIOUS POTENTIAL IN THE WORKPLACE

DE GRUYTER

ISBN 978-3-11-138462-7
e-ISBN (PDF) 978-3-11-138470-2
e-ISBN (EPUB) 978-3-11-138488-7

Library of Congress Control Number: 2024951480

Bibliographic information published by the Deutsche Nationalbibliothek
The Deutsche Nationalbibliothek lists this publication in the Deutsche Nationalbibliografie;
detailed bibliographic data are available on the internet at http://dnb.dnb.de.

© 2025 Walter de Gruyter GmbH, Berlin/Boston, Genthiner Straße 13, 10785 Berlin
Cover image: Katherine Glenday; Cover design: Ion Jonas, Berlin

www.degruyter.com

Questions about General Product Safety Regulation:
productsafety@degruyterbrill.com

To Sylvan, my son, a man of integrity who works beneath, between and beyond for a thriving psyche, community and planet.

CONTENTS

CHAPTER 3
DEPTH PSYCHOLOGY – THE INDIVIDUAL

CHAPTER 4
DEPTH PSYCHOLOGY – THE GROUP

CHAPTER 6
MANAGING YOUR OWN PSYCHOLOGY

CHAPTER 7
DEPTH RELATIONSHIPS   159

CHAPTER 11
A DEPTH WORLD

PREFACE

This book brings to fruition a process that started about thirty-five years ago. At that time, as an idealistic young adult, and as a response to my own wounding, I dreamt of a world in which people no longer hurt themselves, each other, or the other living creatures on the planet. My personal history, and my participation as a South African in our collective history, meant that I was outraged when I encountered what I perceived to be oppression – the silencing and injuring of others in order to build and protect personal privilege. I was naively judgemental of people who exploited their power over others. Like many young people, I was acutely aware of the injustices I saw around me but didn't know what to do about it. I had a big dream and a great deal of passion, but I didn't have a method.

The dream is still there, but it is less infused with idealism and judgement. I now understand that people who oppress others have almost always been oppressed themselves. Breaking the ongoing cycle of oppression is a complicated process and it requires many psychological and environmental conditions and resources that are not always easy to find. Wanting it to be different is not enough. I understand that living in a way that respects our fellow human beings and other life forms requires hard work, knowledge, insight, and sacrifice. It does bring joy and deep fulfilment, but it also requires compassion, commitment and the courage to confront one's own fallibility and frailty, which is always a painful process.

However, after thirty-five years, I am pleased to say that I have a method or rather a set of methods that I have refined over time. It is, of course, not the only approach for achieving the dream, or necessarily even the best one, but in my experience, it is one that works. As my knowledge and practice of the approach have developed over time, I have learnt to apply it in a range of settings with increasing success. Obviously, this approach to leadership (and living as a whole) does not address all difficulties, but I can say that I have found it to be highly effective in unleashing potential and resolving chronic conflict in groups.

This book describes the underlying theory and the group of methods in detail. It illustrates the application of a blend of depth psychology and systems thinking principles and practices to leadership. This book is aimed at anyone who leads a group, whether it be a formal organisational group or an informal social one. Potentially, this book can help CEOs, chairpersons, directors, project managers, teachers, police officers, nurses, municipality managers, preachers, sports coaches, choirmasters and even parents in their leadership practice.

The ideas in this book are based on academically sound theory, but they are discussed from a layperson's perspective. The reader should not need a formal psychological or academic background to make sense of it. Many of the theoretical concepts come from the discipline of depth psychology, which is based on the work of people such as Sigmund Freud, Carl Jung and their colleagues. The book takes a contemporary view of depth psychology, which transcends some of the cultural and era-based limitations of the original work. The academic theories are practically applied and are not presented in their technical form. Mostly, I have used non-technical language and where I have used the technical terminology, I explain it. All the concepts discussed have been applied in real situations over the years and have been modified and refined by practice and feedback from the people I worked with. Also, many of the ideas included are still evolving and may be very different in years to come. Finally, from a technical perspective, I have addressed the issue of gender by using non-binary terminology unless there are specific examples. The concepts described apply to all genders.

WHY THE ILLUSTRATIONS?

I am privileged to have a long-standing friendship with award-winning artist Katherine Glenday. I have always loved her art, but also her conversation, as she is one of the few people I know who holds many different perspectives in her mind at one time. Katherine has an unusual depth of understanding of psychological processes, and we share a passion and interest in the mysteries of the unconscious mind.

Somewhere along the line, an idea was born that combining Katherine's drawings with the text that I had written would serve an important psychological purpose in communicating the message. Illustrations engage the unconscious mind and its symbolic capacity, and this helps our rational minds make sense of complex concepts. Katherine's unusual ability to visually represent abstract ideas in a multilayered, symbolically rich, yet whimsical way allows additional access to the theory. Katherine read the book and illustrated phrases or sentences that evoked images in her mind. Of course, Katherine always added her own meaning and often took the somewhat technical explanation into a world of fantasy, surrealism, and mostly, humour, beyond anything that I could have conceived of as the author. I would like to thank Katherine for the extraordinary effort, time and boundless creativity she brought to the project.

ACKNOWLEDGEMENTS

I would like to acknowledge the important people who do not get their name on the cover, but without whom the book would never have been published.

Thank you to the staff at De Gruyter for helping to make this publication a reality. In particular, thank you to Steve Hardman, who had the vision that this book would have international appeal, and to Jaya Dalal and the team for implementing the vision.

Thank you to Gillian Coetzee, the layout artist, who worked many long hours to integrate the different layers and elements of the book, for her talent, perseverance and perfectionism.

Thank you to all my clients, who helped me to refine the theory and practice of depth leadership by sharing their experiences, and having the courage and fortitude to pursue the often painful, courageous and arduous labour of deep self-reflection and care of others and the environment.

Thank you to my father, James Smit, for his generous support of my work and my projects over many years.

Thank you to my husband, Bodo Wenz, for his deep commitment to me, and taking care of many large and small tasks with love and rigour, enabling me to focus on the work that I am so passionate about.

Thank you to my children Sylvan and Sophia, for understanding and challenging my approaches to work and life, always embracing and further evolving the values and principles that make our (terrible and) wonderful world a better place for all living beings.

CHAPTER

I

WHY THIS APPROACH TO LEADERSHIP?

INTRODUCTION

All groups have leaders, whether they are tribes, communities, organisations, gangs, soccer teams, families, or even couples. We live and function in groups all the time and to achieve group goals, group members naturally expect both formal and informal leaders to direct and coordinate the way they behave.

But ideas of what makes good leadership vary enormously. Should our leaders tell us what to do, or should they guide us invisibly? Should a leader be forceful or gentle? Should leadership be centralised or should it be shared? How should conflict be addressed? Well, it all depends. The appropriate nature of leadership required by a group depends on the context and culture of the group, including the demands, constraints and opportunities of the times. Deciding what makes for effective and healthy leadership is a complex and difficult task for which there is no simple recipe.

There are many theories about what constitutes good leadership. These have evolved over time as the world changes and knowledge develops. This book presents one more of these theories, that of *Depth Leadership*, which will be defined a little later. The decision to offer this theory is based on the notion that to lead groups to thrive sustainably under current world conditions, certain leadership imperatives arise that must be addressed. To better understand these imperatives, an overview of prevailing global conditions is necessary.

AN OVERVIEW OF WORLD TRENDS AND THEIR IMPLICATIONS FOR LEADERSHIP

It is not possible to offer an objective summary of world trends without a dedicated study, but it is possible to describe a few of the trends at a high level and to briefly consider their implications for theories of leadership. Amongst others, they are:

INCREASED HUMAN INTERDEPENDENCE

Various global changes including population growth, urbanisation, advances in transportation, communication and technology, mean that most humans are more connected and live more densely together than ever before. If we want to live constructively, we must acknowledge our interdependence and get on with one another. This means understanding one another better, as well as understanding the mutual impact between humans and the systems of which they are part.

INCREASED DIVERSITY

Increased globalisation and an increase in population movements and migration, mean that many communities, groups and, therefore, organisations are characterised by greater heterogeneity and diversity. This requires the capacity to lead inclusively, avoid polarisation, and manage the intricate dynamics of human demographic and psychographic diversity within their planetary context.

A GREATER SAY

There is a general move towards greater democratisation in the workplace. This means that individuals expect to have a greater say in the policies and rules that affect their lives (notwithstanding the ongoing dictatorships and autocracies that prevail in many parts of the world). Also, an increase in human rights awareness has awakened a greater sense of entitlement in many individuals and groups, and less tolerance of oppressive behaviours at all levels in the workplace. This requires leadership engagement in the complexity of human psychology and relationships, rather than simply relying on command-and-control approaches to power.

CLIMATE CHANGE AND MASS EXTINCTION

Both the burgeoning evidence of accelerating climate change and the negative environmental impact of humans on the planet have escalated to the extent that they can no longer be ignored. The rising threat of mass extinction and the consequences of environmental degradation on the functioning of planetary ecosystems need urgent attention. Increased systemic awareness and systemic intelligence are both critical skills for leaders. In addition, we are now more obviously at the mercy of one another's decisions, and so it is critical to create constructive, life-preserving cultures in our communities and organisations.

GREATER PSYCHOLOGICAL AWARENESS

The popularisation of the discipline of psychology, the general availability of information and the resulting growth in psychological knowledge worldwide have culminated in a greater focus on individual personal development and self-actualisation. Individuals are more aware of themselves and their potential to develop psychologically. The Covid pandemic also accelerated general awareness of the impact of physical and psychological trauma. This requires psychologically literate leadership.

A TRAUMATISED WORLD

Linked to the idea above, many people have been victims of various kinds of trauma. Covid caused widespread trauma which included the illness and death of loved ones, the trauma of one's own illness (with many living with long Covid symptoms), the social isolation of lockdowns, or alternatively, the experience of being trapped in homes where poor or abusive relationships prevailed. Many people suffered economically and lost their livelihood.

In addition, many people have been part of wars, emigration and displacement, and affected by catastrophic weather events. Psychologically, whole generations have suffered from developmental trauma when parents are unable to provide an environment conducive to healthy development. Trauma has an indelible impact on human functionality and wellbeing, and leaders who do not understand this are likely to take counterproductive action instead of helping people to cope and heal. This requires an in-depth understanding of the impact of trauma on human psychology.

INCREASE IN TECHNOLOGY AND INTELLIGENT MACHINES

With the acceleration of the development of artificial intelligence, technology is replacing many of the traditional functions of leadership such as data processing, system regulation and even decision making. This requires an awareness and understanding of the systemic nature of human relationships with technology, and it requires more emphasis on interpersonal and social skills for leaders as their roles change.

THE RISE IN POPULISM

For a variety of good reasons, many people in the working class, and in poorer countries the unemployed class, are feeling powerless and are at the mercy of charismatic leaders who promise, often falsely, that they will restore control to them. Many people have lost faith in the ability or willingness of the established elite to take care of them. Leaders who ignore or do not understand human defences against anxiety and helplessness do so at their peril, and leave this sector of the population alienated and vulnerable to exploitation.

New and ongoing economic and environmental difficulties mean that it is critical to optimise the productivity of resources, particularly human resources. This places even greater emphasis on the need to help people express their full potential while working cooperatively with others. The deepest individual and collective human potential needs to be tapped to ensure that we survive the challenges of our times. It also means that problems can only be solved if underlying multiple, systemic, interconnected causal relationships are understood.

These changes have multiple and far-reaching implications for leadership in organisations and communities. All of this means that leaders need to understand how people work, what motivates them, how relationships work, what causes conflict, what causes suffering and dysfunction and what builds cooperation, including understanding themselves as well as possible. Leaders must base their actions on the deepest possible understanding of human psychology – that is, the theories that explain the drivers beneath human behaviour. It also means that leaders need to understand how larger systems work and must have an integrated and ethical approach to all the systems of which they are part.

Many of the ideas above can be summarised by two quotes. The first is from Carl Jung. Although it comes from almost fifty years ago, it seems as true now, as then:

> "The world today hangs by a thin thread, and that thread is the psyche of man." CG Jung, from the film documentary *A Matter of the Heart*, 1986

The second comes from Reynolds and Piirto (2009, p. 198) who introduce the idea of a complex psyche with a conscious and unconscious part:

> [B]ecause the self-destructive forces within the human psyche [have] reached world-annihilating proportions, there is a moral obligation to acknowledge the power of and enter into a relationship with the unconscious, especially in order to confront and admit the evil that finds shelter in our own attitudes, assumptions, and self-esteem.

These two quotes refer to the importance of the human psyche, with both its conscious and unconscious parts. Further detail is given in the next chapter.

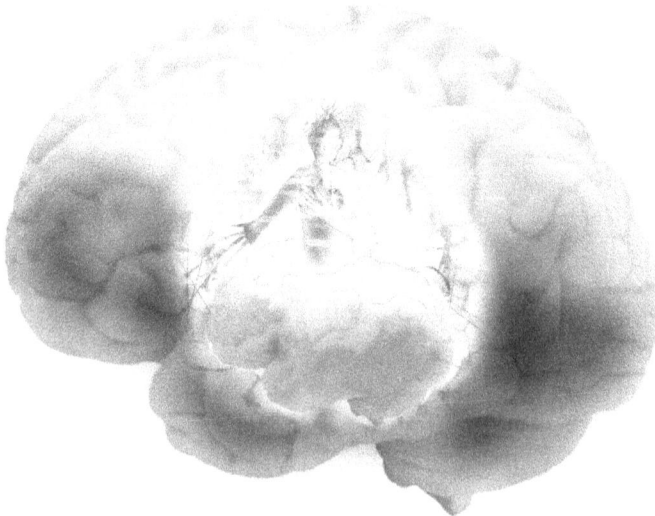

To better understand the evolution of thinking behind the approach suggested in this book, it is helpful to consider briefly an overview of theories of human behaviour.

THEORIES OF HUMAN BEHAVIOUR

Much of human activity is concerned with trying to influence, control, manipulate, protect or support human behaviour. A great deal of theory has been produced in human history about the origins and determinants of human behaviour. The theories span many cultures and disciplines, which have varying degrees of overlap and agreement. Some of these disciplines have begun to integrate as a direct result of the increasing interconnectedness of social and other systems in an increasingly global environment. Technological, intellectual, social, political and environmental factors have all played a role in this increasing interconnectedness.

For those who study leadership theory, it is particularly relevant that in this process of theory integration, several of the academic disciplines that have developed over the past few centuries in the western world – including those of psychology, politics, sociology and management – have increasingly overlapped in their areas of study. These disciplines attempted to solve different problems. Broadly speaking, politics concerned itself with power arrangements and governance. Sociology addressed the nature, structure and functioning of society. Psychology originally concerned itself with understanding mental illness and human development and functioning. Management (or leadership) theory (the youngest of these disciplines) concerned itself with the processes of harnessing human behaviour in the interest of producing wealth and managing power. These disciplines have all melded together to produce a set of theories and practices for leading organisations. It is helpful to understand how these disciplines have informed one another. Many of our current leadership approaches have their roots in an eclectic mixture of all the original disciplines, but we rarely remember or talk about this. In particular, a leadership approach is always explicitly or implicitly based on a view of what drives behaviour psychologically. Therefore, to build the argument in this book, we will take a closer look at the evolution of psychological theories and resulting leadership theories.

THE DIFFERENT SCHOOLS OF PSYCHOLOGY

The evolution of psychology as a discipline led to a variety of schools of thought, each to some extent reacting to or building on the limitations of its predecessors. Each offers a focus on a particular set of determinants of human behaviour. Some of the main schools of thought are described below.

THE BEHAVIOURAL SCHOOL OF PSYCHOLOGY (BEHAVIOURISM)

Behaviourism, one of the earliest formal academic schools of psychology, was established in the early 20th century, a time in which the emphasis was on the development of theory through laboratory experimentation. Scientists such as Skinner (1985) and Pavlov (2020) demonstrated the impact of conditioning on behaviour. In keeping with the interest in scientific approaches, behaviourism studied the impact of the environment on observable behaviour, viewing external factors as the main drivers for human behaviour. In other words, behaviour is determined by the perceived reward or punishment the person experiences in response to that behaviour. Behaviourism contends that behaviour can be modified by changing environmental factors, particularly the consequences of behaviour.

Although true in many cases (individuals do change their behaviour based on the consequences elicited by what they do), it is, of course, also a theory with limitations. As most of us know intuitively, other factors also play a role, and at some point, consequences no longer have an impact on behaviour. For example, although eating too much makes you feel uncomfortable, it might not stop the tendency to eat too much.

THE COGNITIVE SCHOOL OF PSYCHOLOGY

The cognitive school of psychology was, to some extent, a reaction to the reductionism of behaviourism, which ignored the human capacity to think and reason. This school emphasises the role of human intelligence and internal mental processes. It focuses specifically on the cognitive processing of environmental stimuli and thinking processes and how these can be modified to change behaviour. Neisser (2014) was considered the father of cognitive psychology, and Piaget (1997) made a significant contribution with his stages of cognitive development. A variation of this is the cognitive-behavioural school, which broadens the thinking behind the behavioural school and incorporates the knowledge of cognitive psychology into understanding and managing problems.

Many leadership actions are based on the ideas of cognitive psychology. Any interaction between leaders and followers that tries to change the way people think is essentially cognitive in nature. Like behaviourism, this approach produces results. But it also has limitations because even when people know what the right thing to do is, they sometimes do not do it. A smoker knows that smoking damages health, but this knowledge is often not enough to stop the smoking behaviour.

HUMANISM, PHENOMENOLOGY AND GESTALT PSYCHOLOGY

Humanism, phenomenology and gestalt psychology are a general grouping of theories that developed as a reaction against behaviourism, which reduced humans to machines that are at the mercy of external stimuli. Maslow (1943) and Rogers (1975) were proponents of humanistic psychology and believed in the inherent human capacity for development and self-actualisation. Humanism and phenomenology were interested in the individual's internal experience and emotional wellbeing and the exercise of free will. Gestalt psychology was interested in the internal experiences of the individual, but particularly in the human capacity for perceiving wholes as more than the sum of the parts. These theories focused on the internal experience of the individual and emphasised the constructive qualities of humankind. They are based on a system of pro-social values and beliefs that emphasises the human drive to develop potential. Rogers focused on the idea that if you provide individuals with a positive, affirming environment, which he called unconditional positive regard, their behaviour will be productive and constructive.

Of course, this basic premise is true up to a point, but it too has limitations in that even individuals in a very supportive environment will sometimes behave counterproductively. An employee may have a well-paid job with good working conditions and a leader who is supportive, but may still not work effectively because of personal reasons.

THE DEVELOPMENTAL SCHOOL OF PSYCHOLOGY

Developmental psychology is a grouping of all the theories that pertain to the developmental stages of being human. The theories in this school describe a variety of developmental phases, stemming from early childhood all the way through adolescence, adulthood and old age, and the way they affect behaviour. The phases give an indication of the progression and maturity in the developmental process.

For example, some theorists such as Piaget (1997) and Vygotsky (1987) have been concerned primarily with cognitive development. Others, such as Kohlberg (1969)and Erikson (1963), have been concerned with moral development. Theorists from other schools such as Freud (2017), Bowlby (1982), Winnicott (1992)and Klein (2017) have been concerned with aspects of identity development and their theories can also be placed in this category, although they are regarded as primarily representing the schools of depth psychology.

Although developmental stages certainly provide an indication of the behavioural outcomes of certain levels of development, there are many other factors that also play a role. So again, there are limitations to the ability of this to explain human behaviour.

DEPTH PSYCHOLOGY

Depth psychology refers to the sub-group of psychological theories that are characterised by the notion that each human mind includes a part that is unconscious, and that an individual's behaviour is significantly affected by the contents of his or her unconscious mind. The discipline is concerned with the influence of early childhood relationships with caregivers and the effect that these have on psychological development, particularly in terms of psychological compartmentalisation. The original theories were developed by individuals, such as Pierre Janet (1925), William James (1890), Sigmund Freud (2017), Carl Jung (2012), Alfred Adler (2005), Otto Rank (1971), Melanie Klein (2017) and others. The term 'depth psychology' or the original German 'Tiefenpsychologie', was coined by Eugen Bleuler (2013), a contemporary of Sigmund Freud's and, according to Craig (2008, p. 230), both Freud and Jung agreed that it was an appropriate term for this sub-group of theories.

SOCIAL PSYCHOLOGY

Social psychology refers to the interaction between the individual and the social environment. Lewin (1939) is considered one of the founders of this field. The work of social psychologists is concerned with understanding the impact of the social environment on the individual and how individuals are able to construct meaning from social situations. This is comparable to the idea of 'interactionism' in sociology (Mead, 1934). Social psychology is also concerned with the group dynamics that arise socially. As such, social psychology focuses on the interaction between the individual and the social environment, rather than only on the internal functioning of the individual.

TRANSPERSONAL PSYCHOLOGY

The body of theory known as transpersonal psychology arose out of the humanistic school and much of the theory was developed by Ken Wilber (1999). Wilber was particularly interested in individual spiritual development and the effect it has on behaviour. Wilber drew together religious faiths and practices from around the world and considered their influence on psychology and, therefore, the behaviour of individuals. This approach argues that humans need to transcend their egos and integrate all aspects of their humanity. He argued that the spiritual orientation and the level of spiritual development of an individual will have a great influence on the individual's ability to engage with the world.

NEUROSCIENCE

Neuroscience is the study of the nervous system including the brain and the spinal cord. It is concerned with biochemical brain functioning and how different parts of the brain perform specific functions. Hippocrates was one of the earliest thinkers to identify the brain as the centre of thought and consciousness (Breitenfeld et al., 2014). Neuroscience offers insight into the way individuals process their experiences and offers an understanding of how different approaches are processed in distinctly different parts of the brain. Neuroscience also offers the possibility of biochemical interventions to alter human experience and behaviour.

TRAUMA PSYCHOLOGY

Trauma refers to the experience of being physically and psychologically wounded, shocked and/or injured. There are a set of theories that consider the impacts of trauma on individuals and groups, and suggest various interventions that can help people recover and heal. Two of the earliest trauma theorists are Pierre Janet (1925) and Sigmund Freud (2017). Trauma psychology has become particularly relevant since the pandemic. Current trauma experts include Bessel van der Kolk (2014) and Gabor Maté (2018) and they have done good work in bringing trauma theory and practice to the general public.

ATTACHMENT THEORY

Attachment theory was developed by British psychologist John Bowlby (1982) and was concerned with the relationship or bond that a child forms with their primary caregiver. Bowlby developed the notion of secure attachment, which is an ideal kind of relationship between the child and the caregiver. In this ideal state, the caregiver is both a secure base from which the child can explore the world, but also a safe haven to return to when the world becomes dangerous or frightening. Research shows that secure attachment is an important factor in many other parts of psychological development, even influencing the child's later ability to behave ethically.

All the above schools of psychology are helpful in better understanding human functioning, and each contributes an element in the picture of the whole person. The diagram below illustrates each school and its area of focus, as well the main vehicle for intervention in the square blocks. Many leadership theories already embrace the wisdom of behaviourism, cognitive psychology, human-ism and even the developmental school, in many instances without explicitly acknowledging their influence. The contribution of each of the schools is considered in the theory of depth leadership. However, depth psychology offers the deepest level of insight and, therefore, is used as one of the most important focal areas for the ideas in this book. Depth psychology is not generally included in leadership thinking, although this is changing in some sectors. If leaders need to understand the deepest drivers of human behaviour, then it is essential to add an understanding of depth psychol-ogy to the leadership knowledge base. However, as the rest of the book will explain, doing this as a leader may significantly change the way you lead.

PSYCHOLOGY THEORIES

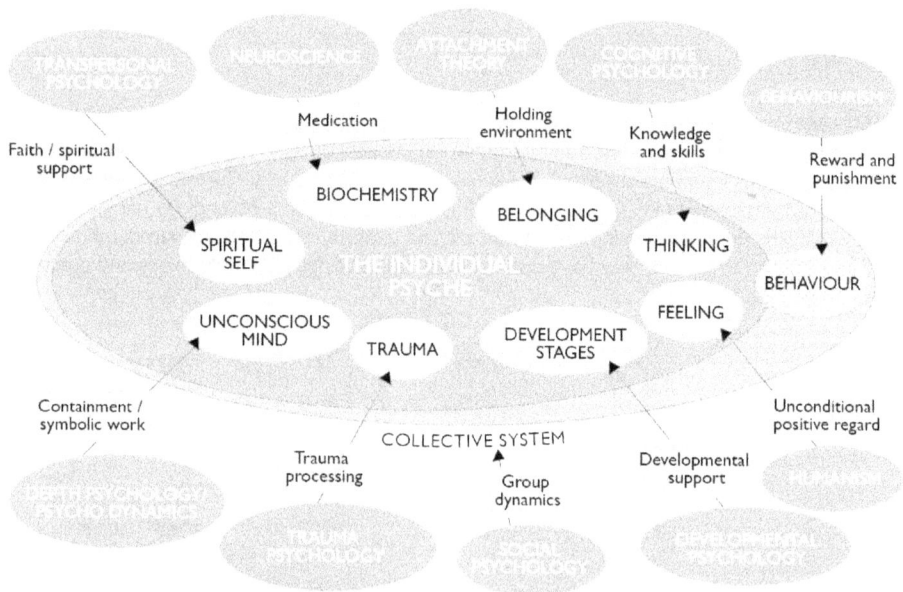

SYSTEMS THINKING

In addition to the theories of human behaviour in the different schools of psychology, there is anoth-er school of thought that comes from the natural sciences, which also informs leadership approach-es. It is broadly known as systems thinking, a loose meta-discipline that insists that different levels of attention are required when thinking about our world. A system is a collection of relationships between various components which interact with each other and the environment, and systems thinking means paying attention to the whole as well as the relationships and dynamics between all the parts.

From approximately AD 1600 to the late 1800s, reductionism dominated scientific thinking. Most problem solving was seen to be within a linear cause-and-effect framework – in other words, a mechanistic system. Thinking mechanistically means thinking of a system as an elementary machine in which problems can be solved by breaking the system into its components and identifying the component that is problematic. It relies on analysing simple linear cause–effect relationships and essentially 'fixing' the part that is causing the problem.

In the last 120 years, it has become apparent that not all problems can be solved by adopting a mechanistic approach. Some problems are context-dependent, i.e., the entire system needs to be evaluated. More sophisticated than mechanistic thinking, systems thinking considers the dynamic relationships that exist within complex systems and the system as a whole. There are many original thinkers in systems thinking. The first was Norbert Weiner (2019) who published a book in 1948 (republished in 2019) on what he called 'cybernetics'. He was followed by, amongst others, Ludwig von Bertalanffy (1969), who was interested in overcoming mechanistic reductionism in biology. More recent theorists include Jay Forrester (1991), who developed Systems Dynamics theory at MIT, Russell L. Ackoff (1974) who claimed that systems thinking is a better alternative to what he called 'Machine Age' thinking and Fritjof Capra (1997), who argued for including ecosystem properties in all our thinking. Most famously, Peter Senge (1990) in his book, *The Fifth Discipline*, popularised the approach of systems thinking for leadership, seeing it as an essential discipline in its own right.

Different kinds of problems require different kinds of thinking. For example, when a car breaks down, it is obvious that mechanistic thinking is the appropriate path to take. However, when the problem is how to address growing absenteeism in an organisation, systems thinking provides the more appropriate approach. Systems thinking is based on some key concepts that essentially challenge a more mechanistic approach and these are outlined below.

- Cause-and-effect relationships in complex systems, which all human systems are, are not linear. This means that outcomes have multiple causes that may be non-linearly related to one another. For example, demotivation in a group may be because of a complicated combination of factors, rather than simply the remuneration they receive.

- Complex systems should always be considered in terms of the context in which they occur. In other words, the larger systems around an individual, a group or an organisation should always be considered. Systems thinking implies seeing actions and relationships in terms of the greater system of which they are part, as well as the smaller sub-systems. For example, when working with a business, it may be important to consider the broader economic climate as well as the immediate business environment.

- The past and future of any complex system are as important as the present. Events should be seen as part of a process where change is continually occurring. For example, a group that is demotivated may be partially affected by a past retrenchment, or a future merger with another organisation. 'Snapshot' views of systems should be avoided.

- Systems thinking means seeing the underlying structures of situations. In other words, events are often the result of underlying patterns, and these patterns are the result of underlying structures. This could mean that the physical environment may be affecting system behaviour. In a group, an individual coming late for a meeting may, in fact, be reflecting a greater pattern in which certain members of the organisation feel less included. This may be because the head office is situated far away from the regions, or because a certain part of the system has access to more resources than other parts.

- As a result of the fact that everything is connected to everything else in a complex system, it is possible to use leverage to effect change. The principle of leverage is that you can find simple actions and changes in structure that can lead to significant, enduring improvements. For example, changing one high-leverage thing – such as the extent to which the person exercises – may change many other aspects of the individual's life. Leverage points, also known as points of high leverage, are those elements in the system that, if changed, have multiple ripple effects throughout the system and produce wide-scale change (Meadows, 1999). Systems thinking embraces the notion of causal complexity, but as Meadows (1999, p. 1) describes, "[t]hese are places within a complex system (a corporation, an economy, a living body, a city, an ecosystem) where a small shift in one thing can produce big changes in everything."

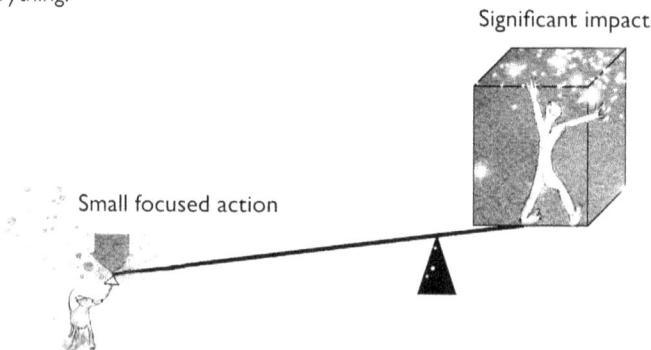

Significant impact

Small focused action

- Systems thinking means understanding that complex systems are so, both in the nature of the detail in the system and in the nature of the processes. In other words, systems have both detail and dynamic complexity, and both must be managed. Dynamic complexity implies that human behaviour operates in a set of self-reinforcing patterns and these patterns can change over time. For systems to shift, the complexity of the relationship dynamics must be recognised. For example, in a strategic planning session, it is not only necessary to consider the different business areas, but also the overt and subtle influences that the actions of the different areas have on one another.

- If you take a systemic perspective, it also means that there are not always clear right or wrong answers to questions. The answers to various problems depend on the perspective you hold, and many different perspectives are possible in a system. For example, in a group that is facing a dilemma, you often have to explore both polarities at length before a new perspective emerges that encompasses the wisdom of both sides. All members are part of the blame and the responsibility in a group.

- When dealing with complex systems, it is important to realise that quick change is usually not sustainable. It is also not possible to speed up growth and development in a system beyond a certain point. Systems that grow too quickly often develop problems at the same speed. This characteristic of systems means that great patience is needed. For example, for a group to break out of destructive psychological patterns often requires a thorough examination of how those patterns work and particularly how they are maintained by responses that individuals are not necessarily aware of. Occasionally, you may find a quick fix that appears to work, but usually, it only works in the short term. Beware the easiest, fastest solution because the easiest way out will lead back into the problem, although it may have taken a different form. All systems grow at an optimal pace and real, sustainable change takes time.

- There is always a period of disruption when a system changes, and this may mean that symptoms worsen before they improve, but the disruption and short-term instability may be necessary to achieve system improvement.

- Closely linked to the idea mentioned above is the fact that solutions that do not address the core problems in a system may, in fact, cause further complications. The logic of the solution and the logic of the problem are seldom the same.

- Analysis alone will not provide sustainable solutions; synthesis is needed too, and multiple perspectives are required.

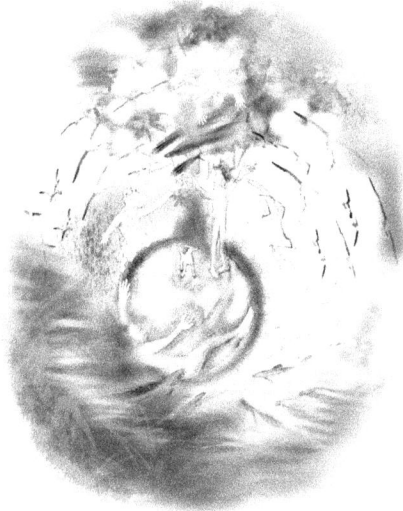

A DEFINITION OF DEPTH LEADERSHIP

Based on the above ideas, it is possible to provide an early definition of depth leadership. We will then consider its theoretical origins and its relationship with other leadership theories. In the following chapter, we will consider the detailed principles behind the depth leadership approach. Depth leadership is defined as leadership in which leaders are: "Working beneath, between and beyond for a thriving psyche, community and planet."

The core ideas are briefly explained below and will be developed further in Chapter 2:

Beneath: the leader actively pursues integration of the whole self or psyche, both the conscious (on-the-surface) self and the unconscious (under-the-surface) self, which includes the body and the imagination, in order to help the individual psyche to thrive.

Between: the leader pursues integration between people to help groups and communities thrive.

Beyond: the leader considers factors beyond the entity of concern, using an integrative approach towards larger systems, including governance systems and the natural environment, to ensure a thriving planet

Working towards thriving: the leader has an ethical attitude towards the self, others and the planet, and works to ensure that people and systems can flourish in coexistence.

The definition implies that a leader has the ethical responsibility to ensure that individuals, communities and the planet are all helped to develop their creative and constructive potential, and to co-exist as sustainably as possible. This definition can also be viewed as a vision, as it is aspirational in nature and is an ideal, rather than a reality. The approach in this book is a blend and an extension of a range of disciplines, based on a foundation of depth psychology and systems thinking, allowing a transformative worldview that strives for the vision of a thriving planet and all who live on it.

LEADERSHIP THEORIES

A review of the evolution of leadership theories is necessary to distinguish the unique contribution of depth leadership. A plethora of leadership theories exist in the world. Some theories have prevailed for some time, while others became short-lived fads for management scientists. As the list of leadership theories is extensive, a selection of the most enduring theories or high-level groups of theories (where appropriate) was made. Each of these theories can be considered for the extent to which they meet the definition of depth leadership. The definition was further broken down into eight related criteria against which each leadership theory was evaluated. They are listed below:

- an integration of the whole self (including the unconscious)
- an integration of the community
- an integration of larger systems
- an integration of the natural environment
- an ethical approach to the whole self
- an ethical approach to other and the community
- an ethical approach to larger systems
- an ethical approach to the natural environment

THE 'GREAT MAN' THEORY

One of the first leadership theories is that of the 'great man' described by Thomas Carlyle in the 1840s. It was later subsumed by the trait theories, which are discussed in the next section. The great man theory is essentially based on the idea that certain men (it was a time when women were not considered leaders) were given special qualities and, therefore, ordained by a deity to lead the world. In this theory, the leader is a hero who has special inherent qualities and who leads a group as a result.

The idea of 'great man' leadership theory does not speak explicitly about an ethical approach to the self. By implication, the individual may be moral, but this is not an explicit requirement. In this theory, there is no indication of the integration of an ethical approach to others and the community. There is an implication that the hero saves the community, but it is not explicitly stated. There is no indication in this theory that the leader has an ethical approach to, nor pursues integration of, larger systems and the environment.

TRAIT THEORIES

Between the 1920s and 1940s, the dominant idea about leadership was that leaders had specific traits, which predisposed them to lead. Various attempts were made to list a range of traits, but this was not sustainably successful as trait theory soon fell out of favour after an expensive study established that effective leaders were either tall or short (Goleman, 1998). The history of trait theories is somewhat chequered, and it is difficult to find a succinct description of the core components, but indications are that trait theories do not speak about an integration of the whole self. There is also no indication that an integration of the community is considered, nor an integration of the system or the environment. There are no indications that trait theories include ethical considerations.

BEHAVIOURAL THEORIES

In the 1940s, Ralph Stogdill (1948) conducted a study to identify leadership traits. He identified 32 of these and concluded that a leader's characteristics do not determine leadership behaviour alone, but rather, leadership is situationally dependent. This and similar studies changed the nature of leadership research. There was a new focus on the behaviour of leaders and on situations where certain behaviours would be appropriate, and this gave rise to a series of behavioural theories, such as the Blake and Mouton managerial grid (Blake et al., 1962). These theories also became known as style theory. A great deal of work was done by Ohio State University on the mixture between task and relationship activities of leaders. Although this theory takes the influence of the situation into account, there is no emphasis on an integration of the whole self, the community or the environment. Nor was there any explicit inclusion of an ethical approach to the self, community, the system or the environment, although some measure of ethics is implied in that the theories regard the leader as being responsible for the psychosocial growth of a group.

CONTINGENCY THEORIES

Contingency theories are closely associated with the behavioural theories and are concerned with matching the leader's behaviour with the situation appropriately. The first and most dominant theory is Fiedler's contingency theory, closely followed by the well-known Hersey and Blanchard situational leadership model. Although these theories considered the impact of the situation, they were not explicitly or implicitly concerned with ethical behaviour at any level, nor was there an explicit concern with an integration of the whole self, the community, the system or the environment.

CHARISMATIC LEADERSHIP

The 1980s brought the development of theories concerned with charismatic leadership. Charismatic leaders have the ability to offer an inspirational vision and to convince others that they and their leadership are extraordinary. The difficulty with these theories is that they do not expressly include the idea of ethics. Some charismatic leaders may well be ethical, but the theory is not concerned with ethics. It is possible that leaders described by this theory might imply integration at all levels in all their activities, but the theory itself is not concerned with whether they do or don't.

TRANSACTIONAL LEADERSHIP

The theory of transactional leadership was developed in the 1980s by Bass (1990) and has as its focus the exchanges between leaders and their followers. The theory saw the relationships between leaders and followers as a series of transactions aimed at maximizing the achievement of individual and organisational goals. The theory was criticised by Burns as focusing on short-term gratification for both parties. The theory also does not take any contextual factors into account. As such, the theory does not consider integration of the whole self, the community, the system or the environment, although relationships with others are taken into account superficially. The theory does not explicitly include ethics as important.

TRANSFORMATIONAL LEADERSHIP

Transformational leadership theory was the first leadership theory to include morals and ethics explicitly in the study of leadership. This theory was developed by Burns (1978), and was concerned with motivating followers to conduct themselves ethically. It involved understanding follower motivation and caring for the follower as a whole person. Transformational leadership theory includes ideas such as concern for others, leaders as role models, and consistency between the values and the behaviour of a leader. These indicate both an ethical approach and a relationship with the self, but a relationship with the unconscious mind is not included. The approach comprises an ethical approach to others (or the community) but is not explicit about developing an integrated relationship with the community. The approach also does not discuss an integration, ethical or otherwise, with the system or the environment.

AUTHENTIC LEADERSHIP

The theory of authentic leadership was introduced by Bill George, a Harvard professor, in the early 2000s. It is an interesting step in the development of leadership theories in that it explicitly includes the ethics of the individual. Authentic leadership promotes ethical self-awareness, and an ethical approach to relationships with others. According to this theory, authentic leaders are clear about their values, and act in accordance with them. However, despite this unambiguous inclusion of ethics, the theory of authentic leadership received strong criticism, namely that it requires the individual to favour their organisational self over their true self. Authentic leadership does not acknowledge the dark side of all leaders and followers, i.e., acknowledging the leader's imperfections. Therefore, although the theory insists on a relationship with the self, it ignores unconscious elements, which precludes the full integration of the psyche. The theory is concerned with an ethical approach to the organisation, but it does not have anything to say about an ethical approach to the larger system and the environment.

SERVANT LEADERSHIP

The idea of servant leadership was developed by Robert K. Greenleaf in 1970, but he did not empirically define it. It also did not attract much interest until 30 years later. A servant leader is primarily interested in helping followers to grow.

- listening
- empathy
- healing – the ability to make whole
- awareness
- persuasion
- conceptualisation – thinking beyond the present-day need and stretching this need into a possible future
- foresight – foreseeing outcomes of situations and working with intuition
- stewardship – holding something in trust and serving the needs of others
- commitment to the growth of people, nurturing the personal, professional and spiritual growth of others; and
- building community

This list indicates that servant leadership addresses more of the elements of the definition of depth leadership than the theories listed thus far. The list shows that the individual is interested in and concerned about ethical relationships with others, the community and the broader system, including an interest in the future. However, the theory does not emphasise an ethical relationship with the self, whether conscious or unconscious, nor does it explicitly include an ethical relationship with the natural environment.

ETHICAL LEADERSHIP

The concept of ethical leadership was developed by Brown et al. (2005), who defined it as ethical conduct in one's personal actions and interpersonal relationships, and the promotion of similar conduct in one's followers. The theory of ethical leadership is based on social learning theory and the idea that leaders need to be credible role models for followers and able to influence followers to behave ethically too. It makes sense that a post-Enron world saw the emergence of a leadership theory that is explicitly and unashamedly about ethics. However, as a theory, ethical leadership does not define the subtleties of ethics but is rather interested in the influence of the idea. The theory therefore implies an ethical approach to the self, the community, the system and the environment, but it does not explicitly state that all those levels need to be taken into account.

EMOTIONALLY INTELLIGENT LEADERSHIP

The idea of emotionally intelligent leadership was developed as an offshoot of Goleman's (1996) work on emotional intelligence. Allen et al. (2012) propose that emotionally intelligent leadership needs to work at three levels: the context, the self and others. They outline a set of twenty-one capacities that operate at these different levels. The capacities include, amongst others, environmental awareness, honest self-understanding, emotional self-control, empathy, authenticity, influence, citizenship and the development of relationships. Emotionally intelligent leadership theory therefore includes the perspectives of the self, the other (the community) and the broader system and environment, but does not explicitly include ethics, although ethical behaviour is implied. The approach further does not explicitly include an approach of building relationships with all systemic levels. There is no indication that unconscious processes should be considered, although there is a focus on intrapsychic processes, such as self-regulation.

SPIRITUAL LEADERSHIP

The notion of leading with a spiritual foundation is not new in the world. However, it became part of mainstream leadership theory when described in detail by Fry in the early 2000s. Fry (2003) defines spiritual leadership as an approach in which leaders are able to motivate themselves and others to have a sense of spiritual connection and calling. To achieve this, the leader needs to communicate a vision, which allows employees to have a sense of calling, which imbues their lives with meaning and needs to create an organisational culture premised on the idea of altruistic love, where both the self and others are cared for and appreciated. Fry also suggests that spiritual leadership offers a holistic approach that integrates the body, mind, heart and spirit.

Spiritual leadership is therefore explicitly concerned with ethics, although it does not specify an ethical approach beyond the individual leader, fellow organisational members and the organisation. There is a sense of a relationship with the self and others, although this relationship does not extend to intrapsychic integration of an unconscious self. Spiritual leadership, as framed by Fry, does not include an ethical approach to the environment.

PSYCHODYNAMIC OR PSYCHOANALYTIC APPROACH TO LEADERSHIP

The idea of the unconscious has been around for centuries, but Sigmund Freud (2017) formalised it as a discipline and became the father of psychoanalysis. However, his work spawned many related theories about the role of the unconscious mind in human functioning, more commonly known as a psychodynamic group of theories, and these have been taken variously by leadership and management theorists. Notably, the psychodynamic approach to leadership was popularised by Manfred Kets de Vries (2015) during his time at the Insead Business School, after his tutelage under Abraham Zaleznik at Harvard in the 1970s. More recently, the work of Petrieglieri and Petrieglieri (2020), Gabriel and Carr (2002), and others has brought psychodynamic thinking to leadership. A psychodynamic or psychoanalytic approach to leadership explicitly includes the idea of a relationship with and integration of the psyche, and is concerned about an ethical approach to the self and others, but does not extend explicitly to an ethical relationship with the community, the larger system or the environment.

SYSTEMS PSYCHODYNAMIC APPROACH

The failure of psychodynamics to extend to include the system was remedied by the later development of a systems psychodynamic approach to organisations and leadership. The parallel endeavours of Kurt Lewin (1935) and Wilfred Bion (1961), who studied the psyche in its social systems on different ends of the Atlantic Ocean, became known as systems psychodynamics. Systems psycho-dynamics is grounded in four principles:

- the first considers the influence of the unconscious mind on human functioning
- the second is a focus on the interactive nature of the psychology of the individual and the collective or the group
- the third is concerned with producing theory in a participative way, and
- the fourth is a challenge to the authority of detached scientists and autocratic leaders and organisations

Therefore, a systems psychodynamic approach to leadership takes an explicit approach of focusing on relationships with the self (including the unconscious self), the community and the system. An ethical approach to all the levels is not spelled out, but it is inherent in the underlying psychodynamic theory. The systems psychodynamic approach, however, does not include a relationship with the natural environment, although this is implied through certain offshoots of the theory, such as in the work done by McCallum (2005).

CRITICAL LEADERSHIP STUDIES

Based on Collinson and Tourish (2015), the leadership theories discussed thus far do not question the politics of the notion of leadership and, therefore, the ethics of the power relationships in lead-ership relationships. The approach known as critical leadership studies (CLS) aims to remedy this by – as the name indicates – critically examining the power relationships between leaders and so-called followers, and the importance of ensuring follower agency and the capacity to be dissenting. This approach is concerned with the use of power and authority. Practitioners of CLS use other theories, such as systems psychodynamics, to evaluate traditional leader–follower relationships. CLS does not explicitly take an ethical or integrated approach to the self, the community or larger systems or the environment, but it includes the notion of ethical power relationships between the self, the community and the system.

Integral leadership is an approach developed by Ken Wilber (1999) who combined individual and collective approaches with internal and external landscapes. This comprises multiple areas of theory, ranging from psychology to culture studies to the physical sciences and sociology. Wilber's theory also considers levels or stages of development, depending on the consciousness of the individual. Wilber further includes the idea of multiple selves that combine into a larger self, which is continually in relationship with larger systems. His approach is holistic but complex and draws extensively on deep philosophical and psychological theory. Integral leadership, therefore, implies a holistic approach to the self, the community and larger systems, but does not have an explicit ethical component. However, an ethical approach to the self and all other systems is implicit in the approach. Integral leadership does not spell out a particular relationship with the natural environment (see Wilber, 1999).

A GAP IN LEADERSHIP

As shown in the figure below, an overview of the leadership theories indicated several gaps with regard to various aspects of depth leadership as described above. No single other leadership theory encompasses all the aspects of the definition of depth leadership.

Leadership theories and Depth Leadership

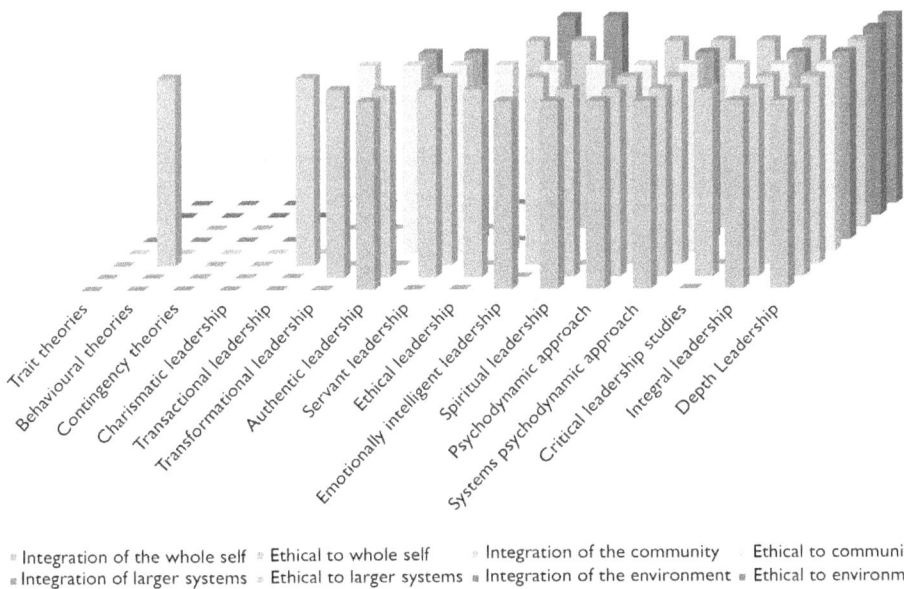

- Integration of the whole self
- Ethical to whole self
- Integration of the community
- Ethical to community
- Integration of larger systems
- Ethical to larger systems
- Integration of the environment
- Ethical to environmen

None of the leadership theories mentioned include an understanding of the interconnectedness of all systems with an explicit inclusion of the natural environment. Systems thinking is included in the systems psychodynamics approach to leadership, but a focus on the natural environment is not specifically included.

Depth leadership is, therefore, an approach in which the leader integrates all internal and external systems and approaches this interconnected world ethically, ensuring that people and systems can flourish in coexistence.

CONCLUSION

Leadership theories abound, and have roots in a variety of other disciplines, particularly the discipline of psychology. An overview of world trends, psychological theories and leadership theories indicates that depth leadership is well suited theoretically to the challenges of the world we live in.

This book discusses an approach that has the potential to be transformative for groups. As with anything that results in true transformation, it requires new ways of thinking and significant effort. This approach will also not result in the greatest financial returns in the short term, but it will significantly reduce the psychological costs of group functioning and result in more creative and sustainable outcomes in the long term.

PERSONAL EXERCISES

At the end of each chapter, there is a set of exercises or questions you can work through to develop your insight and skills. You can complete them on your own, with a partner or fellow learner, or with a therapist, coach or mentor. The exercises are designed to stimulate your thinking and there are no right or wrong answers. It would be useful to keep your answers in some form of a journal for later reference. The first set of exercises are given below:

1. Many of our basic assumptions or beliefs about the world are implicitly developed through our early relationships. Consider your basic assumptions or beliefs. Can you identify where you learnt some of them? Are they still valid?

2. Consider the formal theories that inform your general worldview and where they came from. Are these still valid? Do they still fit the current context that you find yourself in?

3. Consider the current context of your leadership. What are the main trends and challenges of your current environment?

4. What kind of leadership do you think is needed in this environment?

CHAPTER

2

WHAT IS DEPTH LEADERSHIP?

INTRODUCTION

Because of the changes in the world that we looked at in the previous chapter, leaders now need to have an integrated approach to all systems, including the psychological systems of people and the larger institutional and natural systems of the environment. This means an explicit inclusion of the wisdom of the psychological theories that exist, but specifically depth psychology, as well as a capacity for systems thinking at all levels. An introduction to depth psychology is given below.

THE ORIGINS OF DEPTH PSYCHOLOGY

The term depth psychology (originally in German 'Tiefenpsychologie') was coined by Swiss psychiatrist Eugen Bleuler (1857–1939) to refer to any psychological approach that incorporated the idea of an unconscious mind. Bleuler's contemporaries – such as Pierre Janet, Joseph Breuer, Sigmund Freud, Alfred Adler, Otto Rank and Carl Jung – all contributed to our current understanding of the unconscious mind as they created and developed the academic discipline of depth psychology. Although Sigmund Freud was not the first to consider the idea of the unconscious, he is commonly regarded as the founder of depth psychology, which studies the unconscious and its effect on human behaviour. Carl Jung, originally a student of Freud's work and later a rival in some respects, developed Freud's idea of the unconscious further.

The idea of depth as a factor in human behaviour did not start with Freud and his colleagues. The idea that there is more to human functioning than we are conscious or aware of has been around for centuries. Guy Claxton (2005), in his excellent book called *The Wayward Mind: An Intimate History of the Unconscious,* argues that:

> "… before the seventeenth century, the fact that people were not entirely transparent to themselves was so commonplace that it had not needed stressing. Only in the aftermath of Descartes' rejection of the very idea of 'unconscious intelligence' was a special word required, to point insistently at all the phenomena that had been quietly airbrushed out of the mental picture. An old idea that had been implicit in a host of images and myths and ways of talking was suddenly explicitly reasserted." Claxton, *The Wayward Mind,* 2005

Claxton goes on to argue that many ancient cultures, such as those of the Egyptians and Greeks, incorporated the idea of the existence of a realm beyond the conscious mind that influences human behaviour. For instance, the capacity to dream (while sleeping) has been embraced in many cultures over the centuries. The main achievement of Freud and his colleagues is that they brought the importance of a depth approach back into our contemporary studies of human behaviour.

KEY PRINCIPLES OF DEPTH PSYCHOLOGY

Depth psychology is an evolving field which has much disagreement within its ranks about some of the details of the functioning of the unconscious mind. However, there are some general principles that are, broadly speaking, held to be true by most theorists in the field:

1.   Human beings have a psyche (from the Greek word for breath) that carries the whole of mental life. It is the faculty for thought, feeling, memory and imagination. The psyche is not just a combination of the body and the mind; it is an integrated system that has a life and language of its own beyond individual conscious control or even awareness.

2.   In addition to carrying all our human potential in the form of inherent biological and psychological predispositions, the psyche processes, records, and stores all our life experi-

ences. Using our earlier experiences, the psyche develops a subjective logical framework for perceiving and further processing ongoing experience.

3.   Life experiences often expose us to social pressures which may run counter to our natural impulses and this results in ambivalence and irreconcilable conflicts that the psyche has to manage. The psyche divides itself into public and private compartments, and into conscious and unconscious compartments to manage internal conflict. To keep us safe, the psyche keeps the socially acceptable part of our complex experience in the public conscious mind and buries the other, more dangerous or unpalatable part either in the private or in the unconscious mind.

4.   The unconscious mind is multilayered in itself. Closer to the surface, one will find individual personal experience and potential that, for a range of reasons, cannot be brought into consciousness. The deeper bedrock of the unconscious mind contains collective predispositions that affect and connect all human beings.

5.   The contents of the unconscious mind continue to influence behaviour, even though such content is buried away from conscious awareness and control.

6.   The divisions in the psyche (caused by internal conflicts) and the deeply buried individual and collective potential all contribute to continual dynamic processes in the psyche. These alternate between developmental, integrative processes and defensive processes. The psyche is continually striving for greater integration (although some debate exists about this idea).

7.   The psyche uses the language of imagery, symbolism and metaphor to express itself. This language allows the simultaneous communication of multiple layers of meaning.

8.   Human experience becomes more meaningful when the psyche's personal aspect encounters the deeper, collective aspect. A depth approach tries to make the connection between the different levels.

9.   Personal difficulties, blockages, and symptoms, as well as interpersonal problems and conflicts, can be viewed as a form of communication from the less conscious parts of the psyche about its developmental process. These can be resolved by interpreting the symbolism inherent in the difficulty and thereby finding the deeper meaning, purpose or essence that our unconscious mind may be seeking to express and integrate. Ignoring or silencing difficulties and symptoms will mean that psychological needs are not being addressed and that these will almost certainly manifest in other ways.

10.   Individual psyches do not remain separate from one another. At the simplest level, when two people come together, they form a third psyche between them that has a life and psychology of its own. This applies to all interactions with others – there is always the creation of a shared psyche which is more than the sum of the individual psyches. The shared psyche will express itself in terms of psychodynamic patterns that will affect individual autonomy. To change the systems around us, we need to understand and intervene in these psychodynamic patterns.

11.   Objectivity in perception, interpretation and action is complex for two main reasons. We do not easily know our unconscious intentions and our unconscious processes always both influence and are affected by the unconscious processes of others.

12.   Like all disciplines, the original thinkers in the discipline of depth psychology operated in and were, to some extent, limited by the culture and era from which they came. As such, some of the original theories were founded on biases and stereotypes that are no longer appropriate. Modern day depth psychology challenges stereotypes that lead to discrimination on demographic bases and helps us to always consider the psyche in its entire context.

13.   Our psyches are inextricably linked to all the forms of life around us. Our inner landscape will, to some extent, be a reflection of our outer landscape and vice versa, so that we are only really as well as our environment.

14.   In order to move towards the greater health of a system, whether it be the individual, the group or the ecosystem, a depth approach suggests that the voices, opinions, and experiences that are repressed, marginalised, silenced or simply ignored, are attended to, considered and integrated in systemic decision-making processes.

These principles have many ethical and practical implications, which will be explored in the rest of this book. Firstly, however, we need to understand why this is regarded as a relatively new approach.

THE DIFFICULTIES OF ADOPTING THE DEPTH LEADERSHIP APPROACH

Although not generally described as depth leadership, many well-developed theories and practices now exist for leading from a depth perspective and are slowly gaining popularity among leaders. But this approach has not yet been widely adopted for several reasons, including the fact that such an approach is not yet part of mainstream leadership training. Prevailing leadership worldviews still value the perception that scientific approaches are only conscious and rational. This is slowly changing.

Also, by its very nature, depth psychology addresses the more difficult parts of being human. Most of us instinctively turn away from the kind of challenging and painful experiences that are sometimes housed in the unconscious mind. The content of the human unconscious is hidden from consciousness precisely because it is potentially disturbing, maybe even dangerous to other parts of the (human or organisational) system. The problems that can result from the unleashing of material from the unconscious can be devastating for a system if it is not managed carefully.

Leaders need knowledge about the nature and functioning of the unconscious to reduce their wariness. Knowledge will help them become more conscious themselves, thus increasing consciousness in the workplace, as well as empowering them to make informed choices when seeking specialist help. The knowledge they need should ideally be grounded in formal theory and practical experience. Too few comprehensive, accessible and formal bridges exist between the theory and practice of depth psychology and the theory and practice of leadership. These need to be built – through research, writing, education and informed practice in the field. Such bridges would ensure that the power of depth leadership for organisations is utilised in a way that is as safe and effective as possible.

These bridges are slowly being built in academia and organisations. There are increasing numbers of professional therapists, consultants, lecturers and coaches who work in the depth area. Equally, leaders who are aware of how depth leadership and its underlying psychology works, can use the approach to help unlock the hidden potential in groups in their organisations. The focus of this book is to help them to do that.

Also, it is onerous to always take an integrative approach to oneself, others, the community, institutional systems, and the environment. It means that the full implications of decisions need to be considered, and this is time consuming, potentially constraining and burdensome.

WHEN IS DEPTH LEADERSHIP NEEDED?

Depth leadership may be useful in any situation and at any time in a group's life. It is especially useful when leaders want to unearth the deeper potential in individuals and groups. It is also specifically needed when the usual team-building interventions, training courses, community projects or other organisational development interventions, such as restructuring, fail to produce the required change. Depth leadership is useful when a team is stuck, and it is hard to identify what the problem is.

Examples of the symptoms that may indicate the need for depth leadership are:

- 'wicked' problems (problems that are difficult to solve because of their complex and interconnected nature)
- recurrent conflict between individuals or groups
- unexpected organisational absenteeism, low morale or poor performance

- repeated incidents that indicate an intolerance for diversity, manifesting as racism, sexism or other types of discrimination
- recurring failure to meet deadlines, make or implement decisions
- unexplained organisational or project problems of a chronic nature
- continued failure of change processes and programmes and
- persistent people difficulties after mergers and acquisitions

Increasingly, it has become clear that if leaders do not have the ability to both work at a deeper psychological level (including the unconscious level) with organisations and adopt an integrative approach, many problems will not be solved, and creative potential will be missed.

WHERE DEPTH LEADERSHIP WILL NOT BE APPROPRIATE

There are certain instances where depth leadership will not easily work and address the problems in a system. These include situations where there is a lack of ethics or some measure of dishonesty, which cannot be challenged because the powerful people are unethical themselves. Where the system is corrupt and the people in power are using the system for personal gain in an unethical way, it will be more difficult to derive value from a depth perspective, because individuals will resist any meaningful deeper exploration for fear of exposure.

Depth leadership is most effective when people are operating from a foundation of good faith. This means that they genuinely want to resolve difficulties and develop themselves and others, rather than merely serve their own selfish and short-term interests. If the group is not operating in good faith, depth leadership will not be immediately effective.

Sometimes depth leadership can only become effective over time, where the group gradually develops an attitude of good faith. If a group has a history of poor treatment, it may take some time to build enough trust in a leader before it will experience a depth leadership approach as constructive and transformative.

Depth leadership may not be suitable in a crisis, where quick, targeted action is needed to ensure safety. Once the crisis is addressed, a depth leadership approach will be useful to metabolise the crisis and prevent a re-occurrence in the future.

BENEFITS OF DEPTH LEADERSHIP

In the right situation, there are many potential benefits in using a depth leadership approach. These are outlined below:

- Individuals may know themselves better, can develop more of their potential, and may be more motivated and, therefore, more productive.
- Team members communicate more accurately and clearly, there are fewer misunderstandings, they feel more heard and, as a result, have better and more cooperative relationships.
- Ongoing conflict is handled more constructively and is seen as an opportunity for growth and development. There is less displaced aggression, and less tension and stress.
- Blockages that covertly cause conflict can be identified and resolved.
- Individual and group creativity and untapped systemic potential can be unlocked.
- People are physically and psychologically healthier so there is less absenteeism and higher productivity.
- There is less destructive and dysfunctional behaviour, less politics and therefore better team functioning.
- All these aspects mean fewer disciplinary procedures, fewer dismissals, less industrial action, less sabotage, and less unethical behaviour. Organisations are more effective and successful.
- There is more coordination between differing parts of a system, ensuring greater synergy and more effective resource utilisation.
- The health and longevity of systems are supported, and whole system sustainability becomes possible.
- Systems and projects develop at a sustainable pace.
- Negative unintended consequences are avoided.

COSTS OF DEPTH LEADERSHIP

Depth leadership can be very beneficial to a system, but it will almost always lead to some disruption to the system that may be experienced as costly. The possible costs are outlined below:

- A change of thinking is required, and so existing mindsets may need to be challenged. Decision making may become more complex and time consuming in the short term because an additional range of perspectives needs to be taken into consideration.
- Depth leadership is built on a set of values that prioritise long-term sustainability; care for the whole system, the whole community and the whole person; the inclusion of minority positions; a focus on emotion as well as cognition; and the inclusion of subtle, unconscious processes are sources of information. These values may be onerous to implement.

- The way success is measured may need to be changed. Depth leadership demands a long-term view of any situation from the combined perspectives of the individual, the community and the environment. Organisational processes will feel more time consuming in the short term. Including a depth leadership approach will often feel as if it goes against the approaches that seemed to work in the past. It requires more involvement of people, more conversation and dialogue, and more introspection and reflection after implementation. Perspectives on issues will no longer be clearly right or wrong, and the real positive results may only be seen later. Also, things may often feel worse before they get better and so commitment and patience are needed.

- The culture of an organisation is closely linked to the psychology of its leadership. The leader carries great psychological importance for the group and will usually be the centre of attention when addressing depth processes. As a result, changing the culture of an organisation through depth work requires greater levels of consciousness from the leadership. It is often very difficult for leaders to become more psychologically aware because they have a lot more at stake. They may also have too little support for the difficult job of increased self-awareness. To practise depth leadership, leaders will need to be open to receiving painful and difficult feedback. This may leave the leaders feeling exposed, so good support systems are needed.

- Often, group members unconsciously participate in psychological collusions, and these cannot continue once the group or team becomes more conscious. Established relationships may be disrupted. Leaders may also be part of these unconscious collusions and dysfunctional patterns of relating and may, therefore, need to change their interactions. Emotions that may have been buried for a long time are sometimes unleashed and this can be disruptive and upsetting.

- Depth leadership will change the culture of the group or the organisation in sometimes strange and unpredictable ways. This leads to greater uncertainty in the short term.

As a result of the implications above, implementing a depth leadership approach may be arduous, especially if leaders are not surrounded by others in the organisation with similar approaches who are able to offer support. To implement this kind of approach, leaders will need to actively develop their self-awareness and capacity for psychological self-management. They will also need to extend their awareness and consideration to systems outside of their immediate environment. This will require the commitment of practical and emotional resources to build awareness, develop new skills, acquire information, develop understanding, and collaborate.

LEARNING DEPTH LEADERSHIP SKILLS

As explained, depth leadership may require additional knowledge and a new skill set. As with any new skill, it takes time to really become competent. Good theory helps, but ultimately practice provides the real teaching.

Depth leadership is a great deal more complex than it may look because people and systems are a lot more complex than they appear on the surface. As a group leader practising depth leadership, you will need to manage yourself and your psychology to prevent it from contaminating the group. To help groups work together, leaders will need to manage the individuals in the group, and identify and manage group dynamics, as well as system dynamics. This requires a continuous intricate cycle of insight and intervention. Depth leadership of people and systems means that leaders must continually confront themselves, develop their self-awareness and manage their own psychology. This requires courage and emotional resilience.

To work successfully with the complexity of groups or teams, the leader needs the ability to understand what is happening through a variety of lenses. It is important to develop an understanding of a variety of approaches and lenses and to move flexibly between them. Many of us tend to fall in love with one approach and use it to the exclusion of all others, but this leads to a myopia that does not serve our organisations in the long run. Also, it is essential that leaders actively test any theories that they may embrace against personal experience. It is important to supplement the theories and ideas given in this book with any of your own, and to continue developing your theoretical knowledge throughout your leadership life.

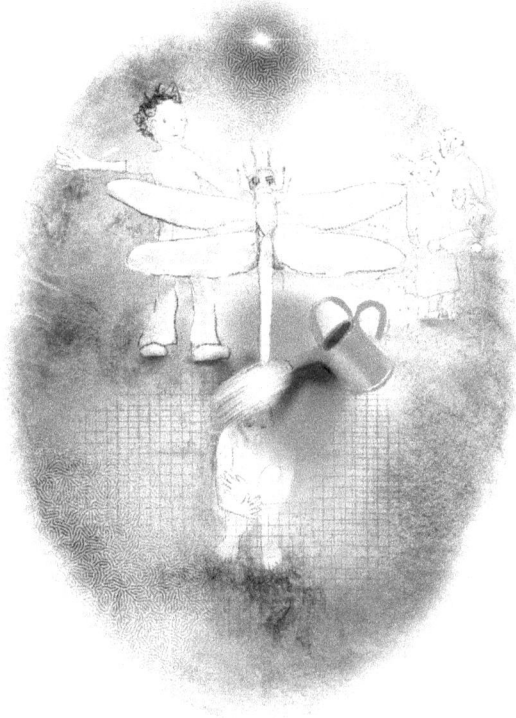

WHAT DO WE MEAN BY DEPTH?

The theory of depth leadership has its roots in depth psychology, but it is also possible to understand the idea of depth from a layperson's point of view. Before discussing the theory more technically, it is useful to distinguish between the ideas of surface and depth and what they mean from a leadership perspective.

Broadly speaking, the word depth can be thought of as referring to the deeper, often unnoticed or unattended to, levels of functional, psychological and emotional activity within a person, or a relationship between people, or in a system. The different levels can be illustrated with the example of a relationship between two people. In any interaction between two people, there is a range of different levels at which they can engage with one another.

At the most superficial level, there can be an arbitrary or ad hoc interaction in which neither individual engages emotionally or psychologically – neither is dependent on the other in any way. They have no requirements of one another as for instance, when two people share a lift without taking much notice of one another.

At the next level, the two people engage in a transaction of some kind. For example, a customer and a shop assistant conclude a sale. They may even have a short conversation, but there is no requirement from one another apart from concluding the transaction.

At the next level, the two people begin to cooperate with one another and a certain amount of dependency occurs. They have expectations of one another at this level, although there may be no emotional investment. When they start experiencing an emotional reaction towards each other, they are at the level of emotional investment. An example would be two members of a project committee who have been tasked to organise an end-of-year function. The way they work together starts to have an impact on the way they feel.

At the deepest level of engagement, the individuals start to have a meaningful psychological and systemic impact on one another, which affects their psychological make up. This level can be thought of as the depth level. Each individual has an impact on the way the other views and experiences the world at a fundamental level.

Each of the levels mentioned can include the previous levels too, but at the deepest psychodynamic level, human interaction becomes very complex. Simple transactions and cooperation are often no longer possible. Conflict may develop over seemingly straightforward decisions. Power battles may occur. Individuals may feel a great sense of belonging or exclusion, which will affect their motivation. The relationship interaction may help individuals to discover untapped potential in themselves. Potentially, both constructive and destructive outcomes might emerge. Finally, at the deepest level, profound individual and group transformation becomes possible.

These depth processes that occur at the deep level of a group's life have important implications for leadership. With the right knowledge and skills, the leader can help the group to harness the potential of the deep level of interaction so that transformation becomes possible. The leader now has to work at both a surface level (e.g., winning the soccer match, or rolling out the new technology in the organisation) and at the deep level (e.g., helping to resolve the diversity issues and the undeveloped potential caused by a lack of confidence in a team). It is helpful to divide group and systemic processes into two broad categories and to consider each in more detail. We will therefore make a distinction between surface processes and depth processes.

SURFACE AND DEPTH PROCESSES IN GROUPS

Surface processes are the explicit and consciously acknowledged tasks, jobs or processes in an organisation. They are the tasks and ideas that are uppermost in people's minds and that can be discussed openly. Individuals identify with those aspects of their tasks and behaviour that seem most comfortable to them. In business, the surface process may well be to generate revenue, either personally or as an organisation.

Although the surface processes are important, they are only part of the total system. For example, you may be in business primarily to generate revenue, but it could also be an avenue for expressing your creativity. As another example, your surface process right now is reading and understanding the concepts written on this page, but that it is probably not all that is occupying your mind. You might also be involved in several other processes that you may or may not immediately be aware of, such as feeling tired or excited about your plans for your evening. These would be called depth processes.

Depth processes are the processes of which we are not necessarily aware. They refer to interactions and dynamics that are happening beneath the surface of the mind. They include anything that occupies us at a deeper level, but that we may not be paying direct attention to. Depth processes exist because we have a psychological and systemic life beyond our conscious minds and the dynamics caused by the different levels in the psyche result in continual emergent psychological and systemic activity. This may result in conflict between the different parts of a person or system.

The internal conflicts in all of us give rise to dynamic tension in our psyches. Depth processes can be more technically known as psychodynamics and we will discuss them in far more detail in Chapters 3 and 4. Briefly, psychodynamics refers to the deep psychological patterns that play out inside the psyche and between different psyches. At their most basic level, these patterns are linked to the underlying duality in human nature. Most systems have an underlying dilemma or conflict that will play itself out in the functioning of that system. A system can be one individual, a group or team, an organisation, or even a country. Here are some examples of such dilemmas:

- being personal versus being professional
- being people-oriented versus being task-oriented
- being artistic versus being scientific
- being risk averse versus being risk-taking and
- focusing on the individual versus focusing on the group

These dilemmas give rise to the psychodynamic patterns in and between people and may play out as recurring problems and relationship difficulties. For example, the surface process between two people may be that one of them is frustrated because the other is often late. The depth process may be that the one who is often late feels dominated by the other and so the lateness may be an unconscious way of resisting dominance.

A depth approach is one of encouraging groups and teams to engage with both the depth and the surface processes – in other words, to address the system psychodynamics of team functioning. It involves taking the time to discuss the "can of worms" with the knowledge that time spent resolving the psychodynamics often pays rewards in the longer term.

We may be actively avoiding the depth process because it provokes anxiety in some way, or it may lie beneath our conscious awareness for some other reason, which we will investigate in later chapters. These underlying dynamics affect the way an organisation functions, but in a way that is not usually acknowledged or sometimes even noticed by the organisation. These dynamics could be counterproductive unless they are addressed; if they are brought to the surface they could offer the potential for new creativity. However, because they are usually unknown or at least not openly discussed, they provoke anxiety, and most individuals and groups will initially resist them. Paradoxically, they often hold the key to the group's advancement or survival.

DISTINGUISHING BETWEEN SURFACE AND DEPTH LEADERSHIP

At the highest level, one way of thinking is that there are basically two approaches to group leadership. The first is to fulfil the roles of direction setting, planning and execution, where the leader helps a team or an organisation to complete a planned process where the outcome is predefined. This will be described as surface leadership in this book. In this case, the leader's job is to help the team or organisation decide what they would like to achieve and then help them to complete the required tasks as effectively and quickly as possible, ensuring that any distractions are avoided and adhering strictly to the planned process.

The second approach, described here as depth leadership, is helping an organisation to deal with – and benefit from – whatever additional processes may emerge, and in fact ensuring space for these additional processes to come to the surface. The leader then needs to be able to help the group carefully negotiate detours from the planned process in order to ensure completion of the task. Sometimes, a detour is needed to enhance the creativity of the group and, therefore, the quality of task completion. Depth leadership becomes especially necessary when the surface process is hijacked or compromised by other unresolved and usually more hidden processes. In other words, depth leadership can help surface leadership. Problematic dynamics will hamper task achievement but if we can address them, we can unleash a great deal of potential and creativity.

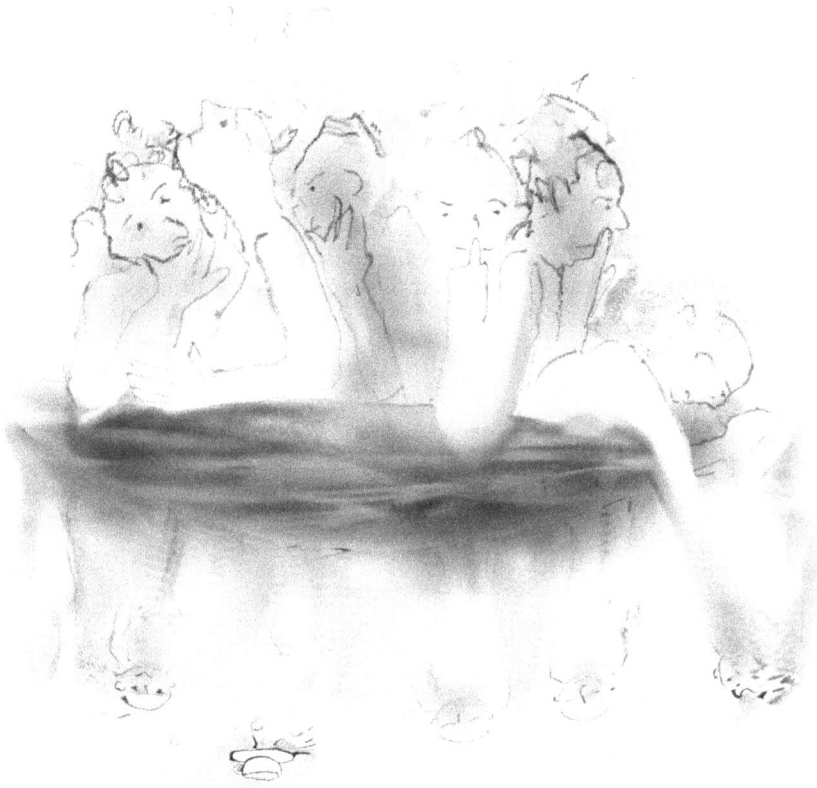

Depth leadership implies that we are working with under-the-surface material. The most important thing about this is that material is under the surface for a reason. The reason for burying issues and ways of seeing them vary in different systems, but there is usually some unspoken injunction or taboo related to discussing or dealing with these issues. Breaking the taboo could be dangerous, but most certainly will feel undesirable or uncomfortable to the majority of group members. Therefore, depth leadership implies working in an area that feels unfamiliar, anxiety-provoking and possibly un-pleasant to people. As a result, this work must be done very carefully and with the explicit consent of the group members. The difficulty with gaining consent is that many people do not understand what it means to work with the under-the-surface material, and so we often have to offer education regarding the nature of the work before we can move into the work itself.

To recap, surface leadership refers to working with the conscious direction and tasks of an organisa-tion, team or group. Its purpose is to help set and meet an objective as quickly and as participatively as possible. An example would be deciding on the brand of new devices to be bought for the sales team. Depth leadership refers to working with a process that is under the surface because it is in some way unacceptable at the surface level. An example would be to address the power struggle in a company, or the need for rest in an overworked team. It could also highlight the need for an opposite, or other, way of being that is not currently supported by the culture of that group – for instance, addressing the underlying fear that exists in an adventure group.

WORKING WITH CAUTION

At this stage it should be clear that depth leadership requires working in uncharted waters for a team. As a result, it is important to take the precautions you would take when entering any unknown territory. Firstly, no one should enter a depth process without the permission of all participants in such a process. This is discussed in more detail later. Secondly, a depth leader must be prepared and equipped with the right skills to manage a process with the appropriate amount of caution. In a sense, depth leadership requires moving behind people's walls – or more technically, behind their defences – which means working in an area where there will be anxiety.

A leader who is intent on reaching a result at all costs will not be sufficiently cautious when moving into a depth process with a team. Remember that if the organisation or team wanted to or knew how to deal with the depth process, it would have done so already. Depth processes are sometimes like radioactive material in the psyche, whether individual or group – something to be handled with extreme care.

Leaders who have not done their own depth work tend to be the most cavalier when taking a team into a depth arena and so can do the most harm. It is important for you as a depth leader to have tapped into and explored your own hidden self, so that you know exactly how disconcerting and disruptive this kind of work is. Exploring one's own unconscious or hidden self is a humbling experience because it means becoming vulnerable and being aware of exactly how defenceless and dependent one can be, even as a functional and apparently in-control adult. Confronting the inner world means facing, enduring and managing anxiety.

This book provides a comprehensive description of the theory, tools and techniques that are needed to work as a depth leader in organisations. It considers the principles and practice of depth leadership in detail. Most importantly, the ideas in this book are designed to emphasise caution above all else. Good leaders work with patience and care, always regarding the needs of the organisation or group as equally, or even more important than their own needs and understand that the leadership task is one of helping to actualise the full potential of the group in its achievement of objectives. It is always important to err on the side of caution. It is never useful to push against a group's resistance with force. A group can only work at its own pace; as one of my students once said in class, "You can't squeeze a banana ripe."

APPROACHES TO DEPTH WORK IN ORGANISATIONS

The depth leadership approach suggested here is based on a variety of theories that are concerned with depth processes in groups and the facilitation of such processes. The main theories include:

- Arnold Mindell's Process Work or Process-Oriented Psychology, based on the work of Carl Jung and systems thinking
- the Tavistock approach, originally based on the work of Wilfred Bion and Sigmund Freud, and
- the work of a broad range of depth psychologists
- my own body of knowledge developed through 35 years of practice

The material in this book draws from as wide a variety of typologies (classifications according to type) and frameworks as possible. The approaches differ in terms of their basic philosophy, and in terms of their methodology. There is a broad split in depth psychology between work based on Sigmund Freud's thinking and that based on Carl Jung's, and this split has carried over to some extent into depth work with groups.

Process Work is Jungian in nature while the Tavistock and group-analytic approaches are more broadly based on Freudian concepts. However, both Process Work and the Tavistock approach have embraced systems thinking – the mindset that developed in the natural sciences at the end of the 20th century, which sees groups as organic, integrated systems, rather than an agglomeration of individuals.

This book does not favour one methodology over another. Rather, it hopes to expose leaders to the strengths of a variety of methodologies, so that they develop a broad-based toolkit.

Ideally, a leader who works at the depth level should subscribe to the equivalent of the Hippocratic Oath for medical practitioners, which is that above all else, you should do no harm. Always remember that the following things may well do harm:

- moving into a depth process without the explicit permission of team members
- moving too quickly into a depth process and
- deciding for the team what it needs to explore or deciding which insights are necessary

DEPTH PSYCHOLOGY EDUCATION

Because of the complex and tricky nature of this kind of work, the group should be prepared as far as possible for its potential experiences. One of the ways of preparing the team for depth work is to provide some education about depth processes. Knowledge about the dynamics of the psyche is not common, although this is changing. The notion of an unconscious mind is still a mysterious idea for many and is not widely accepted as a given. Many people conceive of themselves as only rational and conscious beings who can operate independently within a group and are in full control of their behaviour.

For team members to be better prepared for the unpredictability and unexpected vulnerability that depth work may entail, it is important for them to learn the principles that follow.

- There are processes, thoughts and feelings inside them that they may not know about and may not be able to anticipate.

- They may experience feelings of anxiety and discomfort when dealing with depth material.

- When they are functioning in a group or organisation, they lose at least some of their autonomy over their own responses as they become subject to the group psyche and the larger system.

The extent of depth psychology education varies depending on the group and will be subject to factors such as the scope of the work, the availability of time and money, and the willingness of the group to engage with such education. Even if no separate education process is agreed upon, the leader can include explanations of what may be happening during the process if they may be helpful. Chapters 3 and 4 describe some of the concepts that may be included in any depth psychology education.

CONCLUSION

Depth leadership is a new and evolving field. It does not yet have a comprehensive theory base of its own, and so draws from many related theory bases. To ensure that it is based on a rigorous approach, the roots and underlying assumptions of any leadership practice should be carefully considered. This chapter outlines the important considerations when embarking on depth leadership and emphasises the caution required in this work. Depth leadership can be truly transformative for teams in that it can dismantle destructive patterns and develop latent potential, but only if it is managed with the appropriate care and skill.

PERSONAL EXERCISES

1. Consider the 14 principles behind depth leadership. Do you agree with these principles? Would you add any other principles for your particular philosophy of leadership?

2. Have you done any depth work on yourself? If so, what was particularly rewarding about such work? What was particularly difficult? How does this inform your leadership?

3. Identify some of the leadership challenges you face that may be addressed through the practice of depth leadership.

4. Have you seen anything similar to depth leadership in practice? Was it helpful to the organisation or the group?

CHAPTER
3
DEPTH PSYCHOLOGY – THE INDIVIDUAL

INTRODUCTION

The individual psyche is the foundation from which all individual and group psychodynamics emerge. Therefore, to influence the motivation, effectiveness and progress of organisations and groups from a depth perspective, it is useful for leaders to understand the individual psyche from a depth perspective. This is a complex area of study, and there are many theories that try to explain the functioning of the human psyche and its effect on behaviour. This book does not offer a comprehensive analysis of the various theories, but it does introduce some of the key concepts that will help you to better understand the individual psyche. This chapter considers the psychological development of the individual in more detail from a depth psychology perspective, to help leaders and managers understand not only themselves, but also the members of the groups that they lead.

WHAT IS PSYCHE?

The word psyche comes from the Greek which means life, breath or soul. It can be understood as the mind or the invisible animating entity that occupies the physical body. According to the depth psychologist, Carl Jung, the psyche is the "totality of all psychic processes, conscious as well as unconscious" (Jung, 1971, p. 463). Jung also says that: "The psyche is far from being a homogenous unit – on the contrary, it is a boiling cauldron of contradictory impulses, inhibitions, and affects... (Jung, 1968, p. 104) Therefore, the psyche refers to the complexity that resides in the human mind, the seat of the faculty that results in human behaviour. Psychology is the study of the psyche.

THE PURPOSE OF THE PSYCHE

According to Jung, the human psyche is inherently purposeful, or as he calls it, 'teleological'. The purpose of the psyche, both consciously and unconsciously, is the development of the full potential of the human being. Jung calls this process 'individuation'. The psyche will continue trying to develop and integrate potential parts of the self throughout one's life. The psyche is also a self-regulating system like the body, and it will try to regulate or balance any characteristics or parts that are out of balance.

THE LOGIC OF THE PSYCHE

The human psyche and its functioning can often seem mysterious, but the more we study our psychology, the more it is possible to understand, predict and manage our own behaviour. Depth psychology sheds light on some of the mysterious aspects of human behaviour because it considers the existence and influence of the less conscious drivers of what we as humans do. One of the premises of depth psychology is that human behaviour is fundamentally logical in that there are clear causal relationships between mental processes and behaviour, however the causal relationships are based on subjective experiences, and may not seem objectively logical. Thankfully, although the detail of the logic is subjective and unique, there seem to be certain general mechanisms at work that are useful to understand.

Each person, over time, develops a mental representation of the way the world works based on the proximity and similarity of events and experiences in their life. This mental representation or mental map of the world not only records our experiences, but also influences the way we perceive and therefore experience anything new. This mental map will contain a set of logical paths that organise and group our experiences conceptually and emotionally.

An important aspect of these logic paths is that the mind joins together aspects of experience that are not necessarily closely related in terms of space or time, but rather associated with one another because of psychological similarity. Therefore, a response you have towards an event today may have its roots in events that happened in other places many years ago. Making those links enables you to become aware of associations and therefore identify responses that may no longer be appropriate.

The individual's mental map starts developing in the womb. The first few years are influential because early experiences become the foundation for the mental map. As children live in the world of the caregiver while young, the child will internalise the caregiver's decisions and approaches as the bedrock for their mental map. The child does not distinguish between the caregiver's world and the larger world until later, mainly in adolescence. As the mental map is largely unconscious, the individual also cannot truly distinguish between beliefs that have been absorbed from the caregiver's logic and those that are a result of their own independent discernment about the ways of the world. In other words, the caregiver's logic becomes the logic of the psyche for the child, and therefore the caregiver's logic becomes the psychology of the child.

For example, if a child is exposed to parents who are distant and aloof, the child may expect others to be unapproachable later in life, even when that is not the truth of their behaviour. The child will be reticent and unlikely to approach others naturally; this, in turn, will affect people's availability to the child, who may even appear distant and aloof to them. And so, our early experiences can shape our expectations of and capacity for our later life experiences.

If we are to escape the influences of our early programming, it is useful to understand our early experiences as much as we can, and to reinterpret those through adult eyes. Leaders with a depth orientation will have a reasonable understanding of their own set of logic paths and recognise when they are not appropriate in the present, in their work within their organisations.

THE DEVELOPMENT OF THE PSYCHE FROM A DEPTH PERSPECTIVE

Human development can be viewed as the activation of human potential through interaction with the environment, and the conversion of that potential into character traits that serve individual survival and effectiveness. To understand this process better, it is helpful to consider theory about the nature of human potential.

HUMAN POTENTIAL – ARCHETYPES AND INSTINCTS

Just as trees grow from seeds, a fully-fledged human being develops from a set of 'seeds', or potential ways of being human. Jung introduced the idea that in human beings, these seeds are an inherent set of blueprints or *archetypes*, as he called them, and that these seeds comprise the capacity for the full range of human emotions, thoughts and behaviours. To understand this more easily, we can regard the seeds as containing both our biological and psychological predispositions, or to use more technical language, our instincts and archetypes. Jung defines archetypes as "systems of readiness for action, and at the same time images and emotions" (Jung, 1970, p. 31). He goes on to say that archetypes are not "inherited ideas" but rather "possibilities of ideas", that are not "individual acquisitions" but rather are "common to all, as can be seen from [their] universal occurrence" (Jung, 1968, p. 67). Another way of thinking about an archetype is that it is a "primordial, structural element of the human psyche, an instinctive, universal tendency to form certain ideas and images and to behave in certain ways" (Sharp, 1998, p. 38).

Instincts are the biological versions of archetypes. We are all subject to a set of biological imperatives that drive our behaviour. Psychological thought accepts the existence of inherent instincts in all individuals, but theorists differ about the exact nature and priority of these instincts. The biological blueprints or instincts include, among others, our need for food, shelter, safety, rest and procreation.

TYPES OF ARCHETYPES

Archetypes comprise all potential ways of being human, but it is possible to think of them in different categories to understand them better. The four categories of archetypes are task, political, archetypes and emotional. They can be correlated with the categories of doing, controlling, relating and feeling. These categories are not mutually exclusive or exhaustive; there will be some overlap between them.

1. Task archetypes

Task archetypes refer to the different humans get things done. In many respects, they are the simplest archetype, because they are the clearest, and individuals are usually comfortable discussing them openly. Examples of task archetypes are:

- Cleaner
- Writer
- Programmer
- Creative
- Decorator
- Builder
- Planner
- Designer

- Cook
- Porter
- Troubleshooter
- Coordinator
- Trainer
- Facilitator

2. Political archetypes

Political archetypes refer to the ways of humans relate to power arrangements and politics, including opinions, thoughts and judgements. Often these opinions and thoughts derive from belief systems we formulate in order to better understand and manage the world. The political archetype enables a person to take a particular position on a subject. For example, a conservative archetype would work towards protecting a system in its original state, whereas a revolutionary would work towards transforming that system. Some examples of political archetypes are:

- Autocrat
- Populist
- Democrat
- Liberal
- Conservative
- Rebel
- Feminist
- Activist
- Pacifist

3. Psychological archetypes

Psychological archetypes refer to the different ways human beings have of relating to one another and themselves from an interpersonal and psychological perspective. A psychological archetype will often lie beneath a political archetype, and its roots are most likely to be found in the individual's early history. Psychological archetypes tend to operate in reciprocal patterns. For example, a critic archetype will almost always elicit a victim archetype in another person, and a leader needs a follower in order to lead.

- Critic
- Victim
- Clown
- Rescuer
- Peacemaker
- Disturber
- Perpetrator
- Nurturer
- Protector

- Parent
- Leader
- Follower

4. Emotional archetypes

Emotional archetypes are related to the feelings we have as human beings, which are the ways in which we metabolise and evaluate our experiences. Emotional archetypes are different from the other archetypes in that they cannot be actively chosen, but rather are a result of other choices. In some ways emotional archetypes may be the least spoken of in organisational settings because the expression of emotion may be frowned upon. There may be many defensive processes that prevent the experience and articulation of emotional archetypes. Some of the emotional archetypes are listed below.

- Sadness
- Anger
- Grief
- Jealousy
- Envy
- Affection
- Lust
- Vengefulness
- Bitterness
- Relief
- Anticipation
- Excitement
- Joy
- Love
- Frustration
- Satisfaction

FROM SEED TO CHARACTER TRAIT

As we interact with the world, our seeds or blueprints become activated, and through interaction with the environment develop, personalise, and become part of our experiential and behavioural repertoire. Both our instincts and archetypes will be activated by internal or external stimuli. When they are activated, instincts and archetypes manifest as needs, and will lead to feelings, thoughts and sensations, which then lead to behaviour. The environmental response to our behaviour sets off a process of learning and adaptation. If our initial behavioural expression is approved of, then we learn that the behaviour is positively received by the world, and we are likely to repeat the behaviour. Over time, our blueprints consolidate into behavioural patterns that then become characteristics with which we identify. In addition, individuals will each develop a unique version of these blueprints based on their interactions with the world. For instance, the idea of the hero is an archetype, although individual heroic acts will have a unique flavour. However, sometimes the behaviour is not approved of, and then the psyche must adapt, and the individual must find a different way to meet their needs. This adaptation process results in a divided psyche which is described in the next section.

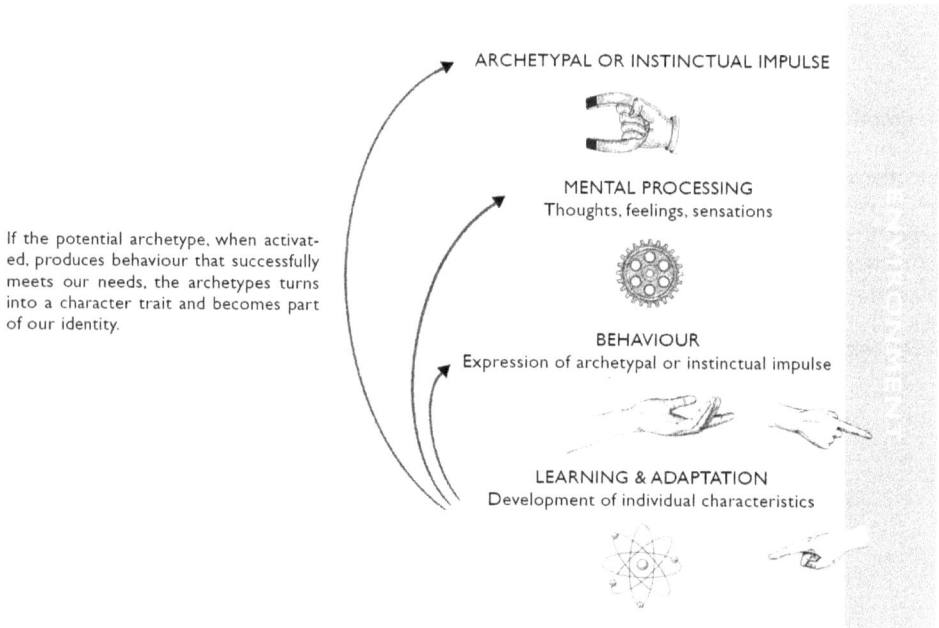

ARCHETYPAL OR INSTINCTUAL IMPULSE

MENTAL PROCESSING
Thoughts, feelings, sensations

If the potential archetype, when activated, produces behaviour that successfully meets our needs, the archetypes turns into a character trait and becomes part of our identity.

BEHAVIOUR
Expression of archetypal or instinctual impulse

LEARNING & ADAPTATION
Development of individual characteristics

FUNDAMENTAL DRIVES – SURVIVAL AND INDIVIDUATION

Sigmund Freud regarded the instinct of self-preservation as a basic human instinct. This is the instinct to take action to preserve one's life in the face of danger. For human infants, survival is dependent on the availability of a capable and willing caregiver. Therefore, to survive, the child and the caregiver need to have an attachment in which the caregiver is committed to caring for the child and protecting them from danger. In other words, for the child, it is imperative to build a relationship with a caregiver in which the caregiver is equally attached, and cares for the wellbeing of the child. Therefore, to fulfil the instinct for self-preservation, the child will be driven to form an attachment with the caregiver and will be strongly motivated to maintain that attachment at all costs. Fortunately, most caregivers will also have an inherent caregiving instinct.

In addition, as mentioned earlier, according to Jung, all humans have a drive towards what he calls individuation. This is the drive that pushes the individual to full psychological development, which means the activation and conscious integration of all the potential instincts and archetypes.

The above two drives, one for survival and attachment and the other for individuation, co-exist in the individual and may sometimes conflict with one another. The impact of this conflict is described in the next section.

CONFLICTING DRIVES IN THE PSYCHE

While the individual develops the archetypal or instinctual potential into behaviours, the responses from the caregivers profoundly influence the way archetypes and instincts are integrated into the person's psychology. The individual is at the mercy of both basic drives simultaneously. If the child must choose between developing an aspect of their potential and maintaining the goodwill of the caregiver, they will be forced to prioritise their survival over the development of their potential. The attachment to the caregiver is necessary for survival, and so the maintenance of the attachment will be the most important driving force in a young child.

Drive to fulfil potential   Drive to survive (and attach)

THERE ARE CONFLICTING FORCES IN THE PSYCHE

As illustrated in the diagram above, our capacity for our full potential (held in our instincts and archetypes) becomes inhibited by our interactions with the world, where we slowly but surely limit our range of conscious and public thoughts, feelings and behaviours to those that are tolerated and/or encouraged by our caregivers and the world around us. In more detail, when the archetypes and instincts are activated, they are expressed as behaviour. If the environmental response to the behaviour is one of disapproval or sanction, the psyche cannot integrate that way of being into the conscious public self and will, therefore, have to find somewhere else to house that aspect of experience. The psyche divides into compartments that house different aspects depending on the level of acceptability or manageability of each way of being human. The psyche creates at least four compartments: the conscious public self, the conscious private self, the unconscious and the persona.

The formation of these compartments is driven by three individual capacities:

1. The first is the capacity to have an experience, to be able to have thoughts, feelings and sensations about a situation experience.

2. The second is the capacity to be aware of that experience, to consciously have the experience.

3. The third is the capacity to express the experience, either verbally or physically or both.

These three capacities can function separately or be combined. We always have the first capacity. However, depending on the degree, intensity, acceptability and manageability of the experience, we have the second and third capacities to a greater or lesser extent. If our experiences are accepted by our caregivers and we are helped to metabolise them when they are overwhelming, then we are able to be both conscious and public about those experiences. If the experience is manageable but rejected by our caregivers when expressed, then we will remain aware of the experience but will keep it private to ourselves and may well develop a mask or persona in which we show a face to the world that has adapted to the world's expectations of us. If the experience is either too over-whelming or seen as unacceptable and rejected, then our psyches will hide that experience from others AND even hide it from our own awareness or consciousness. In other words, the psyche has to create a basement of which the conscious self is no longer aware because its contents are potentially too threatening to the wellbeing, or even the survival of the individual.

This process of hiding something from the self is an ingenious way of coping with a natural impulse that is seen as completely unacceptable by the outside world, particularly to the caregiver. It is im-portant to note, that these compartments are not as simply divided as the diagram suggests. There are a series of complex levels in the psyche. The diagram below is simplified to illustrate the concept and shows the development of the different compartments of the psyche.

DEPENDING ON THE ENVIRONMENTAL RESPONSE, ARCHETYPES ARE ACTIVATED, AND PLACED IN COMPARTMENTS IN THE PSYCHE.

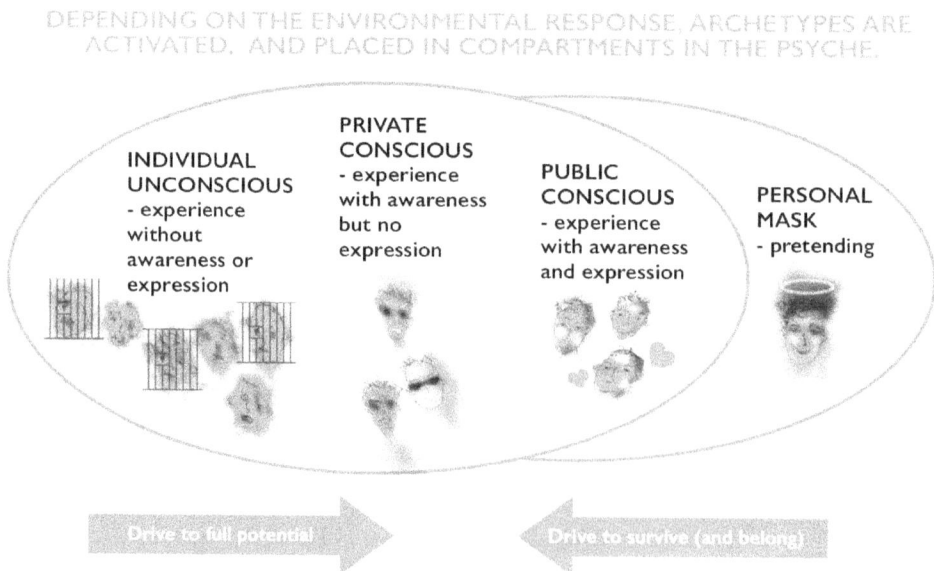

INDIVIDUAL UNCONSCIOUS
- experience without awareness or expression

PRIVATE CONSCIOUS
- experience with awareness but no expression

PUBLIC CONSCIOUS
- experience with awareness and expression

PERSONAL MASK
- pretending

Drive to full potential

Drive to survive (and belong)

According to Jung, the unconscious mind contains:

"Everything of which I know, but of which I am not at the moment thinking; everything of which I was once conscious but have now forgotten; everything perceived by my senses, but

not noted by my conscious mind; everything which, involuntarily and without paying attention to it, I feel, think, remember, want, and do; all the future things which are taking shape
in me and will sometime come to consciousness; all this is the content of the unconscious"
(Jung, 1969, p. 185).

The unconscious also contains any aspect of experience that has been repressed.

The parts that are relegated to the unconscious do not disappear altogether. Instead, they remain
active in the psyche and affect our behaviour. They will appear in our consciousness eventually, often
when we are more able to manage them. Unaddressed, they will escape from the bounds of the
unconscious at unexpected times and cause unpredictable behaviour. Ideally, we need to actively try
to reintegrate these parts by noticing and, in a controlled way allowing them into our consciousness.
According to Jung, we tend to try to recapture the potential of wholeness inherent in our original
being, and the unconscious will, therefore, deliberately remain active in all our relationships, whether we are aware of it or not.

THE ROLE OF ANXIETY

Human anxiety is at the root of most psychodynamic processes. From the moment we are born,
two essential states characterise our being. The first is that we are alive (an obvious but nevertheless
remarkable idea) and the second is that living is not guaranteed. So, life comes with an inbuilt anxiety
about its loss, and this informs the human condition at a fundamental level. We feel anxiety not only
about the loss of life but about anything that threatens a part of the self.

THREAT
Real or perceived internal
or external threat

OUR WHOLE SYSTEM
IS PROGRAMMED TO
DEFEND AGAINST
THREATS AND
ANXIETY.

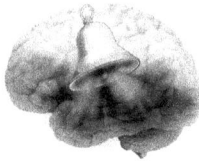

ANXIETY
Activation of a psychological
and/or mental alarm bell
called anxiety

REACTION
Activation of defence
or alternative strategy to
reduce or eliminate the threat

Anxiety is one of the most common human emotions, but it is often hidden or expressed indirectly.
Also, threats to our survival come in many forms. Threats can come from the external world in the
form of disease, violence or accidents. From a psychodynamic perspective, however, internal states
can also be perceived as dangerous. If archetypes are triggered in us that our caregivers would not
approve of, we will experience the internal state as threatening. For example, if we have learnt from
an early age not to be daring, we will experience the impulse to be daring as threatening to our

membership of the family. More technically, survival threats can come in the form of intrapsychic conflict – the conflict between the conscious and unconscious parts of the mind. Potential loss will also trigger anxiety, whether it is loss of a desired object, of love, of identity or of love for the self.

Anxiety can be dealt with in one of two ways.

- It can be dealt with directly by resolving the problem, overcoming obstacles or coming to terms with the loss. This is more likely in the event of an external threat.

- It can be dealt with by distortion or denial in the form of a defence mechanism. This response is likely in the case of internal states that are perceived to threaten our survival.

There are three broad sources of anxiety. Each potentially elicits a defensive response:

- An external threat. This is when the threat to the self comes from the outside in the form of a physical or psychological attack. Our natural response to this threat is to reduce our anxiety by trying to get away from or eliminate the threat. We respond with a natural biological defence mechanism called fight or flight (or freeze). We eventually psychologically internalise perceived threats to our survival.

- An internal threat is when our private self threatens to reveal itself to the public, or there is a risk of exposure of our private thoughts. We respond with a conscious psychological defence mechanism designed to protect us from public exposure.

- An internal threat in the form of unconscious intrapsychic conflict – disturbing thoughts and feelings from our unconscious threatening to come into consciousness. Here we respond with an unconscious psychological defence mechanism such as denial.

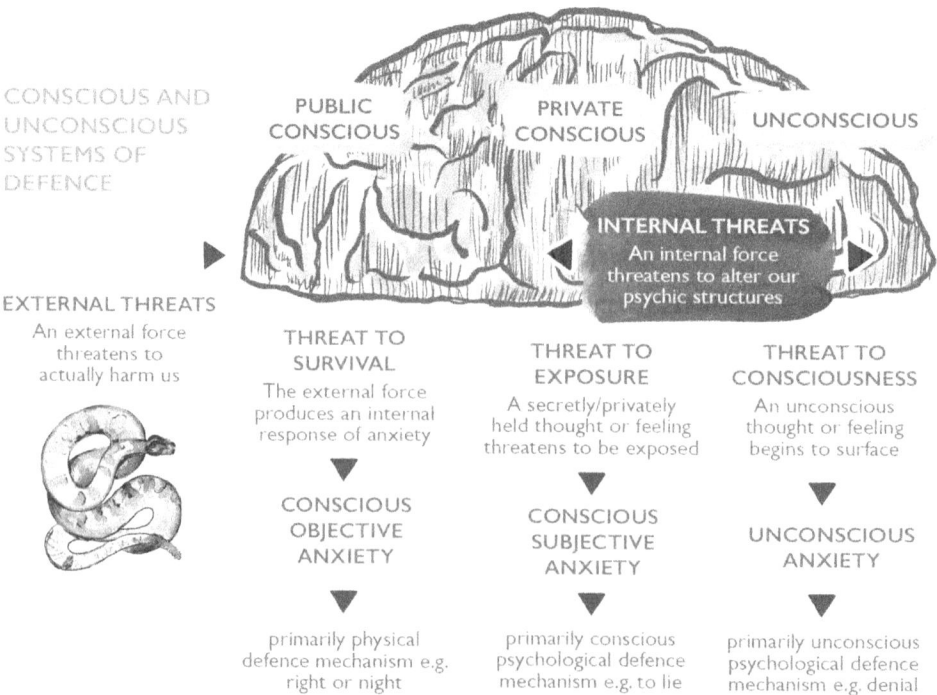

CONSCIOUS AND UNCONSCIOUS SYSTEMS OF DEFENCE

PUBLIC CONSCIOUS

PRIVATE CONSCIOUS

UNCONSCIOUS

INTERNAL THREATS
An internal force threatens to alter our psychic structures

EXTERNAL THREATS
An external force threatens to actually harm us

THREAT TO SURVIVAL
The external force produces an internal response of anxiety

▼

CONSCIOUS OBJECTIVE ANXIETY

▼

primarily physical defence mechanism e.g. right or night

THREAT TO EXPOSURE
A secretly/privately held thought or feeling threatens to be exposed

▼

CONSCIOUS SUBJECTIVE ANXIETY

▼

primarily conscious psychological defence mechanism e.g. to lie

THREAT TO CONSCIOUSNESS
An unconscious thought or feeling begins to surface

▼

UNCONSCIOUS ANXIETY

▼

primarily unconscious psychological defence mechanism e.g. denial

The compartments in the psyche cause continual tension because the split-off ways of being that exist in the unconscious are active, energy-laden entities that need expression. This causes anxiety because the psyche, on the one hand, tries to maintain the compartments to feel safe, but on the other hand, the natural drive for balance and wholeness demands reintegration of the disavowed parts. As a result of these two opposing forces, there is intrapsychic conflict, which is very uncomfortable. The psyche has various ways of trying to lessen the anxiety caused by the conflict, as discussed in the following pages.

The conflict is often characterised by two different and usually opposite ways of being, such as caution versus recklessness, or a task focus versus a people focus, where one way of being is consciously allowed and the other is regarded as unacceptable. Individuals have both archetypal potentialities and each should ideally be developed for use when necessary. For example, we have both the potential to be cautious and to be daring, and each way of being is useful given the appropriate context. However, our parents may favour caution and actively discourage our daring to the extent that we bury our potential and capacity to be daring in our unconscious mind.

INTRAPSYCHIC CONFLICT

The compartments in the psyche cause continual tension because the split-off ways of being that exist in the unconscious are active, energy-laden entities that need expression. This causes anxiety because the psyche, on the one hand, tries to maintain the compartments to feel safe, but on the other hand, the natural drive for balance and wholeness demands reintegration of the disavowed parts. As a result of these two opposing forces, there is intrapsychic conflict, which is very uncomfortable. The psyche has various ways of trying to lessen the anxiety caused by the conflict, as discussed in the following pages.

The conflict is often characterised by two different and usually opposite ways of being, such as caution versus recklessness, or a task focus versus a people focus, where one way of being is consciously allowed and the other is regarded as unacceptable. Individuals have both archetypal potentialities and each should ideally be developed for use when necessary. For example, we have both the potential to be cautious and to be daring, and each way of being is useful given the appropriate context. However, our parents may favour caution and actively discourage our daring to the extent that we bury our potential and capacity to be daring in our unconscious mind.

MINDELL'S CONCEPT OF THE EDGE

Arnold Mindell, a psychologist who started Process-Oriented Psychology (also known as Process Work), defined a concept that describes anxiety and how it works in the psyche. His idea is included here because it provides a useful way of describing and understanding how anxiety functions psychodynamically. Mindell called the internal state that gives rise to anxiety an edge. According to him, an edge is something you cannot bring yourself to say, to think, to do, to feel or to look at because it causes anxiety. One of our edges would be the dividing line between the private and the public parts of our psyche, and another could be the dividing line between the conscious and the unconscious.

We all have different edges – what some of us will comfortably do, others cannot.

Examples of edges

To say: Some kinds of communication can cause anxiety, such as telling people that we are upset with them.

To think:

Some thoughts can provoke anxiety, such as contemplating losing your job.

To do:

Certain actions will provoke anxiety, such as making presentations, engaging in conflict with someone, giving or receiving feedback, or saying no.

To feel:

Certain emotions could provoke anxiety, especially if our caregivers disapproved of those emotions. For example, for some people feeling angry or sad is uncomfortable or provokes anxiety.

To dream:

Visualising or dreaming of some things could cause anxiety. Examples may be moving to a new city or country or dreaming of returning to university to change your career.

To hear:

Receiving certain kinds of communication will cause anxiety such as receiving critical feedback from someone.

To look at:

For many people, looking at certain things provokes anxiety. Some of us find it difficult to make eye contact with others. Many of us are afraid to look at the scene of an accident.

As we approach an edge, our anxiety increases and our internal voices tell us that it would be dangerous to cross the edge. These internal voices are a mixture of reality and perception based on our previous experiences, our culture, our families and our values. We approach an edge because we choose to, or because our life circumstances place us near or over an edge. The edge idea does not imply that all edges should be crossed. Some edges should not be crossed because they are simply too dangerous for that individual. For example, certain comments about the leadership of an organisation may be career-limiting if leaders are not open to feedback.

To move over edges, individuals need support. If leaders are not aware of the edges experienced by individual team members, they can inadvertently push those team members over edges and embarrass or hurt them. It is critical not to push individuals over edges, but rather to support and assist them over an edge. Also, different individuals will approach edges differently. Some leap over edges, others tread slowly. Most individuals are somewhere in between.

There are some ways of crossing edges in an unprepared and uncontrolled manner:

- People may cross edges when under the influence of mind or mood-altering substances. For example, alcohol works as an anaesthetic that silences our internal cautionary voices.

- Strong emotion may cause people to cross edges more quickly and with less preparation than is safe, as the strong emotion could override and silence cautionary voices.

- Peer pressure in groups or crowds may cause people to cross edges too quickly and with too little preparation.

Sometimes, life circumstances push individuals over an edge. Examples include job loss or retrenchment, the death of a loved one, sick children, and the end of a relationship.

REASONS for not crossing the edge in the form of real or perceived internal and external messages cause the anxiety.

Edge symptoms in the form of increased ANXIETY and defence mechanisms appear as the individual approaches or is pushed towards or over an edge.

THE EDGE is something that is hard to do, to say, to feel, to think, or to look at.

SUPPORT AND CONTAINMENT help the individual over the edge.

EDGE BEHAVIOUR

Individuals can decide whether to cross an edge by considering their internal voices and checking which of them are reality-based and which are perceptions. If the internal voices reflect reality, then it is sometimes possible to make contingency plans to avoid those outcomes.

Edges are important for depth leadership because depth processes or psychodynamics are characterised by edge behaviour. It is necessary to recognise when edges are at work. It is possible to notice when an individual is at an edge because certain symptoms of anxiety will be present. Also, the individual may already have started moving towards defending themself from anxiety by moving into a defence mechanism. We will explore defence mechanisms in more detail later. In Chapter 9, we will explore how to safely help individuals and groups move over edges.

The following list may indicate some of the more visible symptoms of anxiety or defences:

- physical symptoms of anxiety such as perspiration or fast breathing
- uncomfortable silences
- mixed messages or double signals (two messages given simultaneously which are conflicting)

- uncharacteristic behaviour

- cycling – going around in circles

- boredom or low energy

- confusion or chaos

- nervous laughter

- incomplete acts or sentences

- gossip or reference to third parties

- anger or frustration and

- withdrawal

DEFENCE MECHANISMS

Defence mechanisms are some of the ways in which the psyche manages the anxiety caused by external threats or intrapsychic conflict. It is important to stress that the presence or use of a defence mechanism is not necessarily dysfunctional and is a natural part of being human. Defence mechanisms, or our defences, have many benign functions. They originate as healthy, creative adaptations that allow us to deal with difficult and stressful periods in our lives. We tend to make use of our defences when we need to manage powerful, threatening emotions or when our self-esteem is feeling threatened. When individuals confront an edge, they usually use defence mechanisms as part of the response to the edge. We also tend to use our defences automatically or without much thought as to what we are doing or saying. We all make use of defence mechanisms at different times, with a greater or lesser awareness of why we are reacting in this way.

There are different levels of defence mechanisms. This is because the type of defence mechanism that an individual develops is related to the general developmental stage at which that person is functioning. The earlier a defence mechanism develops, the more unsophisticated it is. These early defence mechanisms are referred to as 'lower-order' defences. They tend to be used unconsciously and are more likely to remove the existence of a threatening internal state and place it outside of the psyche. Of course, internal states cannot be removed, they can only be buried, but once the defence is active, it will seem to the conscious part of the individual as if the uncomfortable internal state no longer exists within.

The 'higher-order' defence mechanisms that develop later tend to be more mature and are often used more consciously. Rather than remove the uncomfortable internal state, they transform difficult thoughts and feelings into something more palatable or manageable to the individual. The lower-order defence mechanisms tend to be more destructive to our sense of self and interpersonal interactions if used continuously. Ideally, the individual increasingly needs to develop the more constructive, higher-order defences.

THE ROLE OF DEFENCE MECHANISMS

Defence mechanisms remove, reduce or transform threats so that they become more manageable. Defences help the individual reduce, ward off, or escape from external threats. In the case of internal threats, defences expel, bury or transform the threatening aspect of internal responses in order to reduce the anxiety the individual experiences. The following diagram outlines how it works:

Triggers a desire to reduce anxiety and activates a defence

Defence mechanism implemented

ANXIETY

Hides

Produces

unacceptable or unbearable thoughts and feelings

unacceptable or unbearable thoughts and feelings

Reduces

Triggers

Anxiety

SITUATION

Situation becomes manageable

A detailed list of some of the more common defences and their explanations is given in the table on the next few pages. The lower-order defence mechanisms are presented first, followed by increasingly higher-order mechanisms.

Defence mechanisms

Explanation   *Type of defence*

Denial

Distorting our perception of some aspect of   *Tends to be unconscious. Lower order.*
external reality, refusing to accept that something is happening

Repression

Essentially forgetting or ignoring, preventing   *Tends to be unconscious. Lower order.*
painful emotions and memories related to prior
events having an outlet in our consciousness

Splitting

Keeping apart two thoughts or feelings, because   *Tends to be unconscious. Lower order.*
only one can be managed at a time; separating
the world into parts that are either only good
or only bad

Explanation	*Type of defence*

Projection

Attributing our own state of mind, and the internal conflicts it gives rise to, to someone else, thereby freeing ourselves from it

Tends to be unconscious. Lower order.

Conversion

Transforming psychic or emotional conflict into physical symptoms

Tends to be unconscious. Lower order.

Reaction formation

The transformation of a negative, disturbing thought or feeling into a positive, more acceptable response

Tends to be unconscious. Lower order.

Introjection

Attributing the qualities, aspects and feelings of another person to ourselves

Tends to be unconscious. Lower order.

Explanation	Type of defence

Regression

Reverting to former and outgrown behaviours in order to avoid an anxiety-provoking, more mature responsibility, feeling, thought or behaviour

Tends to be unconscious. Lower order.

Displacement

The redirection of an emotion, thought or behaviour from its original object to another less stress-inducing object or person

Tends to be unconscious. Lower order.

Aggression

Resorting to anger when the underlying experience of hurt, fear or vulnerability provokes too much anxiety

Tends to be unconscious. Lower order.

Compensation

Masking a perceived weakness, developing other positive traits to compensate for a weakness

Tends to be unconscious. Lower order.

Explanation

Isolation

Separating the knowing and the feeling out of an experience, such as being able to do something without feeling anything

Can be conscious or unconscious. Lower order when unconscious.

Minimisation

Discounting the actual importance or effect of an object, event or person

Can be conscious or unconscious. Lower order when unconscious.

Suppression

Temporarily removing an unpleasant thought or feeling from our conscious mind

Tends to be more conscious. Higher order.

Rationalisation

Inventing an explanation to justify behaviours or feelings, generally after we have failed to get something we wanted or when something bad has happened

Can be conscious or unconscious. Higher order.

Explanation	*Type of defence*

Intellectualisation

Applying cognitive analysis to threatening emotional content; using theories to manage feelings

Can be conscious or unconscious. Lower order when unconscious.

Sublimation

Finding a creative, useful and socially acceptable way of expressing anxiety-producing impulses and drives

Tends to be unconscious. Lower order.

Humour

Resorting to making jokes or fun about an anxiety producing situation or experience

Can be conscious or unconscious. Higher order when used consciously and constructively.

PROJECTION

Projection is a defence that is so pervasive and has such a great influence on group processes that it is given special treatment here. It is at the root of most of the psychodynamics that happens in groups. Projection is one of the most common defence mechanisms used by all people and one that develops very early in an individual's life. It is the process of attributing our own state of mind, and the internal conflicts it gives rise to, onto someone else, thereby freeing ourselves from it.

The individual may experience an internal state that is intolerable to the self because it represents a significant threat to the psyche. The defence of projection develops in response to the anxiety caused by the internal response or state that is perceived as (or is actually) dangerous to psychic or physical survival.

For example, if a youngster (child) feels angry towards a parent, it may feel too threatening to the relationship with the parent – on whom the youngster depends absolutely – to express or even experience their anger. They bury the anger in the unconscious, but because they cannot fundamentally rid themself of it, it needs to be given away to someone else. Until they can experience (and possibly express) that anger without it seeming or being threatening to their psychic or physical survival, it will have to be projected onto someone outside of themself. Projection happens automatically, unknown to the person doing the projection and seeing the projected qualities in another person.

Similarly, projection can be found in the workplace. For instance, an employee might be exceptionally hardworking, to the extent that they are unable to rest appropriately. They may have learnt to ignore their need to rest because of tough circumstances early on in their life. The need to rest is lodged in their unconscious and regarded as an unacceptable impulse. As a result, they are likely to be critical of other employees who seem less hardworking and may refer to them as lazy. Their unconscious need to rest is projected onto the other as laziness and is attacked as such – with negative effects on team dynamics.

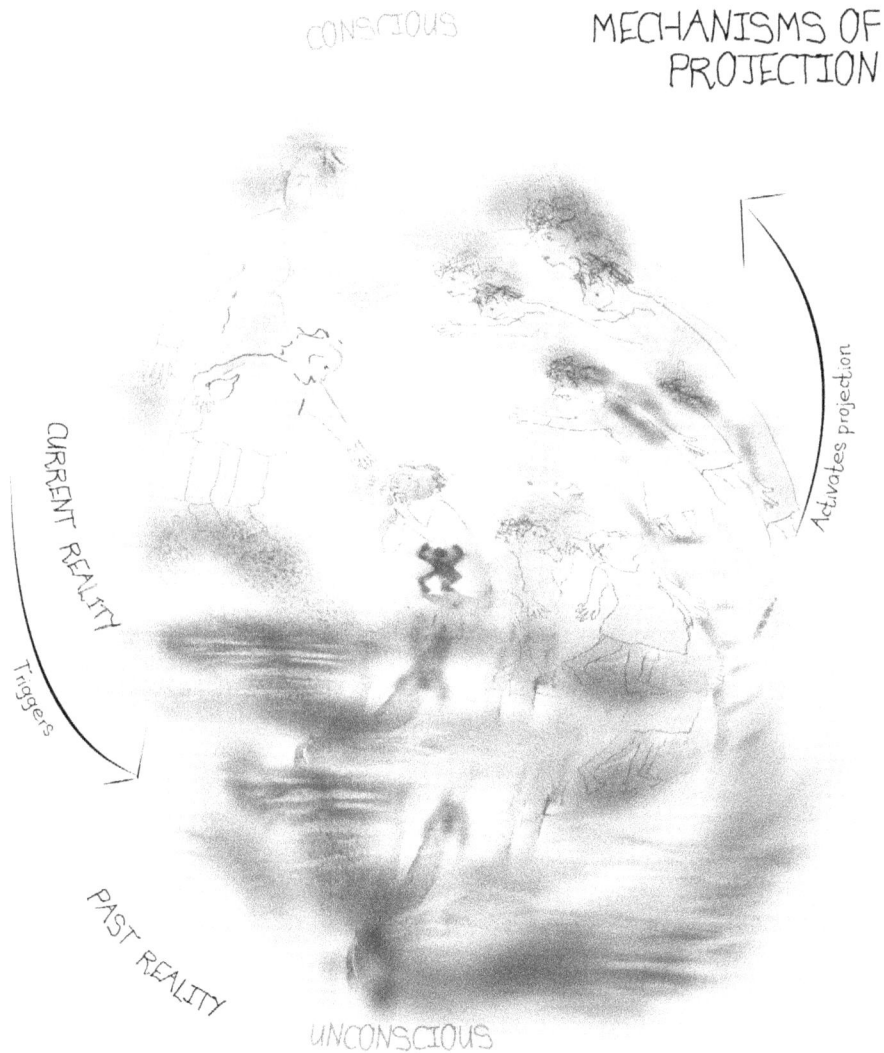

CONSCIOUS

MECHANISMS OF PROJECTION

Activates projection

CURRENT REALITY

Triggers

PAST REALITY

UNCONSCIOUS

There are two different kinds of projection, namely positive and negative projection. Negative projection is when a quality that is regarded as undesirable is projected onto another person. Negative projection can cause great interpersonal conflict. We project because we cannot integrate the quality directly and therefore experience the projected quality as intolerable in the other person. Positive projection is when we do not allow a positive quality in ourselves (possibly because our early circumstances did not allow or value such a quality) and we then see an exaggerated version of that quality in someone else. In a sense, we fall in love with the quality in another person and then suffer huge disappointment when we discover that he or she is simply human and has qualities other than the projected one. This often happens between followers and a new leader. The leader is unconsciously given all the undeveloped positive leadership qualities in the followers, who then admire the leader in an exaggerated way. The leader may then reveal his or her clay feet, much to the disappointment of the followers.

The practical mechanism of projection can be described as follows. An individual will find themself in a current situation where a person or event may trigger a past situation that in some way resonates with the present. The experience of the past situation is unconsciously superimposed on the experience of the present. The individual will project thoughts and feelings from the past onto the people and events in the present.

A good indication that projection is present is when the intensity of the feeling seems incongruent with the situation in some way. In other words, our reactions towards people on whom we have projected certain qualities will seem extreme to others not caught in the projective process in the same way.

PROJECTIVE IDENTIFICATION

Another defence mechanism worth a special mention is that of projective identification. This is a defence that occurs between two people where one is projecting a way of being onto the other and is doing it so effectively – or the other person is so susceptible to experiencing the projected quality – that a dynamic evolves where the receiver of the projection starts experiencing the quality that is being projected.

For example, someone may have felt harmed by their critical mother. The feelings were so intense that they buried them in the unconscious part of their psyche. Unconsciously, as a defence against their own intense and unbearable feelings of being victimised, they become extremely critical of their partner. The partner starts feeling like a helpless victim of the criticism, and as if they are not good enough themself. The two are in the grip of projection and projective identification. This dynamic may be strengthened by the fact that the partner may have had a very critical father and is, therefore, susceptible to feeling criticised but has consciously not identified their own internalised and self-critical nature. They, in turn, project the critical part onto the first partner, and through a process of projective identification, the first partner behaves even more critically towards them. For this type of dynamic to be broken, at least one of the parties must become conscious of the feelings that have been buried within.

A similar scenario could play out in the workplace. Say, for example, a person had a very critical parent who never trusted them to do anything. Years later, in the workplace, they become a manager who needs to delegate a task but constantly feels the need to check on the staff member who has been given the task. They will keep their eye on everything, checking and double-checking all the time. If the staff member has their own history of being continually criticised or micro-managed, the two of them will get hooked into an uneasy dance in which one is the criticiser, and the other is the victim.

Projection and projective identification often work hand in hand. In this example, the manager projects their own anxiety that the staff member is not going to get things right, and the employee absorbs through projective identification the idea of not being good enough. At the same time, the employee projects their inner critic onto the manager and through a process of projective identification the manager behaves even more critically towards the employee. Again, as in the couple example above, at least one of the parties must become conscious of the feelings that have been buried within for this type of dynamic to be broken.

MECHANISMS OF PROJECTIVE IDENTIFICATION

Produces anxiety

Activation of a defence mechanism to reduce anxiety by psychologically getting rid of problem feelings or thoughts

Triggers unacceptable or unbearable thoughts or feelings

Person B displaces unbearable or unacceptable feelings and thoughts through projection onto Person A

THREATENING SITUATION, PERSON(S) OR EVENT

Expresses thought, feeling and resultant behaviour in the situation which reinforces the initial projection

Produces absorption of projection known as projective identification. Starts experiencing the projected thought or feeling as their own

Person A has an inclination and capacity to experience the unacceptable or unbearable thoughts and feelings as a result of previous experience

TRANSFERENCE AND COUNTERTRANSFERENCE

Transference is a particular case of projection over time, used to describe the unconscious emotional bonds that are formed between two people in a long-standing relationship. It refers to the transfer of an entire relationship that originally belonged elsewhere, such as to a mother or a father, to a different authority figure later in life.

Transference is a phenomenon that can occur in the workplace too. It is very likely that team members will experience either positive or negative transference towards a leader. Simplistically, the leader is either seen as the perfect parent, or the terrible parent. The transference relationship will be experienced as reality although it is not the truth of the situation. In Chapter 6, leaders are helped to reduce the negative impact of transference.

Countertransference is where the target individual for the transference starts identifying with the nature of the projection and behaving in accordance with it. This is a great risk for you as a leader because you can get unconsciously hooked and start responding to someone in accordance with their transference. For example, if someone is looking for a parental nurturing figure, you may start feeling compelled to provide more nurturing than would be appropriate for the professional nature of the relationship.

THE IMPACT OF TRAUMA

In addition to the complexities of normal psychological development described above, human beings may also experience trauma, which can be thought of as the mental, emotional, and physiological impact on the person of extreme stress. Trauma comes in many different forms. It can be a single event such as an accident, or it can be a chronic pattern such as dealing with long-term illness. Emotional neglect or abuse in relationships are also traumatic. Some types of trauma may not be recognised, such as surgery, a humiliating experience or the ending of a relationship.

COMPLEXES

According to depth psychologists, a complex is an emotionally charged group of ideas or images. The human psyche is made up of complexes. They are clusters of ideas, feelings and experiences that develop around our original archetypes. Complexes develop over years and centre around certain images, such as those of mother, father, money, power and so on, and arise from our experiences. Trauma affects psychological structures. Depending on our life stories, if we are exposed to trauma, the affected complexes become problematic, and the result is described below.

AUTONOMOUS COMPLEXES

A problematic complex is one that is usually at least partially unconscious and is referred to as an autonomous complex by Carl Jung. The activation of a problematic complex is always marked by the presence of some strong emotion, whether it is love, rage, hate, jealousy, or joy. We all have problematic complexes, which is to say that we all react emotionally when the right buttons are pushed. We cannot rid ourselves totally of our complexes because they are deeply rooted in our personal history. An autonomous complex is one which is functioning beyond consciousness and when triggered, takes control of the psyche. It is emotionally charged because it is usually the result of early trauma or wounding. For example, if we were abandoned by a parent at an early age, we may have an autonomous complex around abandonment and any significant separation thereafter may be experienced as unusually emotionally charged. Autonomous complexes operate as land mines in the human psyche. They can be triggered by present-day events that resemble the trauma from the past, and when they are triggered, the individual may implode or explode as a result. The following experiences, among others, are trauma examples that can result in autonomous complexes or land mines which can be triggered:

Loss

Abandonment

Financial difficulties

Abuse

Humiliation

Bullying

Race and gender discrimination

Other forms of discrimination

Failure

Self-esteem difficulties

Criticism

Betrayal

Political injustice

Violence

Conflict

Social rejection

IMPACT OF TRAUMA CAUSES LANDMINES OR TRIGGERS IN THE PSYCHE

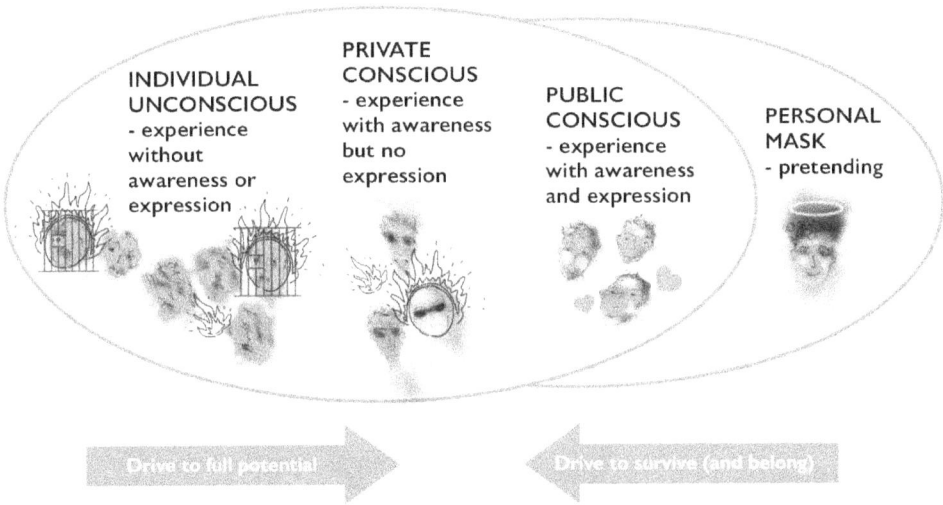

INDIVIDUAL UNCONSCIOUS - experience without awareness or expression

PRIVATE CONSCIOUS - experience with awareness but no expression

PUBLIC CONSCIOUS - experience with awareness and expression

PERSONAL MASK - pretending

Drive to full potential

Drive to survive (and belong)

HEALING TRAUMA AND AUTONOMOUS COMPLEXES

Trauma can be healed by a careful process of treatment, and there are a variety of treatment methodologies available. The book The Body Keeps the Score by Bessel van der Kolk (2014) offers a comprehensive guide to understanding and treating trauma.

At a high level, it helps to become aware of how our history affected us, how complexes and autonomous complexes developed in us, how they influence us and how they interfere with our conscious intentions. As long as we remain unconscious of them, we are prone to being overwhelmed or driven by them. When we understand them, they lose their power to control us. Other people may inadvertently trigger one of our land mines and we will overreact without them understanding the strength of our response. Group psychodynamics are often driven by the interaction between individual or group land mines, where parties may explode or implode and so hamper the relationship. Organisations or even countries could have autonomous complexes that function collectively. For example, a retrenchment process in an organisation could become an autonomous complex for everyone who remains behind, and a political policy such as Apartheid, which wounded a whole nation, could be a land mine in the national psyche. It is unrealistic to expect groups to be able to move on from historical wounding without an active healing process.

REPETITION COMPULSION

The last concept relating to a depth perspective of the individual psyche that we will discuss here is that of 'repetition compulsion', a term coined by Sigmund Freud. It refers to the psychological tendency of human beings to repeat patterns of early distress, trauma or wounding in later situations. Carl Jung developed the idea further by noticing that this behaviour is purposeful because it is, in fact, an effort to heal the original wounding. In other words, we unconsciously recreate certain situations in an attempt to rewrite the original situation and its painful outcome. Friends, partners and colleagues become unwitting characters in a drama played out by the psyche, where individuals other than the original participants in the wounding become actors in a reenactment of early prob-lematic interactions and relationships.

This is a largely unconscious process but will trigger strong and often inexplicable responses in a context that is similar to, but obviously different from, the original context. Projection plays a sig-nificant role in this process because representatives for members of the original cast of characters have to be selected from the available members in the new situation. Our complexes will usually be driving forces behind our repetition compulsion.

Repetition compulsion means that individuals will be attracted unconsciously to participate in dys-functional behaviour patterns in groups. This participation fulfils the need for the reenactment of a historical situation that was psychologically wounding, hoping that the reenactment will transform the outcome of the situation to a more positive one.

In the workplace, for instance, an employee may come from a background where their opinion was not taken seriously by a parent. The employee may unconsciously choose a job where the leader is dismissive of the suggestions of team members. Although the employee unconsciously hopes that, this time, they can get the authority figure to take them seriously and consider their opinion, the likelihood is that their viewpoint will continue to be ignored. This is because the element of repetition compulsion has led them unconsciously to select an authority figure who is unlikely to be persuaded.

Unless an individual can become conscious of the repetition compulsion process, they are often doomed to repeat the pattern in various settings for a long time. Depth leaders will most likely encounter repetition compulsion in themselves and in the groups that they lead. Understanding the associated psychodynamics will often help to resolve chronic interpersonal difficulties.

THE ROLE OF DREAMS

Dreams are the main vehicle for the expression of unconscious experience, and it is necessary for depth work to actively try to remember and make sense of our dreams. This is a difficult and some-what mysterious process, as the unconscious mind communicates symbolically and metaphorically. In other words, our internal dream maker is a poet and will use a variety of poetic strategies to alert us to the parts of ourselves that we are not conscious of. These strategies cannot be too direct, as we will struggle to hear about experiences that we have defended against because they threaten our perceived psychological and social survival. Our dreams will offer both scenarios and feelings which indirectly articulate aspects of our experience that we may not be in touch with consciously.

Dream symbolism is drawn mainly from personal experience and associations, although there are collective elements in all our dreams. Analysing and making sense of our dreams requires paying attention to all the associations we have with the dream figures, events, stories, feelings and symbols that appear. It is important to return to the dream again and again and flesh out all the associations with the dream material rather than follow a tangent of free association. Further discussion about working with symbols and meaning is offered in Chapter 8. It is beyond the scope of this book to offer a definitive guide to dream analysis, but it is important to note that dreams are an essential source of intelligence and information. We, as depth leaders, need to actively pay attention to our own dreams, and be respectfully curious about dreams that others share, without imposing our own interpretations.

THE ROLE OF THE BODY

In addition to the psychic world of dreams, our bodies are also important vehicles for our psyches to express conscious and unconscious experiences. Body sensations and symptoms are often a somatic expression of our deeper processes, and awareness of and reflection about bodily expression can reveal important insights and expose personal blind spots. Our physiology and psyches are inextricably linked and work in unison to try to achieve homeostasis in our systems. When we are one-sided or out of balance, the psyche and the body will try to alert us.

Body sensations and symptoms can be viewed through a symbolic lens but will also be direct expressions of the impacts of our decisions and experiences, and so need to be understood both concretely and symbolically. Often, dreams and body symptoms will be connected, and this deserves notice and attention, as the whole system is trying to communicate a situation that we need to become consciously aware of. For example, a person may become aware of a loud heartbeat, and then a dream symbol appears that mimics the sound of the heartbeat, such as the playing of a drum. Or an individual may be aware of a headache, and then dream of a vice tightening around their skull. More information is given about making sense of symbols in Chapter 8.

CONCLUSION

The individual psyche is a complicated system with conscious and unconscious aspects. It is affected by inner conflict, and much of that inner conflict can be unconscious. The inner conflict causes anxiety, which in turn leads to defence mechanisms. The split in the psyche also leads to interpersonal complications caused by phenomena such as transference, complexes and repetition compulsion. In later chapters, guidelines and steps will be given for addressing these psychological phenomena.

As a leader striving to uncover the buried potential in individuals and groups within your organisation, you need to be aware of the complexity of your own psyche and be able to work with the complications caused by psychic complexity in yourself and in others. If necessary, this may involve getting specialist help.

PERSONAL EXERCISES

1. Consider your own psyche. Are you aware of the different compartments in your mind?

2. Make a list of characteristics with which you consciously identify. In other words, describe your main character traits. Consider the opposite of these character traits. May these undeveloped character traits be useful to you in some way? What parts of yourself may you not have developed because they would not have been supported by the key people in your early environment? Would it be useful to develop some of these characteristics now?

3. Consider your own edges and defence mechanisms. Are there particular areas that you need to address to improve your leadership? Develop a strategy for addressing these areas.

4. Consider how you manage anxiety and identify the symptoms you display to others when you are anxious. What can you do to calm yourself down when you are anxious?

5. Practice observing the edges and defence mechanisms that others around you use. Keep in mind that most people are not aware of their edges and defence mechanisms.

6. Identify any complexes that you are aware of in yourself. Notice whether you may be caught in a process of repetition compulsion where you continually place yourself in an upsetting situation in the hope of being able to produce a better outcome.

7. If you are not already doing so, pay attention to your dreams. Start a dream journal and spend time trying to make sense of the stories, figures and symbols in your dreams. Work with a depth therapist if needed.

8. Pay attention to your body symptoms and sensations and how they change over time. Look out for dreams that may be associated with these bodily experiences. Spend time making sense of the expression of your body.

9. Identify further areas of depth work that you would like to pursue.

CHAPTER

4

DEPTH PSYCHOLOGY – THE GROUP

INTRODUCTION

This chapter considers the functioning of groups from the perspective of depth psychology. It considers some of the general psychological principles in groups, and then discusses the way the group manages the tensions between the various aspects of itself. It considers the way the group plays out its psychodynamics through the allocation of roles to individual group members, as well as the impact of power and privilege on these dynamics.

WHAT IS A GROUP?

The concepts in this chapter form a foundation of knowledge that a leader must understand to manage groups well from a depth perspective. The concepts add up to a multilevel, multifaceted view of what groups are and, as a result, of how they work. Process and structure are inextricably linked. In organisational settings, a group is a collection of individuals who have gathered to execute an explicit task or tasks, or to achieve explicit goals. There are also emerging groups who do not explicitly gather for task execution or goal achievement, but nevertheless end up functioning as if they did.

In more detail, a group is any collection of people who:

- perceive and identify themselves to be a group
- are psychologically aware of one another
- interact with one another on a regular basis
- have interdependent relationships with one another
- have a shared, clear idea of what distinguishes members from nonmembers and
- are recognised as a group by non-members

In a corporate setting, for instance, a group could be anything from an entire organisation of 20,000 people under the leadership of the CEO, to twelve members of the board or even just three participants in a conflict resolution meeting. It could be a small, specific group such as a nursing team in the intensive care unit or a larger, more composite group consisting of all the medical and administrative staff in a hospital. The discussion in this chapter about group dynamics would apply equally to all such groups.

THE NOTION OF THE GROUP PSYCHE

Many theorists (including Wilfred Bion and Arnold Mindell) have discussed the phenomenon that when a collection of individuals comes together as a group, they in fact become part of something that has been called the group mind, the collective mind, or the group psyche. In practice, this means that in a group, you are no longer dealing simply with the individuals and their psychological processes, but with an additional entity, a new being, with its own conscious and unconscious processes. The group behaves as a single psychological unit and uses the individual members to play out the different parts of the group mind.

Attempts to deal with the individual members on their own could cause further problems in the group or might not solve the group difficulties that may exist. The group will unconsciously use different members to play different roles or different aspects of the group psyche, and to a relatively large extent, individual autonomy may be lost.

Many individuals will struggle with the notion of their potential subjugation to the will of the group mind. It is nevertheless essential that as a depth leader, you view and work with groups as entities in their own right, in addition to interacting with the individuals themselves.

TYPES OF GROUPS

The two broad types of groups in organisations are:

- Formal groups – These are explicitly constituted in organisations to fulfil specific tasks clearly related to the overall organisational purpose. These groups can be either temporary or more permanent.
- Informal groups – These groups emerge informally because of psychological, political and other alliances.

Both types of groups are subject to the group dynamics discussed in this chapter. Often informal groups are not explicitly managed or led because they are not explicitly recognised as having an impact on the achievement of organisational tasks. However, informal groups can be immensely powerful and significantly affect an organisation's functioning. For example, a group of employees may meet outside of the work environment for social or other reasons, such as sport or religion. The interactions in these social gatherings may lead to informal decision-making about organisational activities that are then implemented with a formal process.

FUNCTIONS FULFILLED BY GROUPS

Groups fulfil many functions in organisations and society. It is important to recognise that there are formal organisational functions and more informal psychological functions. In fact, leading groups successfully rely on recognising that the psychological functions are sometimes far more important to the individual than the organisational ones.

The formal organisational functions of groups include:

- working on complex, interdependent tasks;
- generating new ideas or creative solutions;

- offering liaison or coordinating functions;
- providing problem-solving mechanisms;
- facilitating the implementation of complex decisions; and
- serving as vehicles of socialisation or training.

The more informal, psychological functions of a group for the individuals include:

- meeting affiliation needs (the need for attachment);
- strengthening and confirming an individual's sense of identity;
- maintaining self-esteem;
- serving as a vehicle for establishing and testing our perceptions of reality;
- offering a psychological holding environment or container which reduces insecurity and anxiety;
- reducing a sense of powerlessness and enhancing the individual's power;
- offering a problem-solving, task-accomplishing mechanism for the individual;
- serving as a lobbying mechanism;
- serving as a vehicle for the individual's projections; and
- providing a place to re-enact unresolved childhood psychodynamics.

Often, group members will stay in an organisational setting because their psychological or emotional needs are being met, even though their job satisfaction needs are not being met. A depth leader may need to recognise and address this to ensure optimal group functioning.

THE GROUP CONTEXT

Understanding the group context is critical when leading a group because the group's behaviour will be dictated largely by the nature of the context. The following systems need to be considered when building an understanding of the group context:

- the global situation in all its aspects;
- the political environment;
- the economic environment;
- the technological environment;
- the natural environment;
- the cultural system in which the group functions;
- any hierarchical systems, including class systems, that operate in the surrounding environment;
- the religious environment;
- the history of the group;
- the industry sector;
- the region in which the group operates;
- the organisation of which the group is a part;
- the department in which the group operates;
- other related departments; and
- the organisation's client group and key stakeholders (if any).

When thinking about these systems, we need to consider the major events and trends in each system. The human psyche – whether individual or group – continually anticipates, monitors and evaluates the events and trends of the context to better position itself for survival. Behaviour is, therefore, context-dependent, and the system's psychodynamics will reflect the psychodynamics of the larger systems within which it functions.

THE GROUP HISTORY

Part of the group context will be its history. Each group will have a history that will predispose it to certain experiences or outcomes in almost a mythical way. For example, if a group has a history of surviving multiple retrenchments, its members may stick together psychologically in the same way as the survivors of a natural catastrophe may do. The history will include both trends over time and critical events or incidences. Of course, all human beings share a common ancestry of being human, so we have all the archetypal possibilities available to us. In other words, all the human stories of our history as a species may be part of how we function today.

However, a particular group history will predispose us to a certain set of archetypal behaviours and, therefore, a particular set of psychodynamics. For example, if the group has a history of oppression, then the behaviours of oppression and submission or rebellion will be part of its psyche and play out during depth processes in the group. The way a group story unfolds will always be connected to the history of the group, and so the history is significant in understanding and processing depth material.

Knowing the group's history will help the leader to anticipate and identify possible psychodynamics. As an example, in South Africa, whether everyone likes it or not, groups share the history of

Apartheid. Often group members will dissociate themselves from an aspect of the history and insist that they have moved on. Whatever the history, however, it is an integral part of the identity of the group and needs to be kept in the leader's mind.

GROUP COMPLEXES

One of the important aspects of group history is that the group may have experienced traumatic events or wounds in its past that may have scarred the group psyche. This type of scarring is referred to as a group complex. A complex is an emotionally charged group of ideas or images. As we saw in Chapter 3, a complex in an individual arises from their experiences over the years and centres on images like mother, father, money, power, and so on. We also saw that strong emotions (love, rage, hate, jealousy, etc.) accompany the activation of a problematic complex. Individuals cannot get rid of their complexes because these are deeply rooted in their personal history, but they can become aware of and less influenced by them.

Just as individuals have complexes, so do groups. It is important for the leader to recognise that complexes are part of group functioning. As mentioned above, Apartheid was part of South Africans' group history, and therefore it is also a complex in the South African group psyche – an area of wounding or trauma in the collective psyche that predisposes South Africans to strong emotion, and affects the group functioning. The Holocaust is a complex in the German psyche. The events of 9/11 form a complex in the American psyche. Group complexes will play themselves out in the psychodynamics of the group and will need attention from a depth leadership perspective.

THE GROUP FIELD

The group context, history and complexes will determine the group field. The group field is the psychological, mental and emotional force field that exists in the group and is derived from the entire set of systems that have an impact on it. This force field will be made up of all the archetypal energies at work in the system. These energies will play themselves out in the group and will influence patterns of behaviour significantly. In other words, the group field determines the psychodynamics of the group.

An example is a group functioning within an organisation that is making a consistent financial loss. This group will be psychologically and practically affected by that context, even if the group itself may be a profitable unit within the organisation. The group will define itself and derive its identity, at least to some extent, from the identity of the larger system.

It is useful if you, as the leader, have some idea of the group field and potential archetypal energies at work. This information may not be apparent initially but will certainly make itself known over time to an alert observer.

PSYCHOLOGICAL LEVELS IN GROUPS

We have considered the superstructures that operate in group life, such as the group context and, therefore, the systems surrounding the group. It is also important to consider the psychologically coherent systems that operate within the group because these are similarly multileveled.

For our purposes, there are three sets of psychological systems operating in a group: the group psyche, the individual psyches of the members, and the subgroups. As a leader, you need to keep all three levels in mind and attend to the interrelationships between them. Ultimately, as a leader, you are attending to the group psyche, but you cannot do this successfully if you are not also attending to the other two levels. Special aspects of each of the three levels are discussed in more detail below.

1. THE GROUP PSYCHE

The group functions as a psychologically integrated unit in which the individual members become subject to the larger psyche of the group. Individual group members will, of course, have distinctive psyches, but the human psyche is a permeable and flexible system, and it easily combines with other psyches to form an integrated larger whole.

This means that the individual psyche is significantly affected by the larger group of which it is part. We can assume that we are both agents and puppets when functioning in groups. Many individuals claim that they can maintain their psychological and practical independence in a group, but this is manifestly not the case. Just as individual rivers become indistinguishably part of the sea, so individual psyches become part of a larger group psyche. The difference between an individual psyche and a river is that the individual psyche can re-form after the group. However, for the time that the individual is part of the group, the individual psyche is unlikely to function completely autonomously.

The role the individual plays in the group is determined by their particular tendency to embody one of the archetypal energies at work in the group. Individuals develop characteristic preferences. Depending on the other members and their availability to take up a particular characteristic of the group, the individual will be used by the group to fulfil a particular psychological or practical purpose. Individuals are often not aware of their role tendencies or of how the group may use their capacity for a certain role. In fact, the whole notion of playing a role for a group may be a foreign idea. This idea is discussed in more detail later in this chapter.

For individuals to work successfully using the perspective of roles, it may be important (if possible and you feel equipped to do so) to offer some education regarding these psychological ideas. If you are working with a group in which the members particularly want to learn about group consciousness and how it works, then it is critical to offer psychological education, or to find someone who can do so. With more knowledge about how groups work and how their own role tendencies operate, individuals can reflect on their behaviour in the group and then it becomes possible to operate less as a puppet and more as an agent. The more clearly one can see the psychodynamics at play, the easier it becomes to develop healthier patterns of interaction.

In order not to be sucked into the undertow of the group psyche, any individual needs to maintain a reflective capacity. This is obviously particularly important for the leader because leading a group successfully at all levels demands a certain measure of psychological independence.

The work of Wilfred Bion was groundbreaking in that it introduced the idea of the group psyche and the idea that individuals have tendencies (or 'valencies', as Bion termed them) for certain roles in the group psyche. We will look at this in more detail later. The Tavistock tradition, which is based on the work of Bion, emphasises a focus on the 'group-as-a- whole', but it is important not to focus on the group-as-a-whole to the exclusion of the individual. The individual psyche still exists and needs to be cared for in a group situation. If the leader focuses only on the group, ignoring the individual psyche, it can become extremely stressful for the individual – and this can be counterproductive to the group process.

2. THE INDIVIDUAL PSYCHE IN THE GROUP

The individual psyche is one of the subsystems of the group but needs special treatment because it operates as a psychologically coherent subsystem. There is a trend in some group leadership approaches where the individual is regarded as merely instrumental in the group psyche, and therefore all individual behaviour is treated as an expression of the group psyche. It is true that the individual is expressing an aspect of the group psyche but remember, ultimately, the individual psyche has to remain intact beyond the group's life. A leadership approach that depersonalises the individual completely may be useful in a training situation where individuals are learning about group life but is not desirable in general leadership situations.

Therefore, the challenge for leaders is to manage the tension between treating the individual as an individual in their own right and simultaneously remembering that the individual is operating as an aspect of the group psyche. The individual must be treated as an individual, but not necessarily as a special individual in the group.

3. SUBGROUPS

All groups are part of larger groups (the largest being the entire human race) and any group larger than two members will have the tendency to divide itself further into subgroups. Group power relations and group dynamics will influence the nature of this subdivision and these mechanisms will be discussed in more detail later. Unlike the individual psyche, the subgroups need to be managed only as part of the group as a whole. Subgroups will try to demand special attention from a leader. Although this may be practically impossible not to give, as in the case of a leadership subgroup, it is important for the leader to remain psychologically equally attentive to all the subgroups. Subgroups represent aspects of the group psyche and it is important to maintain an integrated view of subgroup functioning. It is sometimes tempting to be drawn into a subgroup, especially if you identify with certain aspects of it, but it is important for leaders to guard against this.

THE GROUP IDENTITY

The group identity will be formed by a complex set of factors. The group will overtly identify with the explicit context and task of the group, but there will also be an emergent identity based on its psychological development and the psychological needs that it meets for the individuals. Often, this emergent identity will become more important than the explicit identity. This is because the emergent identity will resonate unconsciously, often with deeply held unconscious needs, and may well be more powerful than the explicit identification. For example, a group of miners may all come from a particular cultural group, and their cultural identity may be more important to them than the identity of their mining shift teams.

As a depth leader, it is helpful for you to assist the group with integrating their explicit and implicit identities as much as possible. In later chapters, we discuss how the emerging identity can be brought to the surface so that the group may identify more consciously with all aspects of itself.

GROUP POWER

Many things determine a group's power, particularly the sum of the power held by individual members and the combination of the variables of the group in its context. A research and development group, for instance, will be powerful if the larger organisation is in need of new technology. That same group will lose its power in an organisation where the current technology is very profitable.

The larger the group, the more powerful it is, both in terms of its own members and the surrounding systems. However, the sheer number of members is not sufficient to determine the levels of power. Other factors such as economic clout, intellectual levels, education levels, access to force and psychological influence will add up to determine the power of the group.

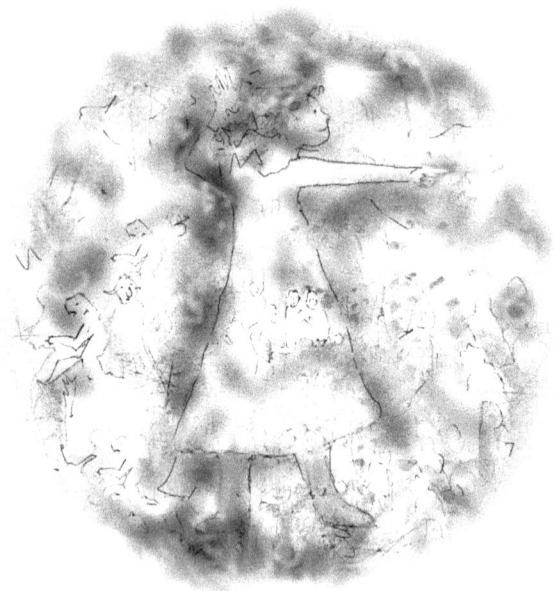

Groups will tend to be more powerful than one individual. However, because you, as the leader, have organisational power – that is, you have been given authority by virtue of organisational status – you have power over the individuals and will even have some power over the group. But if the group chooses to go against you, it may still be able to do so because it may be more powerful psychologically.

As a result of the power dynamic in a group, it is important for leaders to have an awareness of the impact of their power on it. Usually, when a leader is leading, he or she will dominate the group. If you want to apply the depth leadership skills discussed in this book to unlock the group's intelligence and wisdom, occasionally, you may need to step out of the role of leader and temporarily into that of follower. For this to succeed, you need to shed your leader's hat so that the group is not intimidated by your leadership power. If, for instance, you are with your top management team, you might say, "For the rest of this discussion, I'm not going to be setting direction because I'm interested in your views." Then, using general facilitation skills such as asking questions, really listening and paraphrasing, we will bring out the wisdom of the group. In this way, the group's views dominate rather than ours.

A group's power in relation to its members is something that needs to be kept in mind. This will be discussed in more detail later, but it is important to say here that psychologically, groups carry power because they meet or frustrate the unconscious needs of individuals, and often the individual is unaware of this at the conscious level. The leader who is not sufficiently aware will also be subject to this power and may often be taken by surprise by the extent of it. Never underestimate a group's power and remain vigilant to avoid being unduly influenced by it.

GROUP SIZES

Leaders and managers tend to work with groups that range in size. In this case, size does matter because the number of members has an impact on how the group works. If you are a middle-management team leader, you may have ten people reporting to you, and they, in turn, may have another fifty reporting to them. So, you will have to work at different levels: i.e., work with the immediate group that reports to you, and also have a psychological responsibility for the whole group of sixty.

The CEO of a large multinational corporation, for example, is responsible for, say, all 30,000 employees. As a leader, she has to think about the whole group, but she also directly leads her management board, which perhaps has only ten or twelve people on it. Being able to think about the psychological impact of different group sizes is important for a leader. The larger the group, the more complex and burdensome the psychodynamics of the group and the more the individuals are vulnerable to being plagued by those psychodynamics if they are unhealthy. It follows that the larger the group you have to lead, the greater your need for depth leadership skills to be able to think through what the group is doing to the individuals and how to stop the group from swamping individual contributions.

Group size has an impact on the following:

- the degree of face-to-face contact that is possible in the group and with the group leader;
- the amount of psychological energy available to be expressed;
- the impact of proportional relationships between the minority and majority subgroups;
- the psychodynamics that are triggered, e.g., family dynamics versus herd instincts;
- the relative powerlessness experienced by individual members; and
- the relative levels of anonymity experienced by the individual members and, therefore, the levels of responsibility taken.

Group theories differ in their definitions of group sizes, but there tends to be agreement that a small group has a maximum of fifteen members, a medium-sized group fifteen and twenty-five members, and a large group more than twenty-five members. Only a small group can reliably have face-to-face contact, which will mitigate the more destructive aspects of the anonymity that the individual experiences in a large group.

As the leader, you are to some extent, responsible for the psyche of the entire group. The less experience you have of managing the group psyche in depth, the more difficult it is to cope with larger groups, because the psychological force of a bigger group also expands. If you want to be the kind of leader who tries to look at the psyche as a whole rather than just making sure people do tasks – in other words, you are considering not just the task level but the psychodynamic level as well – then you should start small because this is a much bigger responsibility. Inexperienced managers or leaders should ideally have no more than five or six people reporting to them because the complexity of relationships makes it too difficult when working at a depth level.

THE GROUP TASK AND INTENTION

Groups have both explicit and emerging tasks. The explicit task will be the conscious and openly identified one. It is important for us, as leaders, to ensure that we are working towards helping the group achieve this task. The explicit task is, in fact, the most important one. However, if emerging tasks in the form of underlying processes interfere with or prevent the achievement of the explicit task, then we may need to alert the group to the lack of progress and help it to decide whether to address the underlying issues before resuming the work towards the task itself. Depth leadership is a way of helping a group explore depth material when necessary so that it may achieve its explicit task. Without a detour into the underlying processes, the group may not achieve its stated task. Unless explicitly stated, depth leadership is a means to an end, not an end in itself.

Without an explicit task, the group may easily fall into exploring the emergent intentions of the unconscious minds of individual members and the group. This takes the group into a depth process that it has not agreed to address. The most likely outcome of such a process is great dissatisfaction among members and frustration or even anger towards the leader.

According to Wilfred Bion, a group will be successful in an organisational context only if it can stay in touch with the need to perform a joint task, and with the external reality, its constraints, its moderating factors on group functioning, and the inflows in terms of information and resources offered by the external environment.

Failing the existence of a group task that is consciously understood, acknowledged and actively pursued, the group will resort to what Bion terms a 'basic assumption' group, which is more occupied by its psychological needs and will remain organisationally unproductive. Bion divides basic assumption behaviour into three types, called dependency, pairing, and fight/flight. (We will look at this in more detail later in this chapter.)

It is, therefore, very important for a leader to help the group clarify its explicit task and to ensure that all members agree on it, as this will ensure that the group's intention is aligned with the task. If there is misalignment between the group's task and its intention, then a depth process is necessary to achieve alignment.

KEY ELEMENTS OF GROUP PSYCHODYNAMICS

If the group has a psyche that functions as a whole, then its psyche will have thoughts, feelings and behaviours – just as an individual does. These thoughts, feelings and behaviours will be derived from the same archetypes and instincts discussed in terms of the individual psyche in Chapter 3. The archetypes and instincts are the biological and psychological imperatives that drive human functioning, and in groups, the medium of expression of these imperatives is a complex one.

THE GROUP VERSUS THE INDIVIDUAL PSYCHE

An individual has thoughts, feelings and behaviours that identifiably belong to that individual. In a group, the individuals become parts of the whole and so the group can only express itself through those individuals. The group uses the individuals or subgroups to express different aspects of itself, and so the human functions of feeling, thinking and behaving for the group psyche are carried through individuals or subgroups who operate in roles for the group. Therefore, whenever you witness individual or subgroup behaviour in a group, it is important to remember that the individual or subgroup is, at least partially, in a role for the group. Observation of the roles individuals or subgroups take for the group is critical to understanding the functioning of the group psyche.

In the case of an individual, the situation will constellate the archetypal possibilities that can be taken up as ways of being which eventually become character traits. In a group, the situation will constellate a set of archetypes which will then be taken up by the individuals or subgroups and be expressed as roles, as shown in the diagram below.

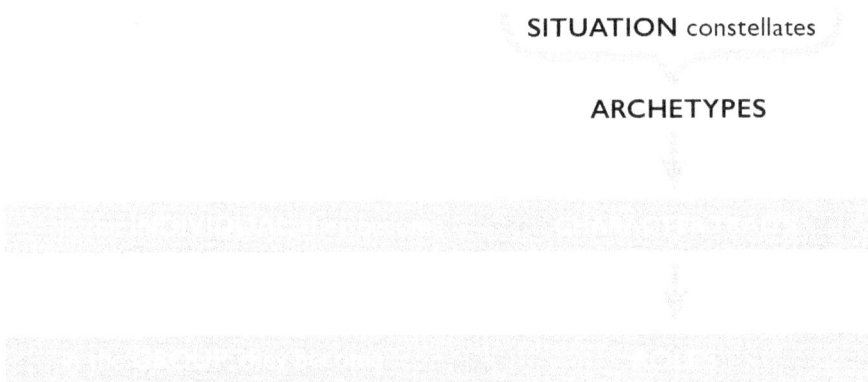

SITUATION constellates

ARCHETYPES

ARCHETYPES AND INSTINCTS IN GROUPS

Role theory has been a part of traditional sociological thinking for at least half a century. A role is a thought, feeling or behaviour that is expressed in a group context to manifest the mental, emotional and psychological life of the group. Roles are the archetypes and instincts in action in a group.

In Chapter 3, I discussed that human beings have the potential for all ways of being human encoded in their beings at birth. These ways of being include instincts, which are our biological predispositions, and archetypes, which are our psychological predispositions. Which of these predispositions will be activated within a group depends on the context in which the group finds itself and the task that the group has in that context. The context and the task are far more important in determining which predispositions will be activated than the nature of the individuals that make up the group. We like to think of the individual behaviour in a group as being personal, and determined by the personality of that individual, but this is not the case. If the group were stranded on a desert island, the likely ways of being would include some of the following:

Protector; Hunter; Leader; Clown; Rebel; Explorer; Nurturer; Entertainer; Nurse; Pragmatist; Observer; Builder; Strategist; Panicker; Organiser

The exact patterns of behaviour that will emerge may differ from group to group, but many of the essential elements would be the same. The individual members take up archetypes and play them out as roles to express the group psyche. As a leader, it is vital to remember that you are not only dealing with individuals in a group, but also with how individuals represent the playing out of human predispositions in it.

Bear in mind that the archetypes and instincts are responses to environmental demands and, are therefore, ways of being that are designed to ensure survival, rather than good or bad in themselves. They are inherent in our natural human responses to our life situations and can be demonstrated by the ways in which human nature plays out in the myths and stories of our various cultures.

There is usually logic behind the activation of a particular role, often as a response to a situation that is out of balance. The instinct or the archetype will manifest itself as an attempt to balance the situation. For example, in a group that is working too hard, the archetype or instinct related to rest and relaxation will start manifesting itself. It is useful to remember that there is some essential human wisdom at work when a new role appears in a group.

ROLE TYPES

Archetypes play themselves out as groups, and therefore there will be similar categories to those listed for the archetypes in Chapter 3. There are four types of roles: task, political, psychological and emotional. They can be also correlated with the categories of doing, controlling, relating and feeling. As with the individual expression of archetypes, these categories are not mutually exclusive or exhaustive; there will be some overlap between them.

THE INDIVIDUAL AND THE ROLE

For a group to express itself, roles will be adopted by the individual members of the group. The group context and task will provide a script for the required roles, and the individuals in the group become actors who are pulled into the available roles. The roles offer a blueprint or a pattern for appropriate behaviour in a particular situation. Certain roles, such as physician or clergyman, require very specific mannerisms, speech patterns, postures, and so forth. The roles themselves carry these emotions and attitudes, and when an individual adopts a particular role, he or she is influenced by it and takes on its characteristics. For example, a person may become wise by being appointed a judge. The person not only begins to act wisely, he or she actually feels it.

In the workplace, a good example might be a programmer in the IT department who has a techie manner and uses tech-speak to communicate. If he is then promoted to team leader, he will find himself embodying a new role that is less technical and requires some people skills as well. He will start implementing his people skills very consciously. People might even laugh at him because the transformation is so obvious. Initially he may feel odd, but will suddenly feel and act insightful about team dynamics.

From the depth perspective, a role is regarded as being greater and more complex than the individual expressing it at the time, and the individual is also recognised as being greater and more complex than the role that he or she is occupying. As we have already seen, it is important that subgroups can also take on roles for the group. In a group, an individual or subgroup is part of a larger psychological field and is used by the field to express an aspect of its essence. In this way, an individual or subgroup becomes a vehicle for the group process.

Roles, not individuals, constitute the basic organs and limbs of the group's body. Role theory also contains the idea that while functioning in a group, the group itself is psychologically whole or complete and, therefore, the individual need not always be whole. Each individual plays a role, which contributes to the group's wholeness, but each individual unit is not expected to be complete in itself.

The roles will have a longer lifespan in a group than the individuals who occupy them, and over time they change more slowly than individuals do. If no individual is available to fill a certain role, the group will have to invent or recruit a person who fulfils the required specifications.

INDIVIDUAL ROLE VALENCY

The process of role allocation is determined by a combination of individual tendencies and group requirements. Each individual has what Wilfred Bion termed a valency for a particular role. Individuals may have more than one valency, and different contexts will activate different valencies. A valency refers to the conscious or unconscious preference or tendency that an individual may have for a certain role in a group. This preference or tendency develops in an individual as a result of a variety of factors in their early childhood, such as:

- a need in the individual's original family;
- birth order;
- inherent talents;
- role models; or
- parental complexes and projections.

An individual's valency for a particular role may be incongruent with the individual's active and conscious choices. A person may become the rescuer in a group even when he or she really does not want to. However, the group's needs and the individual's unconscious preferences will be stronger than the individual's capacity to make rational choices.

ROLE CASTING

Matching the person to the role can be thought of as role allocation or role casting. Sometimes role casting is a conscious, active process, where a group leader or the group members themselves actively allocate a role to an individual. The individual may be explicitly consulted and then voluntarily take up the role. In fact, conscious role casting is how traditional employees are appointed: a job is advertised for a specific role (e.g., systems designer, project manager, etc.) and someone is appointed to the role.

This type of role casting is probably the best way to allocate roles. It is easy to allocate task roles explicitly; but it is less likely that political, psychological or emotional roles are consciously allocated. Most role casting happens in a very different way, without the explicit consent of either the group or the individual, but rather as an unconscious collusion between the individual's psyche and the group psyche. The collusion happens because the group has a need and the individual has a valency that communicates itself subliminally to the group.

Often, such psychological and emotional role casting will happen almost immediately when a new employee enters the team. The first few interactions with other team members will start determining a person's role. For instance, if she cracks a joke or is playful in the first ten minutes or so, there is potential for her to be taken up as the joker in the team. Or, if she looks nervous, the other team members may notice and start role casting her as the anxious person in the team.

In this way, role casting for psychological and emotional roles happens unconsciously because of the subtle signals we give one another. And it can happen incredibly quickly, so first impressions are critical. Of course, you can change your role casting if you are conscious of it, but if not, the first few signals you send out may give the whole group a strong idea of how to use you in the group psyche.

A depth leader should keep an eye on how roles are allocated within a group. The more explicitly all the different role types can be discussed, the healthier the group's functioning will be. In healthy groups, roles are also shared and rotated to avoid group or individual over-identification with a particular role. As a leader you have to be careful to remain flexible with the roles you occupy too.

ROLE SUCTION

When there is no one else to fill a role, an individual may become subject to what can be thought of as role suction, where the individual is subtly (or not so subtly) coerced into taking up a particular role for the group. Through the complex interaction of projection and projective identification mechanisms, the individual will be sucked into playing a particular role within the group. This may feel uncomfortable and an individual may resist it, but the group will tend to be stronger than an individual's will in this situation. What this means is that if there is a variance between what the individual wants to do and what the group wants that individual to do, the group's requirements of the individual may prevail.

ROLE IDENTIFICATION AND SCAPEGOATING

An alternative to role suction (where the individual knows that he or she does not wish to take up a particular role or that the role does not suit) is that of role identification, where the role fits the individual so well that the person becomes psychologically identified with it. In other words, the person feels very comfortable in the role and starts equating it with their own identity.

In this situation, the collusion between the group and individual becomes complete, and everyone starts believing that the role is the person, and the person is the role. This will feel comfortable to everyone in the group, or almost everyone. In the long term, however, it will be destructive to group development because it does not acknowledge the complexity and diversity of the system or the individual.

If, for example, a team notices that a new team member is timid early on, the team will treat the new member as a timid person, who in turn, may start to feel or even behave more timidly, despite that not being their role in other teams. Everyone else in the team may be strong-minded, needing someone who is easier to control. If the new member shows signs of being susceptible to that control, they will strengthen the team's hand. Essentially, there will be collusion between the team and the new member, both working – albeit unconsciously – to make sure the new member is stuck with the role, especially if the group needs that role to balance the psychodynamics.

One of the most problematic psychodynamics which can result from role identification and role suction, is that of scapegoating. After a person has been consciously or unconsciously selected by the group to fill an unpopular role, the rest of the group tends to identify the person with the role. The prevalence of this kind of scapegoating process is one of the reasons why people are often afraid to speak out in groups, especially when they are in minority positions. Scapegoating refers to the situation in which everything that is wrong or bad with a group is considered to belong to one individual (or subgroup). The group believes that if it can rid itself of the problematic individual, all its problems will be solved.

Although some individuals or subgroups are indeed problematic, group problems are rarely solved by excluding an individual or a subgroup. Groups are interconnected and dynamic systems in which the interactions between all the individual psyches result in functional or dysfunctional behaviour. As long as parts of the group – certain individuals or subgroups – are available to take an unpopular role, the rest of the group can scapegoat that part and avoid the experience of the position them selves. A holistic view of the individual recognises that all the roles are present in all of us

The picture on the next page shows how the person with the greatest tendency to express a particular thought or feeling does so for the whole group.

This person has the greatest
inclination or tendency to
express sadness. They are,
therefore, expressing sadness
with the combined force of their
own energy as well as that of
everyone else present, who may
be feeling sad, but not
expressing it.

BELOW THE SURFACE
Deeply held thoughts and feelings

THE GHOST ROLE

Sometimes, a role is so unpopular or unacceptable that no one in the group feels able or willing to take on that role. Usually, such a role is then allocated explicitly to someone or something outside of the group. Whether expressed or not, psychologically, the role is still part of the group psyche and affects the entire functioning of the group. The way of being or archetype represented by the role will be talked about by the group and will have a significant psychological impact on everything the group does.

When the role is not occupied in person, it becomes difficult or almost impossible to work with the psychodynamics expressed by that role in the group psyche. In this instance, the Process Work methodology (as developed by Arnold Mindell) refers to the role as a ghost role in the group. Your task as a leader is to ensure that the ghost role is in some way actively expressed so that it can be addressed if necessary and integrated into the larger psyche.

A classic workplace example of a psychodynamic with a ghost role is evident in South Africa with its history of racism and the legacy of Apartheid. Few people will admit to being racist, yet there may be racism in all of us. Our history has not allowed us to escape it. But it is such an unpopular role that it floats around in the ether and few people are able to consciously own it. Coworkers will accuse each other of racism, but no one will actually admit to having racist feelings. The truth is that most of us have experienced racist impulses at some level or another, and this causes huge difficulties if we do not acknowledge it. In diversity and transformation work, it is invaluable if someone is prepared to acknowledge their own racist impulses. It requires great courage for a group member to do so, but if well handled by the leader, it can be transformative for the functioning of the group. Once a prejudice is acknowledged, it can be neutralised. When someone takes on such a ghost role in a group, a new and different conversation becomes possible. As the leader you need to ensure that the group does not scapegoat the individual who has taken on the ghost role.

We can see this in another example of the ghost role, where teams from the regions or branches of an organisation are complaining about the head office. Although head office is not represented in the room, the team members have strong feelings about head office and want to express them. In this scenario, head office is the ghost role because no one is representing it in the meeting. Since you cannot resolve the conflict with the ghost role because head office is not represented in the room, the only way to start trying to address it is for someone to take the perspective of the ghost role in the room. To work with this, a depth leader may say, "Let us all pretend that I represent head office. What would you want to say to me? Then I will try to give you an answer from head office's perspective." In this way, you can move towards conflict resolution. This is far more constructive than allowing a one-sided conversation to prevail.

PSYCHODYNAMIC PATTERNS

Psychodynamic theory suggests that psychic life tends to be interactive rather than unidirectional. As a result of the split between the conscious and unconscious parts within us, psychic processes are characterised by duality, in which a particular way of being elicits its opposite or complimentary way of being. The more one-sided a way of being is, the more likely it is to evoke the opposite way of being unconsciously in the self or in another. Roles tend to operate in reciprocal patterns. For example, a critic will almost always elicit a victim, and a leader needs a follower.

When a way of being or behaving in the world is simplistically one-sided, the psyche will, often unconsciously, search for or manifest the other side to allow for the possibility of a more integrated position. The more the psyche is split, the more unacceptable the other way of being will tend to be. In a more integrated position, polarities are complementary rather than adversarial. To resolve the conflict caused by adversarial polarities, the psyche needs to encounter the value of the other way of being and find a way of integrating it.

The group psyche seems to work according to the same principles. But contrary to the psychic dance that is created between the conscious and unconscious in an individual, the group can play out the psychic dance between individuals occupying opposing roles or between subgroups in the group. The purpose behind the dance is to allow a conversation and interaction between the polar opposite ways of being so that a more integrated position can emerge. For this to happen, though, the tension between the two ways of being needs to be held long enough and with sufficient containment for the more integrated position to emerge.

These role psychodynamics can also be thought of as Harriet Lerner (2014) calls them – 'role dances'. One of the most common psychological dances is one in which one of the roles is the critic, and the other role is at the receiving end of criticism, and therefore becomes the victim.

The diagram on the next page illustrates how the role of critic has its pair in the role of victim. The role of critic cannot exist without the role of victim, so the minute there is a critic, a critic-victim dynamic develops. Intrapsychic conflict in each person becomes interpersonal conflict as a result of mutual projection between them. In a group psyche, an individual or subgroup will take up the critic role. Similarly, in response, a different individual or subgroup will occupy the victim role. However, whatever role an individual takes up, the unconscious carries the opposite archetypal possibility. The dance is only complete when the criticvictim dance develops a transcendent third position. Here, a new way of relating, which is developmental rather than defensive, becomes possible. This process will be described in Chapter 9. There are many examples of these psychodynamics or dances, and in each case they reflect the duality of one way of being versus another.

Some examples are provided below:

- pursuer – distancer
- hard-working – lazy
- independent – dependent
- responsible – irresponsible
- playful – serious
- task-focused – people-focused

Paradoxically, opposing roles reinforce one another's existence – they reinforce the psychodynamics. The more one person takes up one role, the more the other is forced into the opposing role. Many group processes will end up, especially in a polarising process, in a role dance. A strong leader needs to help the full expression of each role, allowing the value behind each role to emerge for the group. This allows the other side to see the value of the opposing side and be moved to a position of integrating the opposing role.

CRITIC-VICTIM DANCE

HOLDING THE TENSION

LINES OF PROJECTION

CONSCIOUS VICTIM (Unconscious critic)

CONSCIOUS CRITIC (Unconscious victim)

GROUP PROCESSES

Here we consider the group processes that result from the psychodynamics described above. Obviously, there are as many group processes as there are groups. To have a meaningful discussion about some key concepts of group processes, therefore, it is useful to define some categories. From a depth perspective, at the broadest level, there are essentially two sets of processes in groups:

- defensive processes
- developmental processes

Both of these types of important processes are needed in a healthy group. A depth leader will be more interested in the second set of processes, but it is necessary to appreciate the value of defensive processes too – and sometimes actively support them. The two sets of processes are discussed in more detail below. We will, however, first examine anxiety, which is one of the most important driving factors behind these processes. Groups will use defensive processes when they are in situations that are threatening and provoke anxiety. The nature of group anxiety and group defence mechanisms is discussed in detail below.

GROUP ANXIETY

In Chapter 3, I discussed in detail how individuals manage anxiety. Here we are concerned with how groups manage anxiety, because as a leader you need to help groups move through states of anxiety to achieve their tasks.

Individuals experience anxiety in groups on two levels. The first is individual anxiety about group membership and group issues; the second is anxiety on behalf of the group as a part of the group psyche. Regardless of the level at which the individual is experiencing anxiety, it is important to remember that anxiety is always uncomfortable and that the psyche will do everything it can to get rid of it. This means getting rid of the source of anxiety, and groups and individuals in groups will use a variety of more or less sophisticated means to do so. We will consider these group defensive processes in detail in the following pages.

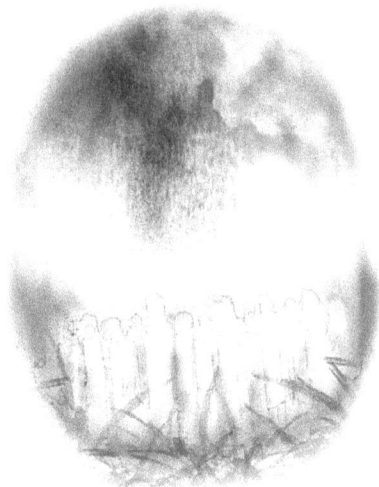

GROUP DEFENSIVE PROCESSES

Just as individuals have defence mechanisms, as we learned in Chapter 3, so do groups. Defence mechanisms are strategies that the group uses to reduce anxiety, essentially by obscuring, hiding or ignoring the source of it. Any impulse, way of being, feeling, or set of ideas that the group finds difficult to deal with – and therefore could cause anxiety in the group – will be suppressed or eliminated in some way if possible.

For example, openly discussing issues of incompetence could cause anxiety, so the group may defend itself against such discussions by focusing on the problems caused by demanding clients. The cause of non-delivery is then laid at the door of the clients rather than the staff members themselves. There are many more or less sophisticated ways in which groups will unconsciously or consciously work together to avoid confronting painful, embarrassing or difficult subjects. Everyone in the group will be involved in these self-deceptions, but they will usually not be openly planned or discussed as such.

Organisational defences vary but will often be reflected in organisational processes and systems, and will determine what can and cannot be spoken about openly. Organisational defences are difficult to dismantle. These defences will interfere with task achievement and are often reinforced by the power arrangements in the organisation.

Examples of organisational defences are:

- continual restructuring, rather than addressing power blocs;
- continuing with unproductive activities, such as closing meetings with next steps that are never implemented;
- having a culture of meetings that seems to suggest an organisation that communicates well, but few of the important issues are discussed;
- an unbalanced focus on one part of the organisation, such as the Finance Department.

Different group methodologies have different ideas about the nature of group defences against anxiety, as well as the sources of anxiety. A more psychoanalytic approach (based on Freud's work) will be concerned with the fact that individuals experience groups as being similar to parental figures; primarily mother figures. Individuals in a group situation will, therefore, experience a state of regression, in which they are plunged back into an infantile state. Depending on the nature of the infantile experiences, they may need to activate a variety of mechanisms to protect themselves in that regressed state. As we saw earlier, Wilfred Bion (1961) suggested that without a clearly defined task and accessible external reality, the group would resort to dealing with this anxiety through what he calls 'basic assumption' functioning. He described three basic defensive structures that groups would use:

- Pairing – here the group will divide itself into sets of pairs where, in one or more instances, two group members bond together. The group will view the sets of pairs as important to survival, and there is hope that the pairs will produce a symbolic offspring that in some way offers salvation for the group.

- Fight or flight – in this defensive process the group chooses an enemy from which it needs to withdraw or flee or fight to survive. The group will choose various things to be defined as the enemy. It may be someone outside the group, or in fact the group task itself. For example, the group can decide that head office is the enemy.

- Dependency – here the group looks for one individual on whom they can depend to reduce the anxiety. They will look for a particular person who has a strong leadership capacity, who they hope will protect them from potential or actual threats that cause anxiety. This individual is left with all the responsibility for looking after the group.

Bion's defensive processes listed above are interesting to keep in mind. Some leaders work specifically with this formulation, but other theorists have added to Bion's list, and there does seem to be a variety of other ways in which groups deal with anxiety. Nonetheless, the principle that groups will find psychological defence mechanisms to deal with anxiety is important.

From a Jungian standpoint, people will develop defensive processes to manage the anxiety caused by the conflicting demands on an individual – usually to manage the conflict between inherent drives and the assurance of perceived or actual survival. Therefore, groups and members of groups will find ways of avoiding confrontation, either with their inner worlds or with the systems around them. Intragroup versus intergroup defensive processes

Some groups will be preoccupied with intragroup defences, while others will be preoccupied with intergroup defences. The differences are listed in the following table:

Intra-group defensive processes	Inter-group defensive processes
The group regards problems as being within the group	The group regards problems as being outside the group
A member or a sub-group is held responsible for difficulties	Individuals or groups outside the group are held responsible for difficulties
The group will struggle with its diversity	The group will regard itself as homogeneous in important aspects

Projective versus denial processes

Essentially, defensive processes will either place the undesirable way of being on one individual or subgroup, or will help the group to pretend in some way that it is not a problem. These can be categorised broadly into projective and denial processes. Sometimes both processes are used together. Some details of these processes are given below:

	Projective processes	Denial processes
Main activity	Scapegoating	Avoidance
View of the problem	Someone is to blame	The problem does not exist
Main symptoms	Conflict Lack of cooperation Membership turnover Incongruities	Superficial harmony and covert tension Rigidity in behaviour
Main defensive mechanisms	Projection Projective identification	Denial Groupthink

Mechanisms for group projective processes

There are two essential mechanisms at work in projective processes: Projection and projective identification, and they operate in conjunction with one another and are dependent on one another. Projection is the process by which anything that is unacceptable to the psyche is attributed to something or someone outside of the psyche. Groups will identify with a certain set of values and ways of being, and reject any way of being that is seen as unacceptable. However, in the process of rejection, the undesirable way of being will be associated with someone or some subgroup, and this individual or subgroup will also be rejected. This can apply to an individual within the group or to someone or something outside of the group. Projection is the mechanism that underlies scapego-ating. If we can view an undesirable way of being as belonging to someone else, and that someone else can be eliminated, then the problem is solved. Groups regularly choose scapegoats as a way of dealing with the existence of undesirable ways of being.

As discussed in Chapter 3, the difficulty with projection is that it operates in conjunction with a twin mechanism called projective identification. In this mechanism, as we have seen, the recipient of the projection cooperates with the mechanism by living out the behaviour that is being projected onto him or her. It is particularly likely for projective identification to work if the recipient identifies with some aspect of the projection. Together, the projecting party and the recipient collude in the success of the defensive process. Projective identification is often present in a group that is engaged in projecting undesirable ways of being onto one individual in a group. This mechanism makes the individual susceptible to the projection, and in a way, the individual volunteers (albeit unconsciously) to be the scapegoat. For example, a highly-driven group may eventually convince the least-driven member that he or she is holding the group back from achievement and is, in fact, responsible for the group's failure in some way. The truth may be that the group is not functioning optimally be-cause there is not enough balance in the way it operates.

Mechanisms for denial processes

Similarly, there are two mechanisms at work to ensure the success of denial processes. Firstly, the group has to deny the existence of an undesirable way of being and, secondly, everybody has to agree.

In some way, the group has to have the ability to maintain the illusion that a way of being, or a set of thoughts or impulses does not exist. Some groups do this by focusing excessively on the opposite of that way of being. This will often be visible in a consciously constructed culture, such as: "We are all part of one big happy family here." These groups will actively construct a belief system and an identity that excludes unacceptable ways of being.

For denial processes to be successful, everyone in the group has to agree. This agreement will take the form of a voluntary process, where everyone is seen as like-minded, and it would be unthinka-ble and certainly not possible to discuss the fact that everyone is expected to agree. There will be a strong unspoken taboo against questioning the validity of the identity. Belonging and agreement become the overall driving forces.

Groups that use denial processes are less likely to volunteer for depth work because the very agreement to do depth work would nullify the defence. As a leader, you must work very carefully when encountering denial processes in a group. Where you identify such a problem, be alert to the possible need to engage a professional facilitator to work through such denial to improve group dynamics and the efficacy of the organisation as a whole.

Maintenance of defences over time

Of course, no defensive strategy will work indefinitely, so many of the strategies have an inbuilt conclusion for which a new strategy is needed. One example is that idealisation (the making of somebody into a messiah) cannot last indefinitely because, inevitably, the messiah turns out to be a real person. The psyche copes with this by going through continual cycles of idealisation and deni-gration, or in organisational terms through a messiah/scapegoat cycle. Therefore, group defences will play themselves out in patterns over time. In learning about the history of the group, the leader can help the group to identify the pattern.

GROUP DEVELOPMENTAL PROCESSES

Group defensive and developmental processes do not operate in isolation from one another. Groups will often vacillate between the two, as their anxiety fluctuates over time. Also, there will be many varieties of group developmental processes, and so any ideas offered here will be generalisations at best. From a depth perspective, however, group developmental processes can be broadly described in terms of four types: relationship-building, polarising, cathartic and reconciliation. These four broad categories are described in more detail below. In each case, the group process is described. We will look at these again later in the book when we discuss the interventions a depth leader can use.

1. Relationship-building processes

All groups go through a variety of stages in terms of the development of their relationships and their ability to function cohesively. These stages can be understood in terms of the natural progression of the relationships between them. Of course, closely tied to that is the development of trust and acceptance between the members.

The different stages of group development are summarised below.

Courting   This is the stage of politeness, where the group members do not know one another. Individuals may avoid being confrontational at this stage. The task during this stage is for individual members to get to know one another.

Asserting   This is the stage where individuals start asserting themselves and expressing their differences in terms of opinions and beliefs. The task here is for members to risk expressing difference and see whether their differences are included in the group's functioning.

Revealing   In this stage, the group members move beyond opinions and beliefs and start revealing their preferences and feelings in a personal way. They will reveal their underlying vulnerabilities by providing the underlying reasons for their preferences.

Fully   In this final stage, the group members have accepted one another and their differences, functioning   and have found an inclusive way of working together.

When individuals initially come together, they come together as strangers. This means that they do not know much about each other, and certainly do not trust each other yet. Any knowledge they may have about each other will be based either on the opinions of others or on their own stereotypes that will be activated by superficial information. For example, group members may draw conclusions about one another based on their gender, race, age, profession, general appearance and a myriad of other clues that may be misinterpreted when viewed subjectively.

Most models of group development indicate that if the group is to become a fully functioning unit, it will need to go through a stage of conflict. This does not have to involve overt and acrimonious conflict, but it will involve disagreement and a negotiation between diverse points of view and ways of doing things. In order for the group to pass successfully through this stage, there has to be a sense that there is mutual benefit in continuing through the difficulty together. The existence of an objective task can provide the sense of mutual benefit.

The other important stage in a group's development is the time where individuals move beyond individual viewpoints and opinions to revealing their feelings and areas of vulnerability and developing greater intimacy. It is very unlikely that a group will achieve tasks successfully over time if group members have not been able to acknowledge and respect one another's vulnerabilities.

Once a group has reached the fully functioning stage of group development, it will not stay there indefinitely. If it functions within an open system where change is inevitable, then new issues will continually arise. New issues will present new challenges in terms of possible differences of opinion, and the group may have to resolve these to become fully functioning again.

Consider, for example, a maintenance team in the IT department. The members have become a fully functioning team and have resolved their destructive psychodynamics. But, of course, nothing ever stays the same. They might be given a new development project that requires innovative thinking. As a maintenance team, they did not need the role of innovation, but now they do. This will cause huge disruption in allocated psychological or emotional roles because now some members have to become innovators. Perhaps three members of the team think that they are innovative and start competing for the role. This shows how, every time there is a change in the external environment, the role allocation for the team will require changes. There will need to be a transition or learning period before the team becomes stable and fully functional again.

Importantly, every time the group gains or loses a member, the group has to form as if it is a new one. These changes affect the group dynamics and the stages have to be negotiated from the beginning. If you are a leader of a regularly changing team, you need to keep your eye on re-forming the team properly every time there is a change. Perhaps the person who has left the team carried a few roles; now those roles are unoccupied and the new person joining the team may not necessarily be able to take them on.

2. Polarising processes

One of the subprocesses of relationship-building is that groups will encounter situations in which the group members have differing opinions. This refers to the dynamic in which groups develop two (or sometimes more) opposing viewpoints in their membership regarding particular issues, which then causes tension.

This is a direct result of the intragroup defensive processes discussed earlier (usually the projective processes). As a result of the projections onto one another, the group will tend to divide itself into two groups: the subgroup that is right and one that is wrong (at least in the mind of the subgroup). Although this is a result of the defensive process, it provides the opportunity for development. In fact, without this polarising process, it is hard to ensure that transformation happens.

The group seems inevitably to head into a dilemma, disagreement or conflict and then possible resolution. The dilemma is a necessary precursor to innovative solutions.

Obviously, the actual steps taken by each group will differ, but there are similar elements between groups. A rough guide to the steps in such a process is as follows:

1.   a general discussion of the situation, the task, establishing and maintaining relationships
2.   surfacing or introduction of issues/listing of preoccupations
3.   sorting of issues, prioritisation of one issue either directly or indirectly
4.   a move either into avoidance, which takes the group back to step 1 or 2, or deeper int the issue, which makes resolution possible

5.	development of views on the issue – many different views initially

6.	polarisation into two opposing views

7.	exploring further, defining the polarities (the two different views in the dilemma or con-
flict), entering into the awakening of what Jung called the transcendent function (which
produces the transcendent third position and results in innovative solutions, or a break-
through of some kind)

To move beyond this polarisation, the group may need help from a depth perspective. A good leader will understand this and take the appropriate action, whether this is to help the group through
a process in which resolution becomes possible or to bring in an outside facilitator who can do so.
The depth theory discussed in Chapter 3 suggests that whatever else we may be engaged in our
conscious lives, an invisible autonomous process exists inside us in which the psyche is trying to
integrate the split between the conscious and unconscious parts of ourselves.

This underlying split inside all of us means that there tend to be two possible parts or views on
any given issue. The psyche wants to resolve the dilemma and will produce ways of interacting that
manifests the duality inside us. This often results in a conflict where there are two sides. In a group,
the split between the two opposing views manifests as a group conflict. This brings the possibility of
integration or, to use the technical term, the possibility for a transcendent third position to emerge,
which resolves the conflict in a winwin.

This third position is only possible if the opportunity is provided for a deeper conversation in which
the tension of opposites is allowed. Usually, groups need some support to manage such a process,
but the results can be truly transformational. Depth leadership would provide the support necessary
for such a process.

3. Cathartic processes

Catharsis comes from the Greek word 'katharos' meaning pure or purified. It refers to a process
whereby an individual or a group releases pent-up emotions and repressed thoughts by bringing
them to the surface of consciousness. This is a very important process for groups because without
it the group life can become septic and unwell. Catharsis can also refer to the release of positive
emotions such as pride or laughter, and celebrations may also be cathartic.

The human psyche (and body, for that matter) has an inbuilt ability to process experiences, or digest
and metabolise the things that happen to it. If we are able to express emotions, we are able to move
on to new activities. However, many of the more modern cultures have chosen a way of being that
discourages the expression of emotion. In particular, injunctions to think positively or move on may
prevent the appropriate expression of emotion. Our capacity to heal depends on the metabolising
function of emotions.

For many reasons, the need to express emotions or certain thoughts may cause anxiety in a group
and lead to the activation of defensive processes. The resulting suppressed thoughts and feelings
become problematic for the group and will interfere with task execution. For example, a team that
has lost a member to a car accident may be unable to express their grief in the organisational setting.
A depth leader would help the group through the initiation of some appropriate ritual to recognise
and express their grief. Sometimes a team does not need to resolve or change anything. It simply
needs to let off steam about what has happened.

Another example is a team that has been in a very stressful situation, working long hours to meet
deadlines. When the task is complete and there is some breathing space, you as team leader need

to acknowledge that this team is exhausted and probably has a lot of stress, anger or resentment bottled up. It is helpful if you can allow them an opportunity to express that emotion. If you do not, it stays blocked in the system, and unexpressed emotion eventually causes demotivation by sapping psychological energy. Once you allow them the space to express emotion, that energy comes back. An important group process, then, is to allow for and encourage catharsis so that the group can purify itself. Cathartic processes may be related to past events or situations, or to the here and now that the group finds itself in. The leader needs to identify that a cathartic process may be needed, and provide a suitable environment and process to ensure that such a catharsis can happen.

4. Reconciliation processes

Sometimes, a group surface process becomes blocked because group members have been harmed by each other, and the relationships between them have been damaged. In this instance, the group has to enter a reconciliation process before the group can successfully complete its task. A reconciliation process will include cathartic and polarising processes, but it has additional stages.

A reconciliation process requires an encounter between two parties, where one party has explicitly harmed the other. This produces a complex psychodynamic because it evokes very strong and painful emotions. It is usually associated with trauma which has a profound impact on the psyche. The victim of the trauma has to be in the presence of the perpetrator, which may be experienced as adding to the trauma. The victim has to be given an opportunity to give expression to their experience and the perpetrator has to be able to withstand the emotional intensity and pain of taking accountability for causing harm. This requires the capacity to survive unpleasant emotions such as shame and guilt, and requires both the perpetrator and the victim to withstand profound feelings of powerlessness.

Reconciliation processes require the individuals involved to exercise two very sophisticated human capacities. The first is that of accepting culpability and the second is that of forgiveness. Both parties have to exercise both capacities to allow true reconciliation to happen. In other words, the perpetrator has to accept culpability for harming another, and has to find a way for self-forgiveness. This requires a great deal of emotional courage. The victim has to forgive which requires an understanding of the potential culpability in all of us. Reconciliation processes can be extremely powerful and transformative but require emotional strength and skill from everyone involved. The interventions required by the depth leader are described in Chapter 9.

POWER DYNAMICS IN GROUPS

One of the biggest complicating factors in groups is the fact that different people or subgroups hold power and others hold less or no power. Power differences account for the most common and most complex psychodynamics in groups. Leaders will invariably encounter the dynamics produced by power and difference. Here we consider in detail how power inequalities and other differences have an impact on group dynamics. Most under-the-surface processes are related in some way to the complexities caused by power and difference.

There is much theoretical literature written about power and authority and related concepts. Many definitions are given, and there is great complexity in the field. For our purposes, the terms below will be used in the following way:

Power	The capacity to have an effect or an influence.
Privilege	An advantage, right, favour or freedom from a burden.
Authority	Power derived from office, character or prestige.
Difference	Dissimilarity, carrying a distinguishing quality.
Rank	The differentiated status afforded to an individual or a subgroup in a group as a result of the combination of power and privilege.

If power is defined as the capacity to have an effect or influence, then it is easy to see that human beings are at their most vulnerable when they are surrounded by others who have more power than they do. Power differences evoke very strong feelings, and create a dynamic that may completely obliterate the group's capacity to fulfil a task. Group behaviour is so greatly influenced by differences in power that you can regard it as a given that power dynamics exist.

Importantly, power dynamics that are not managed consciously almost always cause conflict and, in many instances, can cause wars. It is, therefore, a critical but difficult task to help groups manage the psychodynamics caused by power differences.

TYPES OF RANK

We can think of rank as the effect that the power and privilege held by an individual or subgroup has on its status in the group. Rank gives an individual or a subgroup influence in a group. There are many types of rank possible in groups, and rank is a relative term.

Examples of different types of rank are listed below.

Social, cultural and organisational rank

Race
Gender
Culture
Religion
Age
Sexual orientation
Class
Organisational position
Education level
Expertise
Language
Connections to influential people
Connections to networks

Economic rank

Income level
Family wealth
Employability
Financial worth

Physical rank

Able-bodiedness
Health
Strength
Athleticism
Agility
Physical talent

Local rank

Familiarity with a community or a neighbourhood
Living in one's country of birth
Long service in an organisation

Psychological and spiritual rank

Confidence
Experience
Assertiveness
Self-awareness
Emotional intelligence
Creativity
A spiritual or religious foundation
Sense of humour
Intelligence
Authority

An aspect that will give an individual or subgroup rank in one group will not necessarily do so in another group in a different context. Think, for instance, of a janitor or a cleaner at a school. At work, he has a lowly rank, but when he goes home, he may hold a high rank in the family as the breadwinner of ten people. Similarly, in an organisational setting, a branch manager has rank at the branch, but at head office is a junior person without much rank.

Rank can change according to the demands on a company too. For instance, someone with a lot of technical understanding of a manufacturing process might be given a lot of power when the company is rolling out a massive project for export. But if the technology in which he is an expert changes, he is no longer as valuable – or as powerful.

Of the types of rank above, the social, cultural and organisational rank is the most context-dependent, and the type of rank most likely to play itself out in a group situation. Group members will usually seek out subgroups to join in terms of their social, cultural and organisational rank. Psychological rank is the most reliable form of rank, and the one over which the individual has most control.

EARLY CIRCUMSTANCES AND RANK

Everyone has an experience of rank differences. However, depending on early experiences, where an individual was at the mercy of a powerful caregiver, he or she may be more or less comfortable in the presence of somebody who has more rank. Individuals whose early experience was of being well cared for by a powerful figure are likely to be more comfortable with rank differences. If, however, an individual had a general experience of frustration of their needs and general lack of care, or even an abuse of care, then that individual would be less likely to accept rank differences. Also, whatever the individual's experience, human beings instinctively know the incredible danger of large power differences. Power differences cause anxiety and therefore invariably cause defensive behaviours, which have a massive psychological impact on all the members of the group.

THE PSYCHODYNAMICS OF RANK

Rank differences are responsible for a large proportion of the psychodynamics in groups. All groups will divide into at least two subgroups: those with the rank and those with less or no rank. Arnold Mindell's process work methodology uses the terminology of minority to denote the group with less or no rank, and the term majority to denote the group with more rank. This use of terminology is somewhat confusing because rank does not always belong to the subgroup that is greater in numbers. In many instances, the group with more rank is, in fact, a smaller group. Sometimes, the minority in numbers will also be the minority in power, but this is not reliably the case. It is, therefore, useful to be explicit when using terms like minority and majority. The psychodynamics of rank are outlined in the diagram below.

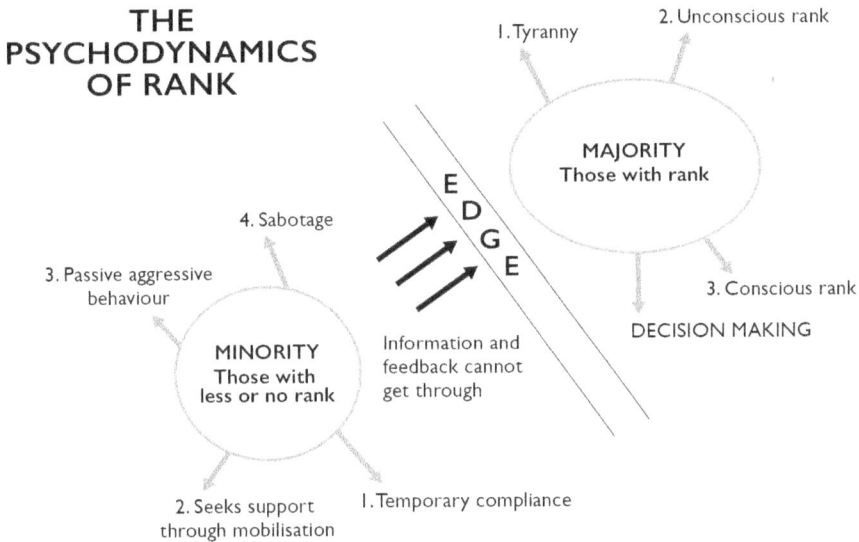

THE PSYCHODYNAMICS OF RANK

1. Tyranny

2. Unconscious rank

MAJORITY
Those with rank

E
D
G
E

4. Sabotage

3. Passive aggressive behaviour

3. Conscious rank

DECISION MAKING

MINORITY
Those with less or no rank

Information and feedback cannot get through

2. Seeks support through mobilisation

1. Temporary compliance

The individual or subgroup that has more rank will tend to be the decision-making body in the group. Individuals or subgroups with little or no rank will be excluded from decision-making processes, if not actively, then by a lack of inclusion. The group with less power will experience an edge (as described in Chapter 3) and their views will not be able to get through to those with power.

The group with little or no rank experiences the exclusion as problematic, rightly so, and eventually starts taking action to address the exclusion. The excluded subgroup may begin with temporary compliance with the powerful group and wait to see if the exclusion is indeed temporary, but after a certain period, it will decide to start acting to rectify the situation. However, because the individual or subgroup does not have power, it is difficult to confront the exclusion directly.

The second step towards gaining some power would be for members of the subgroup to band together or to seek out individuals who are having a similar experience. They will start having offline (subgroup) discussions about the exclusion and how to rectify it. Subgroups may also start banding together more formally. The most formal example of this is that a group may unionise. Once a subgroup has banded together, the members may try to challenge the group with rank to be included in the decision-making.

A third step will occur if the banding together process does not lead to results. The minority subgroup may then resort to passive-aggressive behaviour, resisting the decisions of the group with rank but not doing it overtly. This may take the form of a go-slow situation, or of chronic lateness, or a refusal to engage actively with the majority group.

If the above three strategies do not work, the subgroup may take a fourth step which would be some form of sabotage to undermine the power of the dominant group. The resistance is still covert because the minority group has less power than the majority group.

The majority group also has different ways to approach the management of its rank. In the first instance, some individuals or groups with rank are explicitly oppressive and may behave in a tyrannical fashion. This will usually lead to a conflictual relationship with the group with less rank. However, sometimes, it may be necessary for a leader to be autocratic, especially in a dangerous situation where people can be harmed, such as a fire on a factory floor. In general, however, oppressive behaviour will be counterproductive.

The second possible approach for people with power is that they may exert their power unconsciously, without the awareness that others find them to be oppressive. They are not being consciously oppressive, they are simply unaware of the impact of their power.

The best approach for individuals with power is to become aware of the impact of their power on others and to use their power consciously to empower those with less rank to speak up, thereby including the minority group in decision-making processes.

An example of rank dynamics would be that of an over-controlling manager who, unaware of how to use her rank in a respectful rather than demeaning way, has made herself unpopular with an individual employee. If she asks that employee to prepare an important report for her to present to a major client, the employee may leave out some vital information in the hope of exposing her as a fool in front of the client. This is individual sabotage.

A leader who demotivates his staff by misusing his rank can also inspire sabotage by a wider group. When the manager is absent, the team will gang up and play games instead of doing their work. Their anger may even lead them to resort to white-collar crime because they see stealing as a way of getting even.

An added dynamic in a situation of rank differences is that individuals with little or no rank may exclude themselves from decision-making processes because they do not feel confident enough to make themselves heard. This form of internalised oppression can be as debilitating as explicit oppression. Sometimes the group needs help to develop the confidence to speak up, and a person with more power, such as a facilitator, may support them to speak up. It is important that such a facilitator does not provide artificial strength in this situation. The subgroup should only be encouraged to speak up if it will be able to sustain its challenge in the absence of the supporter.

RANK AND RESPONSIBILITY

Rank differences are a fact of life: there will always be taller and shorter people in the world. However, the way individuals with rank handle rank differences makes a big difference to the psychological impact on those with less or no rank. For rank differences to be palatable to those with little or no rank, the individuals or subgroup that hold rank need to use that rank responsibly. Since leaders enjoy high rank, it is crucial for them to understand this to get the best from people of all ranks who work for them.

An example of irresponsible use of rank is when a parent enjoys beating a child at a simple game, such as a card game, or a game of sport. Another is when people who have resources waste them. Most often, an irresponsible use of rank is when a powerful individual is not aware of how he or she affects others of lower rank. For example, a hotel manager might be walking around with guests when she rudely confronts a junior cleaner in the corridor about a dirty wastepaper basket. A better course of action would be to address the cleaner in private about the problem. By humiliating the cleaner, the manager abuses her rank and does not inspire a desire in the cleaner to do a better job. She needs to remember to address everyone with respect regardless of rank, bearing in mind that the cleaner is probably terrified of the rank and power difference.

People or subgroups who use their rank responsibly do some of or all of the following:

- they are aware of the rank they hold and the privilege that it gives them
- they value the privilege that it gives them
- they are conservative with the use of the privilege
- they do not flaunt the use of their privilege
- where possible, they share their power and privilege
- they work towards developing power and privilege in others
- they are aware of the psychological impact of the privilege

RANK AWARENESS

Many people, in fact most of us, are not aware of the privileges we hold. Human beings are more interested in the areas where they do not hold privilege and are more aware of feelings of deprivation than they are of feelings of satisfaction. We all tend to focus on the areas where we do not hold privilege and to be acutely aware of those people around us who have rank.

When working with groups, you can expect that rank awareness and the responsible use of rank may not exist. As a result, one of the key depth dynamics that a leader would work with is the psychological impact on the group of a lack of rank awareness.

In order for a group to be successful, it is important to minimise the negative impact of rank differences on the group. The only way to ensure that this happens is to try and make those with rank aware of the impact that their rank has on the group. As leader, you can offer psychoeducation and teach people about the rank concept, or gently try to lead the individual or subgroup to an awareness of privilege in the situation. You need to use your own psychological rank to bring awareness in an acceptable way to those who are exercising unconscious rank in a group.

To do this, you could sit down with your team and explain rank theory to them. It is very useful for everybody to understand that we unconsciously carry rank, that rank comes with privilege, and that if we abuse our privilege, it will make other people angry. As a team-building exercise, it might even be useful to have a discussion about who holds what rank in the team. One person might have organisational rank because he or she is the leader, but someone else may have been there for many years and have a great deal of organisational knowledge, which gives rank in another way. If a third person is a respected figure in their community, he or she will have rank in terms of managing people. Most importantly, you as leader need to be aware of the impact of your rank on the group.

RANK INVERSION

One of the most difficult situations to work with is that of rank inversion. This is where someone or a subgroup that has previously held rank loses that rank, and someone or a subgroup that had previously held little or no rank, now gains rank. Effectively, there is an inversion between the two parties. Not only will the parties have the difficult thoughts and feelings normally associated with the rank position that they occupy, but they will also have to deal with change in rank and its psychological implications.

The South African example of Apartheid illustrates this psychodynamic well. With the change of the political regime, older White males who used to have power suddenly find it difficult to get a job and no longer hold power. They may feel marginalised in an organisation where a number of Black people are now in charge, forgetting that they marginalised people in the past. It takes maturity for them to acknowledge that they enjoyed privilege at the expense of other people for a long time and need to come to terms with the fact that they no longer have it.

There are similar upheavals for people who previously had no privilege and are now in the top ranks of an organisation. The change comes with a great deal of complexity because disempowerment often spawns rage. When they get power, they may no longer identify with the oppressed but abuse their power instead. Of course, many have handled that transition well, where they have retained their dignity and treated with respect those who used to have power or rank and lost it. It takes enormous psychological strength for a previously disadvantaged person not to act on their rage once they have power.

FORMAL VERSUS INFORMAL RANK

Another area of complication is when some members of the group have formal rank and some members have informal rank. Formal rank is often more known and visible than informal rank, yet informal rank could be more powerful. Formal rank refers to explicit, designated group positions that have power attached to them, such as the position of CEO or Chairperson. Informal rank usually refers to an intrinsic quality or a particular connection that an individual has in the organisation that is not explicitly recognised as providing influence, but nevertheless holds great influence, such as the staff member who has been at the organisation the longest. From a depth perspective, informal rank is likely to be more problematic because it is often related to under-the-surface processes that cannot be discussed. Unless informal rank is acknowledged and discussed, the group is unlikely to move past conflict caused by rank difference.

THE ROLE OF RANK IN PROJECTIVE PROCESSES

Rank differences have a major impact on the direction and success of projective processes. Unpopular ways of being will always be projected onto others, if possible, and this projection is more likely to be successful if the receiving group or individual is lacking in rank. A powerful individual or subgroup will usually successfully resist the projection of an unpopular role. However, a subgroup or individual who is already carrying the role of less or no rank is sufficiently disadvantaged psychologically to become a target for other unpopular projections. It is therefore important to notice how a difference in an individual or subgroup that can become a distinguishing feature will, if possible, be used by the rest of the group for the allocation of unpopular roles. This will predispose the individual or subgroup to potential scapegoating. To protect that individual or subgroup, it is the job of the leader to try to prevent this kind of situation or to alert the group if it has already embarked on a scapegoating process.

It requires a lot of awareness from the leader, who may be similarly caught in the same psychodynamics as the group. Let us take investment management firms as an example. They are under a great deal of pressure in a competitive industry where they manage large funds for wealthy individuals and pension funds. Investment managers work very hard for very long hours. Heart attacks, depression and other health issues are not uncommon. As the leader of such a firm, you could work against that by trying to keep a worklife balance among your staff. If one investment manager has a good worklife balance and is leaving the office at 5 p.m., the rest of the team might – only half-jokingly – accuse the person of working a half day. This could easily deteriorate into scapegoating. Instead of jumping on the same bandwagon, you could put a check on it by pointing out that maintaining a worklife balance and protecting one's health is in fact a good thing, because it makes for a more sustainable contribution in the long term. The potential for scapegoating is thus squashed at the outset.

RANK AND GROUP CONSTITUTION

Rank psychodynamics have significant implications for group membership. If leaders have choices about the way a group is constituted, particularly if the group is to be divided into smaller subgroups for the purposes of task completion, it is important to keep in mind the impact of rank and difference as discussed above. Avoid the creation of a demographic rank minority if at all possible. For instance, if you have a choice, avoid having one woman in a group of men, or one young person in a group of older people, or one new techie in a group of very experienced technical people. The fact that a person is one of something makes him or her a target for all the other psychologically unpopular roles.

Two common rank-related depth processes exist in most heterogeneous groups:

- issues of ethnic, class or racial discrimination;
- gender, which is the most obvious fundamental difference between people, and exists in all groups worldwide.

A debate about these two issues will appear, almost without exception, at some stage in the group's life. When it does, the representatives of the different demographic groups end up having to speak from the position of the grouping to which they belong. If there is only one person representing a particular demographic grouping, that person has a very difficult task – either being totally silenced or burdened with having to carry the position alone. The person is often targeted with all the feelings the other members in the group may have about their particular grouping, and that is a particularly heavy burden to carry.

In most societies, strong feelings exist about ethnicity and race, and to a lesser extent gender, so depth work can become complex. Whether you like it or not, ethnic, race and gender issues will emerge at some point. If you are rolling out a new project and the team leader is of a different race to the majority of team members, at some point in the project meeting, there may be undertones around the racial differences. If there is only one woman on the board, at some point in a board meeting, there is going to be a depth process around the gender issue. Sometimes it will be joked about, but a wise leader will help the group to put it on the table so that it is no longer an elephant in the room. Although it may still cause trouble in the future, you have now developed a language and can talk about it more easily.

CONCLUSION

This chapter described the core ideas of a depth or psychodynamic view of a group. It highlighted the fact that a group will work as an integrated entity, thereby lessening the autonomy of the individuals in it. Individuals become parts in service to the whole, rather than important in their own right. I discussed some key group processes and described psychodynamics such as those caused by power or rank imbalances and scapegoating.

PERSONAL EXERCISES

1. Consider a group, or team, to which you belong (whether you are the leader or not). Describe the group size, the group members, the group context, the group history, the group task and intention, and any other salient features.

2. Create a timeline of the group's life, listing particular trends and critical incidents or events. Consider the group dynamics or psychodynamics that may appear as a result of the group context and history.

3. Notice your own particular role inclinations or valencies in groups. Make a list of all the roles you can think of that you actively play out in the world and then consider the specifics below in more detail.

    *   Consider the roles that you are most comfortable taking up in a team.
    *   Identify the roles that you are least comfortable taking up in a team.
    *   Identify any roles that you take up in a team but that you would prefer not to.
    *   Identify the roles that you never take up but would like to.
    *   Plan to become more flexible and agile in the roles that you occupy. Experiment with choosing different emotional, political and psychological roles in groups

4. Consider how you contribute to dysfunctional psychodynamics in groups.

5. Make a list of group complexes that you have seen in operation. Consider the group complexes in your family.

6. Consider the difficulties caused by rank differences in groups, or teams. Identify three examples of problematic situations and document the rank dynamics that occur. Consider possible ways you could help the group or team overcome the problems caused by rank differences in these situations.

7. Consider your own areas of sensitivity in terms of rank. How do you respond when those sensitivities are triggered? Try to relate your own minority feelings to those experienced by people who have less rank than you. Can you develop compassion for their experience?

CHAPTER
5

DEPTH LEADERSHIP METASKILLS AND SKILLS

INTRODUCTION

The previous chapters covered an outline of the important theories behind the idea of depth leadership. Leading from a depth perspective, however, requires that the leader develops a particular set of skills. This book aims to teach these skills by discussing the important principles and concepts, and giving guidance about the tools and techniques we can use. This chapter considers the attitudes (or, as we shall be calling them, metaskills) and skills that a leader should have to practise depth leadership. Many of these cannot be taught, but rather need to develop over time through experience.

DEPTH LEADERSHIP METASKILLS

The idea of metaskills comes from Amy Mindell's book (2001) *Metaskills: The spiritual art of therapy*. According to her, a metaskill is a subtle, yet fundamental attitude that influences the way all skills are implemented and is, therefore, more important than the individual technique or skill. Individuals and teams respond first to our metaskills and only then to the skill or technique. The same technique applied with different metaskills can have very different results. Metaskills will shape the way that we, as leaders, apply all the skills, techniques and methodologies that we have learnt. Without the right metaskills, the tools and techniques will not unleash the potential in an organisation.

INTEGRITY

Being a leader with integrity is a complex process. A leader with integrity is considered to be a person who is ethical and pursues integration in the self, in relationships and the system. Ethics refer both to the values that we as leaders hold, and to our capacity to implement them in all interactions despite difficulties. A leader needs to both have an ethical attitude and to abide by specific ethical guidelines that relate to a depth leadership approach. In this section, I describe the idea of an ethical attitude in detail, and then consider some of the appropriate rules or standards for integrity.

An ethical attitude

The notion of an 'ethical attitude' comes from the work of Hester McFarland Solomon (2007), who was primarily concerned with the type of ethics required by psychotherapists. The fact that, by definition, a therapeutic relationship translates into an unequal power dynamic between the two parties means that, if healing is to occur, special ethics and specific boundary management are required to ensure the safety of the client as the less powerful party. This is also true of leadership. McFarland Solomon suggests that the development of a truly ethical attitude means that one person does not 'use' another person to fulfil any of their unspoken psychological needs. Moreover, ethical behaviour cannot be based on currying favour with another, or by avoiding the alienation of the other, but should be aimed at ensuring the well-being of the other person.

McFarland Solomon does not succinctly define the term ethical attitude but explains the meaning in detail. She argues that being ethical means viewing one's unique and non-reversible responsibility towards the other as necessary regardless of whether the other person sees their duties as the same. She offers a Jungian approach, which uses the terms 'morality' and 'ethics' in specific ways, and says that:

> Morality is indicated by the adherence to a set of stated principles or rules which govern behaviour (for example, the Ten Commandments, or a professional Code of Ethics), whereas ethics implies an attitude achieved through judgement, discernment, unconscious struggle, often between conflicting rights of duty. (McFarland Solomon, 2007, p. 219)

McFarland Solomon quotes Jung as saying that an action only deserves to be called ethical when it is reflective and consciously scrutinised. She, therefore, considers an ethical attitude to be one in which the individual habitually confronts the tensions of a moral dilemma, considering both sides, particularly the side that may be lodged unconsciously, in what Jung referred to as the 'shadow. She describes what is meant by the shadow:

> The shadow, that portion of the self that the ego designates as bad and projects as unwanted, carries what is treacherous and subversive – what is unethical and immoral – within the self and hides it, relegating its contents to unconscious areas within the psyche where it can then be lived out in projection, using and abusing the other as a vehicle for holding the bad aspects of the self. To withdraw shadow projections can require tremendous struggle of an ethical nature, bringing to consciousness what is unconscious and projected. (McFarland Solomon, 2001, p. 445)

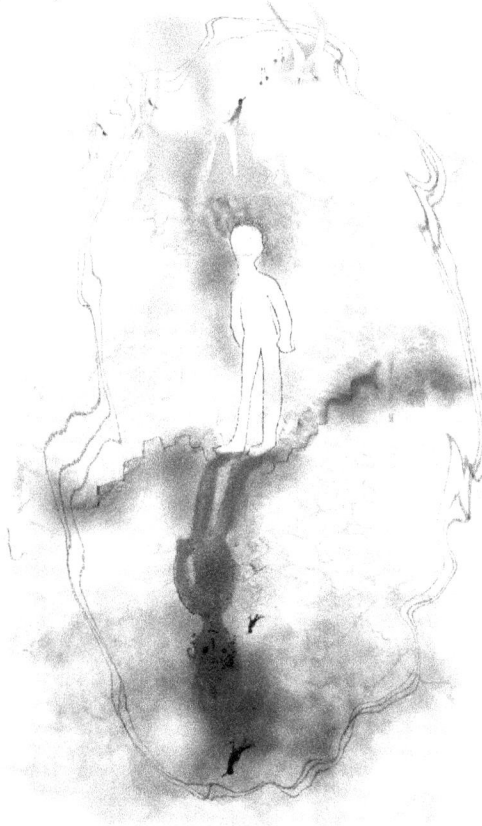

She describes the crux of an ethical attitude as the capacity to confront "the bad" that forms the shadow, which is hidden inside the self. However, this process is challenging, because it requires us to face the difficult and dark parts of the self, and to accept that we may project evil onto others, and that evil comes from our own shadow. Similarly, we as leaders need to recognise our own unresolved negativity that we may project if we are to hold an ethical attitude in our relationships with others and the environment.

Achieving such an ethical attitude is complicated because it is dependent on us having had an experience of being related to ethically by someone else. McFarland Solomon (2007) explains that the type of relationship ideally needed for the ethical attitude to develop in someone is one in which a parent is unconditionally devoted to a child, and in which the parent overcomes their own needs and rages, ensuring that the needs of the child are prioritised. Therefore, the development of the ethical attitude is largely dependent on an early, almost ideal, experience of care in the hands of a mother (or father or other primary caregiver).

There is a positively reinforcing cycle that becomes possible if we work on developing ethics. In other words, the stronger our ethical attitude, the greater our capacity for increased self-awareness, and the greater our self-awareness, the greater our capacity for an ethical attitude. It is therefore important to do inner work regularly, as described in the next chapter.

Specific depth leadership guidelines for integrity

As a depth leader with integrity, it is necessary to be concerned with how we and our organisations can support psychological growth, development and transformation in the workplace and how we can ensure long-term systemic sustainability. For example, it would be important to confront leaders who are tyrannical, to speak up about covert racism or other scapegoating processes, and to interrogate business decisions for their impact on the natural environment. The following specific guidelines should help to develop our integrity, and are based on the definition of depth leadership offered in Chapter 1.

1. We actively pursue integration of our whole self or psyche, both the conscious (on-the-surface) self and the unconscious (under-the-surface) self, which includes the body and the imagination, to achieve the integrity of alignment between values and actions. This means actively engaging in inner work formally and informally, exploring our history and understanding the psychodynamic patterns that have resulted from that history.

2. We develop a moral compass that is sensitive to the needs and limitations of people and the environment, considering divergent views with empathy and interest, even the less powerful and less conscious points of view, and including perspectives from the past, present and future.

3. We treat others with care, respect and fairness, whilst pursuing the truth, and being consistent and trustworthy.

4.   We communicate honestly and transparently avoiding collusion with hidden agendas, but always maintain confidentiality when it is expected and promised.

5.   We are accountable for our actions; admitting and repairing failures; and taking responsibility for honouring and implementing our stated values and commitments.

6.   We strive to behave ethically despite opposition, pressure or adversity.

7.   We use perseverance, collaboration, creativity and holistic sensemaking to balance and meet the complex and conflicting demands of individual, group and systemic well-being.

8.   We inspire and lead others to act with a similar degree of moral consciousness and accountability.

9.   We pursue integration between people to help groups and communities to thrive, and in decision-making processes, ensure that minority voices and their interests are heard and taken into account.

10. We consider factors beyond the entity of concern, using an integrative approach towards larger systems, including governance systems and the natural environment, actively avoiding or minimising the negative impact of decisions on these larger systems.

11. We promote a moral ecosystem in the individual, the community, the organisation and the environment.

COMPASSION

Compassion is probably the next most important metaskill. It refers to the ability to 'suffer with' another person, understanding what they are experiencing, and being motivated to help. It is the capacity to genuinely understand another person's point of view without judging the merits of that point of view. Compassion can also be described as having empathy for the full variety of human experience. According to Amy Mindell, compassion involves nurturing, caring for and attending to those parts of ourselves and others that we like and identify with, while attending equally to and appreciating those parts that we do not like – those parts that we disavow and that are far removed from how we identify ourselves. Therefore, compassion means allowing all aspects of our experience and the experience of others to unfold, and having an attitude of helpfulness to all states.

A compassionate leader also shows compassion for the self, embracing the vulnerability of being human and mortal with kindness. Rogers (1961) introduces the concept of unconditional positive regard in which one accepts others without conditions or qualifications, and we do not criticize but embrace the totality of the other with warm caring.

NEUTRALITY

As depth leaders, it is often necessary to hold an attitude of neutrality towards the different positions that emerge in organisations. When we adopt a neutral stance, we can explore the wisdom of all sides in a situation. To harness the full intelligence of the people around as, we may need to temporarily let go of our own opinions so that we can hear and fully entertain someone else's. This means adopting an attitude of neutrality in that moment, but it does not mean that we may not revert to our own direction and opinion after we have listened. This is a key difference between depth leadership and surface, task-oriented leadership. Although a leader is not essentially neutral, neutrality is an important point of leverage because it significantly changes the dialogue. The ability to wear both hats – that of task-oriented surface leader and that of neutral processoriented depth leader – makes us more effective as leaders. Of course, being neutral requires a fair amount of psychological agility.

PLAYFULNESS

Playfulness may be a helpful metaskill from a depth perspective. It allows a sense of freedom from our ordinary identities and societal rules. Play expert Fred Donaldson (2001) says that true play has two rules:

- everyone is invited; and
- no one gets hurt

Playfulness sometimes helps us to approach experiences that provoke anxiety in a safe way. As children, we have the potential to approach the world with an amazement and joy in the magical and unpredictable elements of life. Through play, we again have access to this worldview, using our senses and acknowledging the sensual information we gather from the world all the time. This gives us access to our broader identity and often provides valuable feedback about depth processes. The energy behind playfulness is best captured in the way young animals play.

HUMOUR

Humour is linked to playfulness and can be a powerful metaskill if we use it to manage ourselves, our idiosyncrasies and our foibles. However, humour is sometimes used inappropriately as a defence mechanism. If we are unsure whether humour would be a good idea, then it is usually better to refrain from it. Humour can help to reduce the illusions others have about us if we can be playful about ourselves and our difficulties in the world. For instance, if we are not strong in a particular area, we could be self-deprecatingly playful. However, we should be careful not to cross the boundaries of political correctness. We need to be sensitive to when certain jokes would be acceptable.

DETACHMENT

Detachment is the ability to maintain clarity and direction amid chaos and not be swept up by the complex dynamics that often characterise group life. It does not, however, only mean being uninvolved, as it is so often interpreted. A more accurate view of detachment is the ability to experience the present so fully that it moves through us swiftly and completely. This may sometimes mean that we will experience emotions with great force.

Detachment becomes possible when you have moved through a feeling or processed it, not when you have avoided it. Amy Mindell says that detachment is a feeling in which we are released from the apparent situation when we step back and discover a meta (or outside) point of view. Allowing ourselves to experience something as fully as possible does not mean, however, that we act on it. Rather, it means allowing ourselves to feel and think about our experience without acting on it. This metaskill does not imply that we never invest in a particular course of action, but it does mean that we invest consciously and deliberately when we do.

FLUIDITY

Fluidity refers to our ability to flow with an unfolding process rather than to control it tightly. This is particularly important when engaging in depth work. If we become rigid about achieving a certain outcome, it is likely that others will sense our resistance and start to push against us. Group energy often ebbs and flows, and we need to be able to manage this movement without becoming anxious or trying to direct the path that the group takes. Of course, if we are leading a surface process only, then it may be important to direct the team more firmly in terms of the path it takes. Depth work, however, requires a far more non-directive style, especially in the early stages of an organisation or group's exploration beneath the surface. The unconscious processes in groups are often circuitous, precisely because they provoke anxiety and the group is negotiating an edge. If we become too directive, the anxiety of a team will rise and become debilitating. Flexibility will help to ensure that we do not become embroiled in the group psychodynamics.

INTELLIGENCE

Intelligence here does not refer to the traditional definition which emphasises intellectual competence. Intelligence can be seen as a holistic ability or metaskill that includes all kinds of knowledge and wisdom. It is the ability to combine resources in new and innovative ways. It involves the capacity to learn though trial and error. Intelligence comes from a breadth of experience and is enhanced by the depth of that experience. The more we expose ourselves to the ways of the world, the better we will live within it. Intelligence involves all the senses, as information comes in many forms. It is essentially the ability of the organism to self-organise in the interest of survival. Therefore, the broader our life experience, the better our ability to consciously self-organise. Also, it seems, as a metaskill, intelligence can be learnt.

DISCIPLINE

Discipline is the ability to manage the self and to do what needs to be done in any given situation. It is the ability to harness the self for appropriate action and follow through, even if it becomes difficult to persevere. Discipline involves having clarity of purpose and a sense of personal responsibility and power. Discipline needs to be self-centred, as an action arising from integrity and therefore an integrated self, rather than the practice of mindlessly adhering to rules. Discipline is not compromised by a lack of resources or a lack of cooperation from others. It is the result of commitment. However, discipline includes careful self-maintenance to ensure balance and sustainability.

COURAGE

Courage refers to the ability to approach difficult interpersonal situations and not shy away from – or use any other defence mechanisms that prevent constructive engagement with – conflict or intense emotions. Human interaction can often be emotionally demanding and we need to be strong in the face of challenging interpersonal interactions. With depth work particularly, we may be exposed to under-the-surface material that can appear in an explosive way. It is important that we stay calm in these situations and maintain a neutral position. This requires a quiet and centred sense of self amidst potential chaos. It becomes increasingly possible to do as we develop our self-awareness. The better we know ourselves, the greater our real courage will be.

HUMILITY

This metaskill refers to the capacity to let go of the need to be the expert in a situation. We need to remember that others ultimately know best what is good and right for themselves, or at least they know best what they can or cannot manage. We need to remember how to learn, that we never know everything, and let go of the need to be the most knowledgeable person in a group. Approach a team with an open mind (what Arnold Mindell calls a 'beginner's mind') because each individual and group story is, at least to some extent, new and unique.

PATIENCE

The metaskill of patience is best captured in the concept of fishing. True fishing is done when we cast our line into the water and then wait, knowing that eventually, if a fish is there, it will bite. It also means knowing and accepting that sometimes there are no fish. Having the ability to be patient means having the knowledge that the process is unfolding at its own pace. Often individuals and groups may become impatient because of the anxiety that is involved in human interactions. It is important that we hold individuals back until everyone in the group is ready to confront difficult situations. Ideally, we should avoid being rushed by the urgency of a group. Often it will seem as if the group is stuck, but sometimes this indicates a period of incubation before the depth material can surface.

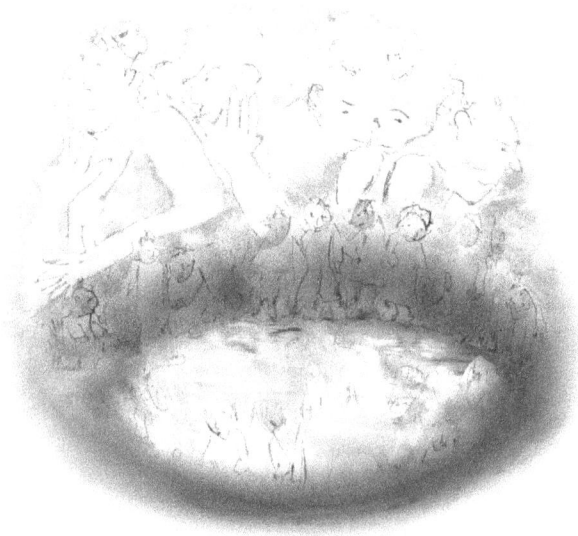

RESOLUTENESS

In all of our lives, it sometimes becomes necessary to take difficult action. Without the ability to do so we would not survive ourselves. We sometimes need to cause pain to others to protect the group and sometimes to protect ourselves. To create sustainability around us, we need to set limits. This will always mean denying the fulfilment of someone's need. Especially in situations of strong transference, it is important to resist meeting needs that will ultimately be detrimental to the group. Well-considered resoluteness benefits the group when it is exercised in conjunction with the metaskill of compassion.

IMAGINATION

Imagination includes seeing the possible and the impossible. It means anticipating the highs and lows of an organisation's life. The ability to continually question and shift the boundaries of the present produces the innovations that improve our quality of life, but we need to imagine the full cost and benefit patterns that can result from our actions. Our imaginations specifically need to include the experiences of others in our world. We need to ask: "What is it like from over there?" "How could it be different?" "What am I refusing to see?" Imagination is most important when ensuring empathy and compassion. Also, to work with unconscious processes, it is important to allow the flow of information from the unconscious to express itself through the vehicle of imagination. By developing our capacity to allow our minds to drift, we will be developing our imaginative capacity, and hence our access to the unconscious mind.

COLLECTIVE CONSCIOUSNESS

Being conscious of our collective experience implies understanding that we are connected to everything around us, that we approach situations with an appreciation of all the parts, even those we cannot sense. Collective consciousness means noticing that the voices of others may also be voices inside ourselves. It also means allowing the disavowed parts in ourselves and others to have a voice. It means noticing the intricate patterns of the relationships around us that interconnect us. Consciousness of our collective experience reminds us that ultimately, we cannot isolate ourselves from our community or our environment.

HARNESSING ENERGY

Our energy is our power. It is the quantity of life force that we have available to live our lives. The ability to harness the energy that is available for our lifework needs to be honed. It is not sufficient to conserve energy. We need to find ways of replenishing our stores and generating enough energy to provide sufficient containment for the individuals and groups we are leading. We waste energy in the following situations: when we are unaware and use the energy of others unnecessarily; when we push against a system blindly; when we do not embrace the fullness of our experience; and when we do not confront ourselves. Unresolved and chronic symptoms rapidly consume our life force. When we find and encourage new parts of our identities, energy is released and becomes available. Continually expanding our consciousness generates new power.

CURIOSITY

An attitude of curiosity is essential for depth leadership. It is necessary to have a spirit of enquiry, to place curiosity and intelligence ahead of action. Curiosity means genuinely wanting to know and not minding being wrong. When we only use the skill of advocacy for telling others what we think, we waste the opportunities offered by relationships. Curiosity means having a genuine interest in what is going on that is not directly related to the self. Depth leadership means appropriately prioritising the processes of others above our own preoccupations. If we are not genuinely interested in the details of the lives of the individuals around us, they will sense it and resist our leadership.

RENEWAL

An attitude that embraces renewal brings the ability to let go of something when it needs to die or end. The life-death-life cycle is found throughout nature, yet we cling to the present and the past. The ability to embrace renewal as part of our existence frees us from an obsession with death. Following the natural cycles of the world ensures continuity. Allowing death brings new life. Individuals and groups will usually resist endings and employ a range of defence mechanisms to avoid facing the necessary grieving processes. If a group has worked together successfully, they will often try to prolong their life together in artificial ways. While they may be able to find a situation that allows them to continue being together, it is important that they confront the end of their current process together. Ensuring that a team faces an ending allows them to acknowledge and honour their common experience explicitly, which allows them closure and the ability to move forward freely. We as leaders need to help groups accept endings, so it is important for us to tolerate ending and the feelings of loss that are evoked in our own life.

REVERENCE

Having reverence means being able to feel awe at the miracle of life in all its forms. It is often linked to loving nature. Reverence powers the breath of life and connects us to our world. Reverence means knowing that regardless of how much we know, we do not know everything and that a great deal of mystery runs beneath our human experience. As leaders, we need the capacity to be moved by the experiences of the people we work with. Without this, we will find it difficult to create an environment in which teams can encounter their own capacity to be deeply moved by their own potential and experiences.

DEPTH LEADERSHIP KNOWLEDGE AND SKILLS

The metaskills described above provide the atmosphere and psychological framework for exercising the skills of depth leadership. There are some general skills and knowledge required as a depth leader and these are listed below.

- General psychology knowledge (covered in Chapter 1)
- Depth psychology knowledge about individuals and groups (covered in Chapters 3 and 4)
- Developing and managing our own psychology (covered in Chapter 6)
  - Emotional self-regulation
  - Managing triggers
  - Maintaining neutrality
  - Inner work
  - Managing projections and transference
  - Managing boundaries
  - Managing the inner critic
  - Self-care as depth leader
- Developing and managing the psychology of others (covered below)
  - Communication skills
  - Awareness and observation skills
  - Group facilitation skills

In previous chapters, I offered a theoretical overview of depth psychology as it applies to the individual and the group. Of course, a book like this cannot do justice to all the knowledge in this field, so I encourage leaders to take the initiative to explore these areas further. The chapter that follows this addresses the skills we need to manage your own psychology (in other words, self-management). The rest of this chapter considers the remaining skills listed above and includes communication skills, awareness and observation skills, and group facilitation skills.

COMMUNICATION SKILLS

There are many texts that deal with general communication skills, so this section will try to highlight those that are essential for depth leadership. Simple misunderstandings cause many difficulties in the world and in increasingly multilingual workplace environments the opportunity for misunderstanding is even greater. Essentially, from a depth point of view, communication is the process of developing shared meaning between people through information exchange and thereby enabling the development of coordinated efforts and relationships. This involves several potentially complex and difficult steps.

1. Clarifying meaning. We must clarify for ourselves the meaning that we wish to articulate.

2. Establishing the medium of communication. We must find the right channel, form and content of communication to express our meaning.

3. Timing and context. An appropriate opportunity for communication must be found or created for us to deliver our message.

4. Message delivery. The message should be delivered in the most accessible way possible.

5. Depth listening. Once the message has been delivered, we must listen, hear and understand the communication from the other, whether it is in the form of a response or an unsolicited new message.

6. Feedback skills. The process of developing shared meaning may require several iterations of the process above and includes giving and receiving feedback. Conflict resolution skills may be required and will be covered in Chapter 9.

The steps are outlined in more detail below, with emphasis given to aspects that are particularly relevant to depth leadership.

1. Clarifying meaning

Depth communication requires the development of insight into our own thoughts and feelings and the expression of those thoughts and feelings. One of the great difficulties in communication generally is that we often do not know what we think or feel. We could assume that all people naturally know what they think and feel, but this is not the case, especially if you consider the compartmentalisation of the psyche into conscious and unconscious parts as a result of the intrapsychic conflict discussed in Chapter 3.

We learn how to know what we think and feel through encouragement and help from our caregivers. Our early expressions of our thoughts and feelings and the responses our caregivers gave us will have resulted in a process of learning about the validity and appropriateness of our expression of our experience in the world. Our earliest forms of expression are simple and sophisticated. Essentially, in the first few months of our lives, all we are able to do is cry, smile, gurgle and move our limbs in an uncoordinated way. Regardless of our limited forms of expression, we receive feedback in terms of the response or lack of response from our caregivers.

Each caregiver response teaches us whether our communication attempts are successful or not – and we adapt accordingly. As we start to express our experiences in slightly more sophisticated ways, we continue to learn from our caregivers whether they regard our responses as appropriate or not. As a result of our absolute early dependency on caregivers, we pay close attention to the messages we receive from them. If we receive messages of strong (overt or covert) disapproval, we may start to hide our thoughts and feelings from others and from ourselves. For example, a child who is continually scolded for crying when hurt may eventually give up feeling hurt by relegating those feelings to the unconscious part of the psyche.

Therefore, it sometimes takes effort to establish exactly what our thoughts and feelings are so that we can clarify the meaning we would like to communicate. If you add to this the natural complexity of the world around us and the difficulty of understanding our situations and then having to solve problems, make decisions and be creative too, clarifying meaning can be an onerous task.

Mirroring

The process of helping children develop a good understanding of their own thoughts and feelings is called mirroring. The importance of this concept was emphasised by Heinz Kohut (2009) in the 1970s and 1980s. It involves acknowledging and affirming the child's experience. If you suspect that as a leader you struggle to know your own thoughts and feelings, you may need to enter into a therapeutic relationship with an appropriately qualified person to develop this capacity.

The role of wounds

It is also important to try to distinguish ordinary feelings and responses from those driven by our wounds and complexes. Such responses are usually characterised by the fact that they are out of proportion to the events that triggered them. For instance, a woman who grew up in a family where her opinions were never considered may have developed a complex that her opinions are worthless. After a meeting where a lot of people are giving opinions (and no one is really listening to anyone else) she is left feeling worthless again. Others in the meeting who do not have the same complex may feel irritated because no one listened to them but, unlike her, they would not experience themselves as worthless.

The role of others

One other difficulty with clarifying meaning for ourselves is that in an interpersonal or group setting the thoughts and feelings of others can infiltrate and amplify our own experience. It is, therefore, important to remember that sometimes we may be experiencing things on behalf of others, albeit unconsciously. Chapter 6 introduces an exercise (page 147) that helps you to clarify your own responses in a given situation, and to establish which thoughts and feelings represent your original and authentic experience.

A note on emotions

A last thought on this matter is that human beings have a vast and complex potential set of responses to their experiences in the world. In addition to the millions of thoughts we could have in response to our interactions with the world, we also have a large range of feelings. Charles Darwin (1998) identified 34 emotions. Robert Plutchik (1982) identified eight emotions, which then extend into other emotions that he depicted in an emotion wheel. Recent research by Cowen and Keltner (2017) indicated that there are 27 emotions. For the purpose of depth leadership, it is important to note that there are a wide range of possible emotions that people experience, and many people do not recognise or name this wide range inside themselves. The more accurate we can be in noticing, identifying and naming our emotions, the clearer we will be in our communication and the more accurately we can clarify meaning for ourselves and others. Also, it is important to recognise that emotions serve an important psychological function: emotions help us to evaluate and metabolise our experiences. Therefore, it is necessary for us as depth leaders to develop our capacity to feel, notice and name our emotions, and to encourage others to do so.

2. The medium of communication

There are of course many different ways of communicating a message. These include the obvious high-level distinctions of verbal or written communication. Modern technology allows a variety of versions of these two main groups and it is worthwhile considering the impact the choice of medium has on the quality of communication. However, there are many subtle ways of communicating, as communication is the result of human expression in all its forms and the observation of such expression. The difficulty of working at a depth level is that our deepest processes communicate themselves in a variety of subtle ways.

There are many channels or pathways, which are described in more detail in Chapter 9, and human communication almost always works through more than one. There will be one dominant channel, such as the verbal channel, and there will be others that are less obvious, but also provide information to the attentive observer. For example, our body language will add to the message being communicated. Often communication from a depth process conflicts with the communication from the surface process and so the more access we have to the various channels of communication, the better we can deliver and receive messages.

Below is a list of possible channels or pathways of communication we can use consciously or unconsciously. Some of them may have to be actively decoded, but many people instinctively decode messages from a variety of channels without doing it consciously.

- Speaking
- Choice of language
- Tone of voice
- Eye contact and expression in the eyes
- Other micro-expressions (such as the unconscious tightening around the eyes while smiling)
- Other general body movements
- Physical touch
- Physical symptoms or sensations
- Human scent
- Writing (ranging from handwritten to various forms of technology-based written communication)
- Symbolic gestures (such as the giving of a gift, the sending of a photograph or the slamming of a door)
- Absence of communication, such as avoidance or withdrawal
- Other actions that send a message, such as not keeping to an arrangement
- The regularity of a type of communication

As mentioned already, many of these channels of communication are used (and received) unconsciously. The more limited our contact with the range of possible channels is while communicating, the more likely it is that the communication will be either misread or misunderstood. It is often only by having access to more than one channel that we can fully transmit or receive a message. Of course, if the people communicating are congruent in their communication (by congruent, I mean that their communication is aligned with their true thoughts and feelings, whether conscious or unconscious), then they can communicate deeply even through limited channels. A short text message of 100 words can communicate deep meaning if there is a clear and well-developed relationship between people.

To check for congruence and resolve any incongruities, our deepest communication should (if possible) happen face-to-face. Face-to-face communication provides the biggest opportunity for reading all the possible channels of communication. Much of our communication is now virtual through video applications. It is necessary that participants maximise the channels available in such situations by keeping their cameras on. However, by its very nature, face-to-face communication can provoke anxiety and so activate our defence mechanisms, which then paradoxically obscure or confuse our true communication. If you are aware that the proposed communication will provoke anxiety, then certain channels can be chosen that will reduce anxiety because they do not require an immediate face-to-face response.

The choice of medium of communication should therefore take several factors into consideration and requires that the whole context is thought about in detail. Depth processes happen on many different levels at once; sometimes switching between channels allows breakthroughs that would otherwise not be possible.

3. Managing timing and context

Considering the detail mentioned above in terms of clarifying meaning and choosing a medium of communication, it should by now have become clear that depth communication is a complex process. If we consider the individual and group psychology concepts in Chapters 3 and 4, it suggests that people communicate most constructively when they are not anxious and when they feel that they will be heard empathetically. A depth leader is aware of this and will consider the timing and context of communication carefully to ensure safety and provide the maximum potential for a positive outcome. The following aspects of timing and context should be considered in any communication exchange.

- The physical space where communication occurs should be conducive. There should be no noise interference, and individuals should be comfortable from an ergonomic point of view.

- Privacy is necessary. If we are to communicate at a deep level, then most people prefer a certain amount of privacy. Ideally, the conversation should be behind a closed door or outside, far away from anyone else to avoid even the possibility of being overheard. If, during important communication, someone is likely to have a strong emotional reaction, privacy extends to them not being seen by others. In group settings this cannot always be achieved, but the group can discuss a set of ground rules to provide the necessary respect for deep conversations where someone may become emotional.

- The right people need to be present for appropriate communication and group constitution is an important consideration in any communication.

- Confidentiality is usually an issue for many of us, so assurances in this regard should be stated (not assumed) and rigorously implemented. Depth leaders should not break confidences unless someone is in danger of hurting themself or others.

- It is useful to have an idea of the major preoccupations of the people involved in the communication process. For example, if someone is about to go for major surgery, he or she is unlikely to engage constructively in a discussion about efficiency improvements at work. Depth processes operate in layers, and those layers are ordered according to the immediate interests and concerns of the people involved in them.

4. Message delivery

Once we have clarified the content, timing and context of communication, we need to deliver the message in as accessible a way as possible. There are some general principles that apply to message delivery when communicating from a depth perspective.

- The style, pace, tone and manner of communication should be authentic, but should also be modified to match (where possible) that of the other person. For example, when communicating with a soft-spoken individual, it is useful to moderate our own volume.

- It is useful to prepare others that the communication is about to happen and to check whether it is an appropriate time and place for a conversation or interaction.

- In a multilingual group, it is important to check that everyone is comfortable and understands the language being used. People need to be invited to give feedback if they are struggling to understand, and we need to organise translation if necessary. If people are not communicating in their mother tongue, accommodation should be made in terms of time and clarification to ensure that messages are being clearly delivered. We need to keep our language usage simple and check for understanding on an ongoing basis.

- The metaskills discussed earlier should inform all our use of language. In other words, the general attitude behind all communication should be carefully considered and applied. It is useful to approach all communication with respect, empathy and compassion.

- Remember that language is powerful and what is heard is often not what is meant. Avoid exaggerations and euphemisms.

- Avoid judgemental language with words like "should" or "must".

- Always invite and suggest rather than demand and insist. It is always useful to be slightly tentative when making observations; this allows others to correct us if we are wrong.

- Speak in the first person – use "I" statements. Do not depersonalise language – avoid "it" and "one" or blame and attack with "you" statements. In any given situation, outline facts first, then explain feelings, followed by needs, and then finally we may need to include the consequences if our needs are not met.

- Do not ask a question instead of making a statement if in fact we intend to make a statement.

- Use people's names if we know them (get to know them as soon as possible). If we have forgotten someone's name or we struggle to pronounce it, we can ask the individual to help us until we get it right.

- Avoid jargon or colloquialisms. If we use colloquial or slang expressions, we need to translate them for the listener.

- Soften language by referring to the positive view of a particular behaviour rather than the negative interpretation: use "forthright" rather than "aggressive", and "independent thinker" rather than "troublemaker".

- Be aware of cultural biases in our language usage. Clarify any local or contextual references even though most people may know them.

5. Depth listening

In addition to delivering our own message with care, one of the most important skills that a leader needs to have is the capacity to listen from a depth perspective. This refers not only to being attentive to others and understanding what they are saying, it also means developing the communication by using techniques that go beyond simply taking in information. There are many different techniques that help us to improve your listening skills. Two types of listening skills that we can apply as a depth leader are reflective listening and empathetic listening.

Reflective listening is a very important skill for building a relationship with a team and helping the team members to clarify their meaning. It involves listening to what is being said and then restating what the person has said. The restatement cannot be mere repetition but needs to reflect the core meaning of the team member's message. To become proficient in this skill we have to listen very carefully to the other person. While listening, we need to try to discover the underlying meaning beneath the person's statement. Once we discover the underlying meaning, we then restate that view using words that pinpoint the underlying meaning. On hearing the restatement, the person will realise that we are listening to the real issue and may then be willing to elaborate on it.

In reflective listening, it is important to reflect both the content and emotion that is being expressed. When reflecting the content, the leader attends to the substance of what the individual is saying and reflects back the basic idea of what has just been said. The person will usually elaborate on their thinking. The leader follows the flow, again reflecting the content by using other words. This ensures that the person will move a little further into the issue.

When reflecting the emotion, the listener notices the emotional tone of the issue. The words used in the restatement should exaggerate the emotional tone, trying to take it a shade deeper. For example, if a person says he or she is "anxious regarding the exams", a reflective comment could be: "You're feeling a bit afraid." Note how the anxiety was exaggerated in the reflection to become afraid.

As a depth leader, start with content and wait for the team member to begin talking about feelings before picking up on the emotional tone. Let the team member lead. Sometimes it is useful to use a metaphor if an apt one springs to mind. The use of metaphor in restatement is a form of combined content and emotion. Metaphors are ambiguous and allow the person to focus on what is important for him or her. For example, if a team member is discussing the recent leadership changes in a team or organisation, we may check whether the team member experiences it as moving into a new house. If the person likes the metaphor, he or she may develop it further and add that it is like moving into a rented house after previously having owned our own house.

Some specific guidelines for reflective listening are given below.

- Use different words. It is important when we reflect that we use words that are different from the ones the person used. For example, if a person says, "I'm feeling miserable about the job" and we restate the exact words, he or she may wonder if we have really heard and are interested, or if we really understand.

- Do not introduce our own views. Limit ourselves to the views expressed by the other person.

- Listen for the issue that has weight. Issues that have weight are emotionally charged and have more relevance than others. If we have emphasised the wrong issue or view, we do not need to be concerned – the person will bring us back to the issue or view that he or she wants to talk about.

- Do not steer the conversation. Follow the person's conversational thread and only reflect back what has been said.

When we use and develop the reflective listening techniques described above, our ability to empathise with people will grow. Empathy is having genuine understanding of what the person has said, together with genuine concern. Empathy is not sympathy. Sympathy is similar but contains a component of pity. Sympathy implies that the person is helpless, cannot cope and is in need of assistance. In most situations sympathy will undermine the person's self-worth and does not acknowledge their own strengths.

Empathetic listening requires that we live ourselves into the message or story being communicated by the other person. We try to psychologically place ourselves in their shoes. One way to do this is to try and remember situations we have been in that may have been similar to the one being described. It also means temporarily suspending our own need to be heard and knowing that our empathy for the situation of the other does not undermine our own position. Once we have listened empathetically, we can once again allow ourselves to take our own side as fully as possible.

6. Feedback skills

Once we have communicated and received communication from another, two (or more) individuals are in an interaction that may give rise to psychodynamics. This usually means that the parties concerned will eventually need to give one another feedback to develop a better interaction or relationship. A leader needs to know how to give feedback so that it can be absorbed, and how to receive feedback without becoming defensive.

Feedback is useful when it is regular, well thought out, specific, accurate and given with compassion and humility. Also, from a depth perspective, feedback is often related to the under-the-surface dynamics that hamper performance in an organisational setting. To resolve a depth process, it is often necessary to embark on an exercise of giving and receiving feedback. For feedback to be of value, follow these simple guidelines.

- We need to give feedback compassionately, trying to focus on the positive intention behind the behaviour. For example, if someone is being disruptive, give feedback that we are aware that this participant may be uncomfortable about the process being followed or the content being discussed.

- Do not generalise, rather comment on specific observable behaviour. When giving feed-back, we need to specifically describe the event we are commenting on. We need to follow this up with reasons for our comments. This is helpful whether the comments are positive or negative.

- If possible, we need to maintain relaxed eye contact with the person we are giving feedback to. Also, keep feedback brief and clear, avoiding extra phrases to pad it out and make it more comfortable.

- We need to take ownership for the feedback we give; use "I" statements. We should not speak as if the feedback is given from a position of greater authority than our own.

- Feedback should be concerned with those things over which an individual or a team can exercise some control and be given in ways which indicate how the feedback can be used for improvement or planning alternative actions. Feedback on behaviours or characteristics that are difficult to change can make an individual or a team anxious and self-conscious.

- Allow people to give input throughout the feedback process. When encountering rising defence mechanisms and emotional reactions, deal with these reactions rather than trying to convince, reason or supply additional information. Recognise that containment is needed.

- Give feedback in a manner that communicates acceptance of others as worthwhile individu-als, and of everyone's right to be different. The motivation of feedback must be to help and not to hurt. In other words, we need to ensure that we are building someone's self-image.

- We need to remember our neutrality when giving feedback. If the group has only agreed to surface process leadership to achieve a specific task, individual feedback can only be given if an individual member is hampering that process. If the team is in a depth process, then the team members themselves will ideally give feedback to individual members. Always allow the member who has received the feedback an opportunity to respond. In a depth process, feedback must be given to the whole group, and both sides (if there are two sides) should be given feedback about their one-sidedness.

It is important to keep in mind that all negative feedback can be perceived as an attack on the individual or the group and produce anxiety that leads to the activation of defence mechanisms. Individuals or groups can use any of the defences mentioned in Chapters 3 and 4. If we as leaders notice a defensive reaction, we need to realise that the feedback may have been given in the wrong way or the individual or team is not ready to hear it. If this happens, we need to move away from the feedback and acknowledge that the feedback may have been wrong.

AWARENESS AND OBSERVATION SKILLS

These skills refer to our ability to be attuned to others and the environment, and to be able to make sense of the messages we are getting. As depth leaders, we need the ability to notice even small changes around us, and to be able to pick up information in a variety of communication channels. These refer to our ability to notice what is happening in a group on various levels: verbal communication, body language, atmosphere, interpersonal relationships and energy level changes. We may need to remain conscious of several different processes at once, and to pick up subtle information about the state of mind of others and the dynamics between other people.

Although we will be concentrating mainly on others, to be an effective depth leader we should also keep an eye on our own behaviour. We need to try to recognise emotional responses and other reactions that may be developing in us. Awareness is one of the most important tasks of leaders – being aware of ourselves and of others. Continual reflection is necessary to maintain awareness. There are many things that could become barriers to awareness, and our own psychological make up is a large factor.

Beware of the following barriers to awareness:

- Feeling tired. We need to ensure that we get enough rest so that we do not become psychologically exhausted as a leader. If necessary, we need to make sure we have a mentor, coach or therapist, or someone else who will offer us support when we become exhausted.

- Losing our neutrality because we have a vested interest or a strong opinion about the team and its process could cause us to lose awareness.

- Thinking that we know what to expect from others and not leaving room for surprises. All individuals and groups have the capacity to behave in an unexpected or unusual manner.

Developing our depth attention

One important aspect of being depth leaders is developing our capacity for observing and paying attention to processes that are less than obvious. It is essential to pay attention to signals from a group that are different from those emanating from the surface process. Surface attention is the awareness needed to accomplish goals, to do our daily work, to appear the way we want to appear. Depth attention focuses on things we may normally neglect, on external and internal subjective, irrational experiences.

This means paying attention to the messages from the unconscious, to incongruous behaviour and the accidents and slips of the tongue that happen every day. A depth leader needs depth attention (an ability to notice messages that occur just below the surface) to work with a team holistically. It is only possible to have this depth attention if we can set aside some of the obvious distractions that demand the most immediate attention.

Awareness and observation guidelines

To develop our awareness and observation skills, we need to be able to look for specific signals in as many different communication channels as possible. All the channels listed above may require our attention, in addition to the nature of interactions and relationships around us. The table below lists aspects of group life that reveal the psychodynamics of the group:

Participation	Who participates in group or organisational activity more than others? Who is quiet? Are there any changes in participation levels? For example, do participative members become quiet, or quiet members suddenly become talkative? How are the silent members treated? How is silence interpreted? Who talks to whom, and who do they look at when they talk? Who interrupts whom during interactions? What is the style of communication used in the team?
Content of a discussion	Who participates in group or organisational activity more than others? Who is quiet? Are there any changes in participation levels? For example, do participative members become quiet, or quiet members suddenly become talkative? How are the silent members treated? How is silence interpreted? Who talks to whom, and who do they look at when they talk? Who interrupts whom during interactions? What is the style of communication used in the team?
Signs of anxiety and defence mechanisms	Do members of the group display signs of anxiety? Is anxiety openly admitted to or talked about? Are there indications of defence mechanisms? Are there efforts to reduce the anxiety? Are the efforts constructive or unhelpful?
Rank and power issues	Which members seem to have a great deal of rank or influence? Which members have less rank or influence? Are the individuals with more rank aware of their rank and do they manage it carefully? Are individuals with less rank encouraged to participate? Is there rivalry in the team, a struggle for leadership? Are rank differences discussed and managed openly? Which members seem to have a great deal of rank or influence? Which members have less rank or influence? Are the individuals with more rank aware of their rank and do they manage it carefully? Are individuals with less rank encouraged to participate? Is there rivalry in the team, a struggle for leadership? Are rank differences discussed and managed openly?

Decision-making procedures	How are decisions made? Do individual members make a decision and carry it through without checking with the other members? Who supports the decisions or suggestions of others? Are attempts made to get all members participating in a decision? Do certain individuals make suggestions that receive no response at all? Are decisions arrived at by calling a vote? Are minority voices ignored or listened to?
Membership issues	Are there any subgroups? Do some people seem outside the group? Do some members move in and out of the group? Do some members of the group pair with or support one another? Is there any scapegoating occurring?

The psychodynamics of groups can take many forms, including the issues above. It is impossible to mention all the signs that may include information about depth processes, but a general list of other things to look for is provided below.

- Body language and changes in body language

- Gut feel, hunches or intuitive signals

- Individual tone of voice, volume and changes in tone and volume

- The nature of eye contact

- Incongruence of any kind

- The appearance of a new role, particularly if the role is disturbing to the group or team

- Any changes in the climate or weather in the room. (This refers to the emotional atmosphere in the room.)

It is always useful if we are unsure, to check our perceptions with the team. For example, we can say, "I am sensing a change in atmosphere in the team. Am I the only one, or is anyone else picking it up too?"

GROUP FACILITATION SKILLS

Group facilitation is a profession in its own right and differs from leadership because the individual does not lead the team or the group on an ongoing basis. However, leaders (especially leaders who work at a depth level) can benefit greatly from using certain facilitation skills. There are many specific skills and techniques which are covered in the rest of the book, but in this last section of the chapter, we will consider three group sets of skills to do with group facilitation.

- Stimulation skills – how to help others to start communicating

- Support skills – how to support individuals and groups through group processes

- Control skills – how to prevent individual group members or the group as a whole from behaving destructively.

Stimulation skills

As leaders, we may need to stimulate team members to participate in group conversations. To begin with, if needed, we do this by providing information on the problem or situation being discussed. We need to provide the objective of the discussion and some of the basic facts.

An effective leader stimulates the members throughout the discussion by asking questions and exploring ideas, and by occasionally summarising the contributions made. We can use expressions like, "Let us get this clear. Are you suggesting that …?" or "Could you give us an example to help us understand your point?" and "It would be helpful to get the views of a few others on this. How do the rest of you feel about that idea?" Some detailed verbal techniques are given below.

Open questions

Open questions encourage people to contribute their ideas and experience. They are used for introducing topics and encouraging participants to talk at length, thus avoiding simple "yes" or "no" answers. Open questions begin with the following words: how, which, when, who, why or what and a few examples are given below.

> "How would you like to begin this part of the process?"
> "Which of these items are the most important to discuss in this meeting?"
> "When would you like to get together again?"
> "How can we investigate this more carefully?"
> "Where would be the best place to try this out?"

Probes

Once someone has started contributing as a result of an open question, it is sometimes useful to pursue the topic by getting more information. This is especially useful if we sense that there is something else the person is trying to say and that he or she may be at an edge. Probes are questions that generally follow open questions to elicit more information about a particular topic or event and some examples are given below.

"Could you tell me more about … ?"
"What do you mean by … ?"
"It would be helpful if you could elaborate on …"

Hypothetical statements

Hypothetical statements are useful to further stimulate thinking and encourage participation in a group. They also provide a way of checking the process to see whether we understand what is happening. These statements help team members to think about a new topic or area or get clarification on an existing area. Examples are:

"What would you do if … ?"
"If x happened, how would the situation be different?"
"How do you think everyone would respond if we decided to do x?"

Support skills

The depth leader provides support for every member of the team and the team as a whole. We do this by ensuring the right of each individual to express their own opinion and by continually drawing attention to the value of considering different points of view. For example:

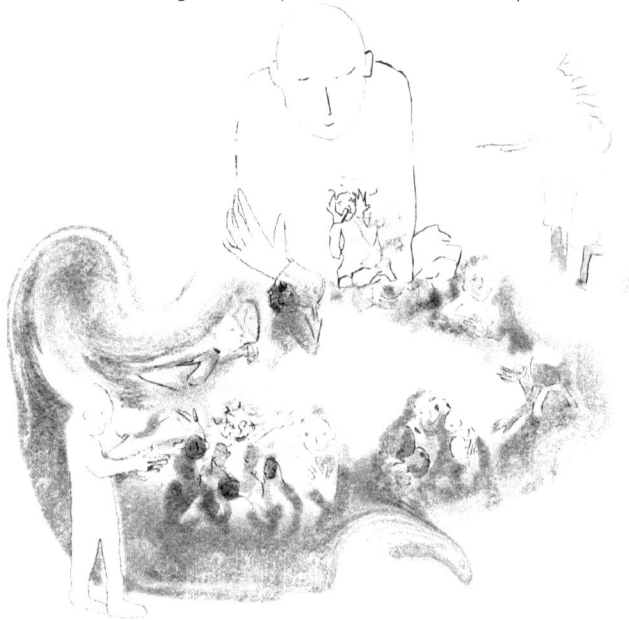

"Both of you have a valid point here. Let's give you both a chance to explain what you have in mind." The depth leader will also provide support to team members by keeping any disagreement or evaluation centred on the problem rather than the individual.

The following verbal techniques will ensure that we understand what has been said, reveal any inaccurate assumptions and help to establish trust.

Reflecting

Reflecting refers to playing back what we have heard to show that we understand and empathise. Its aim is to get team members to acknowledge the emotional content. The rules of reflective and empathetic listening, discussed earlier, apply to this verbal technique. Examples are:

> "It sounds like you were angry when …"
> "That must have been frustrating."

Restatements

Restatements are similar to reflecting statements, but without any amplification or playing back of emotional content. They are designed more to clarify what has been heard than to empathise. The aim of a restatement is to confirm or crystallise ideas and to check that you heard correctly. Examples are:

> "What you seem to be telling me is ..."
> "I am hearing that you need more assistance, is that correct?"

Lubricators

Certain statements encourage the speaker to continue speaking, as they indicate to the speaker that we are listening and want them to continue. Examples are:

> "I understand", "Yes", "Go on", "Mmmm", "Uhuh", "Ah ha", "Tell me more"

Summaries

Summaries are useful to indicate to a group that we are keeping track of the discussion and to help a group pause and reflect on where they are. Summaries draw together the main points of a discussion and avoid emphasising the discrepancies. They are also useful in gaining commitment to action and could be a good precursor to moving on to a new subject. The language used in summaries should always be neutral and try to include the full variety of points that have been made.

> "What we seem to have discussed and decided so far is …"

Control skills

The depth leader controls the group process to ensure that the objectives are achieved. Group members become impatient if they are not making progress and this is likely to occur in surface or task-related leadership if we fail to keep the discussion on course. This does not mean that we must strictly or abruptly control the discussion. Rather, we need to keep the discussion moving forward by gently redirecting members who have strayed from the point and by periodically summing up the progress that is being made.

From a depth perspective, it is important to notice that a lack of progress may be a sign of an unresolved underlying process. In this case, we may feed our observation back to the group by stating that we notice a lack of progress, and that we are wondering what it may be about. More information about this will be given when discussing the leadership of depth processes in detail in Chapter 9.

The verbal techniques listed below are used to control the group process when necessary, and to provide structure to the conversation.

Closed questions are useful in guiding a group in a more directive way because they shorten or discourage further contributions from group members. This may be necessary if we are coming to the end of the agreed time period and need to complete tasks. Closed questions are useful for establishing precise information (dates, numbers, etc.) and receiving simple "yes" or "no" responses. They are also useful when dealing with a talkative, unfocused group member or when closing a session.

Closed questions are questions that can be answered with a simple "yes" or "no". They may start with: "Do you?" "Will you?" or "Have you?" Here are a few examples:

> "Does anyone have anything further to add before we close?"
> "Have we forgotten anything?"
> "Is everyone in agreement about the decisions so far?"
> "How long did it take?"
> "Is everyone happy if we end the meeting here?"

Inhibitors

Inhibiting statements signal to the speaker that enough has been said and that it is time to move on or allow someone else an opportunity to contribute. This is especially useful with talkative group members. Sometimes inhibitors may have to be said firmly. Examples are:

> "Let's move on."
> "Yes, but ..."
> "In the interest of time…"
> "I am going to interrupt you and allow some others to comment."

Bridges

Bridges are statements that provide a smooth link between one topic and another and indicate clearly what the next one is. They help a group that has become stuck on a particular topic to move on. Examples are:

> "It seems that everyone is clear, so let's move on to the next topic."
> "How does this link in with the issue we are discussing?"

Obviously, all the techniques listed above should be used with care and with the metaskills discussed earlier in mind.

SKILLS AND KNOWLEDGE DEVELOPMENT

It takes time and experience to develop our knowledge and skills as a depth leader. It is important that we understand the various tasks required and identify the skills and knowledge we currently lack. Many of the skills mentioned are general in nature and should be developed on an ongoing basis. These include our self-management skills, our general communication skills, our metaskills, our understanding of systems thinking and our psychological knowledge, including our knowledge of depth psychology. Ideally, as a depth leader it would be useful to work on all of these areas in a planned and consistent way.

CONCLUSION

This chapter considered the necessity of an ethical orientation to leadership, showing that without sound ethics, leadership may destroy what it set out to achieve. It also considered the less tangible and more philosophical aspects of leadership in the form of other metaskills. In some ways, metaskills cannot be taught. They can only be developed by individuals themselves or embraced through life experience.

This chapter also provided information about the more specific interaction skills of depth leadership. It is important to note that sometimes the best depth leadership comes from our intuition, and what may work in practice may not necessarily be described anywhere on these pages.

PERSONAL EXERCISES

1. Consider your own ethics. Under what circumstances is it hard to remain ethical? What can you do to ensure that you do not compromise your own ethics?

2. Evaluate yourself in terms of the metaskills listed in this chapter. Develop an action plan to further develop your metaskills.

3. Consider the list of knowledge and skills required for depth leadership under Depth Leadership Knowledge and Skills on page 122. Evaluate your knowledge and skill levels in the different areas. Identify areas in which you may have weaknesses. Develop specific learning processes to develop the areas that require work.

4. Consider the impact of your presence on a team. What first impressions do you make? Practise your communication skills by recording them if possible. Analyse your use of language and consider what needs to be changed.

5. Make an observation list for yourself that you can use to hone your observation skills.

6. Practise reflective and empathetic listening. Notice what makes it difficult for you to keep listening.

7. Practise giving feedback to friends and colleagues. Also ask for them to give you feedback. Notice whether you can manage your defensive reactions when being given difficult feedback.

8. Develop a list of phrases for all the verbal techniques above so that you can have easy access to them when needed.

CHAPTER
6
MANAGING YOUR OWN PSYCHOLOGY

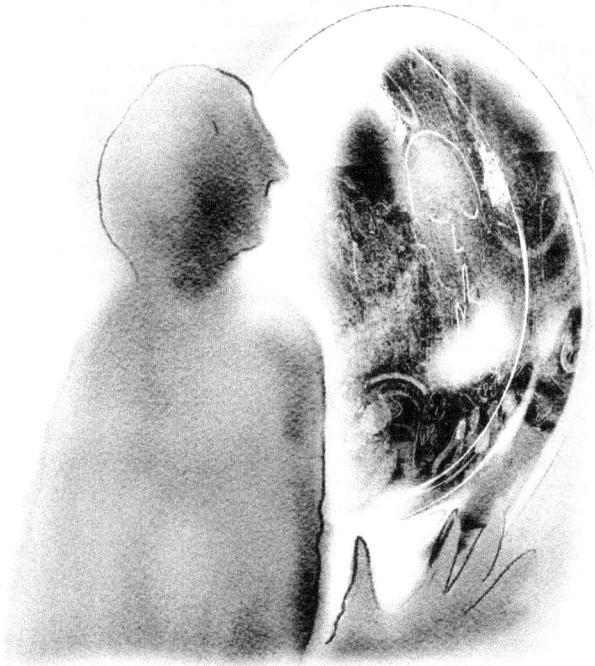

INTRODUCTION

This chapter concentrates on the process of managing ourselves as depth leaders. We are permeable human systems, with our own intrapsychic conflict, role preferences and rank levels, so we will be affected by everything that happens in the organisation that we work with and it, in turn, will be affected by us.

To be an effective depth leader we need to be able to work with ourselves at the depth level first. We cannot help teams to move below the surface if we have not experienced the challenges and difficulties of this kind of work first hand. It is necessary to become sensitive to the issues at the depth level by exploring our own depths and discovering the delicacy of such a process.

THE DEMANDS ON A LEADER

The role of the leader is always potentially difficult, even if we are only working at the surface process level. Whatever the level of work, the full psychological system of the organisation we work with will be active and making demands on us. Team members will project various roles onto us and have a range of psychological expectations of us as leaders.

These demands are even more complex when working with below-the-surface issues. By definition, we will be part of the human interactions in the organisation, and we will participate in the psychodynamics of the group. If we participate unconsciously there will be consequences for the health of the system.

We need great consciousness to intervene meaningfully in organisational and group psychodynamics and there are many components to depth leadership. These range from trying to understand the emerging processes or psychodynamics of the organisational psyche, the power arrangements in the system, and the level of organisational readiness for working under the surface, to the work itself, which involves intervention with either the whole group or subgroups in the organisation. These complex tasks require that we can manage ourselves and our own psychology very carefully. This chapter discusses various aspects related to managing ourselves as depth leaders and provides some tools to help us do so.

THE IMPORTANCE OF SELF-AWARENESS

Self-reflection and the self-awareness that comes from it are critical parts of a leader's role. Without self-awareness, great muddles occur. Self-awareness means greater consciousness of what we are doing, and what we are trying to achieve at the deepest level. Often, we are unaware of our impact on others, and so may not understand why others are being difficult. We may unwittingly be eliciting anxiety, and it is only with self-awareness that we can address this. Often, we feel compelled to achieve something and may be driven by our complexes. The power of the complex blinds us to the need for and validity of other perspectives.

The diagram on the next page indicates that self-reflection and the capacity to relate well to others are linked and work in a self-reinforcing loop. It is desirable to engage in a virtuous cycle of self-development rather than a vicious cycle of self-defence. However, because self-reflection is often hard and painful, it is often avoided. As depth leaders, we must be prepared to confront the difficulty of self-reflection, because without it we are likely to contaminate our organisation with our own psychology. This becomes increasingly problematic the more senior we are in the organisation.

Self-reflection means continually investigating our own behaviour and understanding what is driving us to do what we do. It requires being aware of our own responses and particularly our own feelings. Many of us distract ourselves unwittingly from our experience, especially if we were never taught how to understand and manage ourselves. It is particularly important for us as leaders to explore our unconscious processes because these will affect us in often unpredictable and counter-productive ways if ignored.

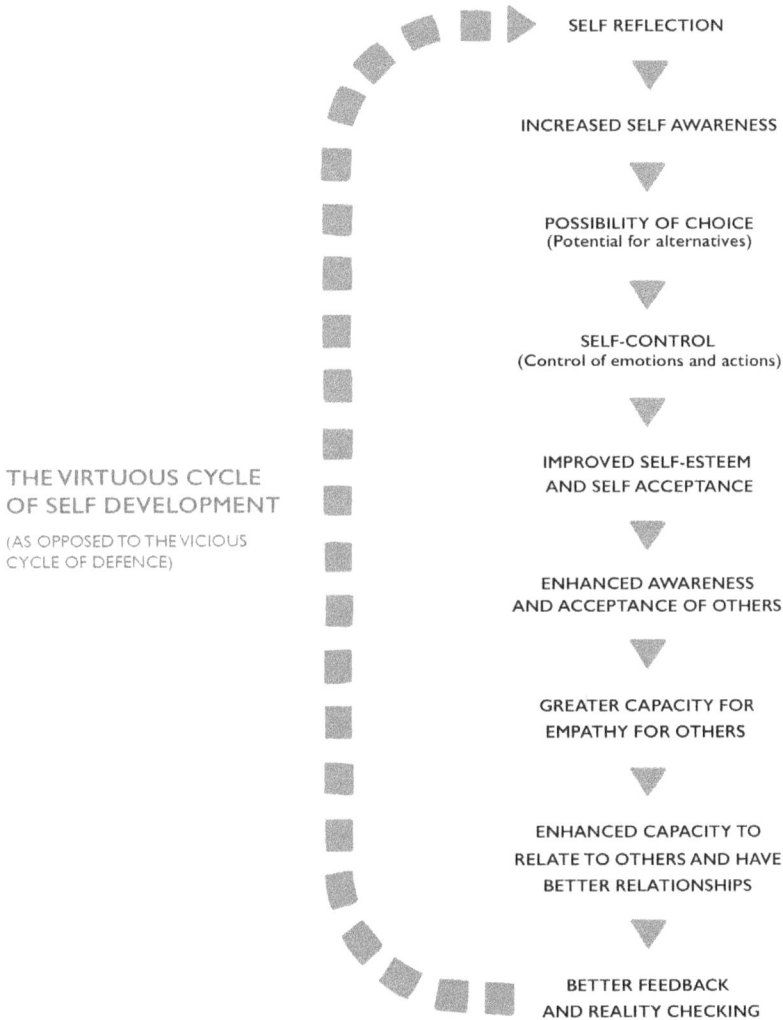

SELF REFLECTION

INCREASED SELF AWARENESS

POSSIBILITY OF CHOICE
(Potential for alternatives)

SELF-CONTROL
(Control of emotions and actions)

IMPROVED SELF-ESTEEM
AND SELF ACCEPTANCE

ENHANCED AWARENESS
AND ACCEPTANCE OF OTHERS

GREATER CAPACITY FOR
EMPATHY FOR OTHERS

ENHANCED CAPACITY TO
RELATE TO OTHERS AND HAVE
BETTER RELATIONSHIPS

BETTER FEEDBACK
AND REALITY CHECKING

THE VIRTUOUS CYCLE
OF SELF DEVELOPMENT

(AS OPPOSED TO THE VICIOUS
CYCLE OF DEFENCE)

AN ATTITUDE OF NEUTRALITY

As leaders who would like to work at the depth level, we will need to develop the ability, at times, to hold a position of neutrality towards the issues discussed by the people in our organisations. Unless we can adopt a neutral stance when necessary, there will be tension when individuals disagree with us. As a good depth leader we need to recognise that a different opinion may bring wisdom to the decision we are making. To harness the full intelligence of the people in our teams, we must temporarily let go of our own opinions so that we can hear and fully entertain the opinions of others. This means adopting an attitude of neutrality in the moment. It does not mean that we might not revert to our own direction and opinion after we have listened, but certainly, an attitude of neutrality is essential in dialogue.

This is the key difference between depth leadership and surface, task-oriented leadership. Although a leader is not essentially neutral, neutrality is an important point of leverage because it significantly changes the dialogue. The ability to wear both hats – that of task-oriented surface leader and that of neutral processoriented depth leader – makes us stronger, more effective leaders. Of course, it needs to be said that it is not easy to wear both hats – it requires a fair amount of psychological agility.

We can only assist the progress of human depth processes if part of the self remains neutral and maintains enough awareness to follow the process impartially as it unfolds. Neutrality is much harder in practice than in theory. However, many people misunderstand the notion of neutrality. Neutrality does not mean not caring about an issue, or not having an opinion about it. It does mean personally exploring both (or more) sides of an issue fully so that we can identify the logic and even wisdom of both sides of the issue.

To ensure this, it is first necessary to allow ourselves to experience our lack of neutrality as fully as possible. This does not mean expressing it in front of others but rather allowing ourselves to internally think and feel as much as we can about our position on an issue. We allow ourselves some space to elaborate on our true experience, but we withhold any expression of the internal process. The more we allow our experience, the easier it will eventually be to see the other side. This requires extensive psychological agility and means exploring as broad a range of archetypes as possible within ourselves and our life experience.

Loss of neutrality can happen for many reasons. We can become identified with a role in a team or become caught in a projection from the team or a subgroup. We can be caught in one of our own complexes. We can develop or hold an opinion about the right course of action for a team and not be able to relinquish our opinion sufficiently to serve the team well. Most leaders will be caught by a lack of neutrality at some point in their interaction with teams. It is not too serious if we lose neutrality for a moment, but it is important to recognise if we are losing it and recover it quickly. Moving back towards neutrality quickly is an advanced skill that develops only through active inner work and a great deal of practice. Although neutrality is an ideal to strive for, rather than a steady state, it is important to hold an attitude of neutrality – at least intellectually – and to notice when we are moving away from it.

The inner work exercise that is described a little later in this chapter will help in the development of our capacity to maintain neutrality. However, first, we will consider the skill and practice of self-regulation.

SELF-REGULATION

Self-regulation is the ability to manage responses within the self. It is both behavioural and biological and means managing physical arousal, attention and emotions. It is the ability to inhibit and delay, flexibly shift and adapt responses. The attribute of temperance or self-regulation is one of Plato's four virtues and refers to the strength to inhibit impulses to behave with integrity. Self-regulation is different to other effortful behaviours because, with it, we must override our own urges, which requires special effort. Our capacity for self-regulation functions in the same way a muscle may function. Muscles get stronger the more they are trained, and so with self-regulation. However, muscles and self-regulation capacities can be depleted in the short term after special exertion. For us as depth leaders, it is essential to invest the effort to develop the capacity for self-regulation because we need to behave with integrity in our depth leadership interactions in organisations. According to Peus et al. (2012), the highest form of regulation in the individual is what they call 'integrated regulation' (p. 334), which according to them, is a quality that is held by authentic leaders, and which occurs when our values are fully integrated into our sense of self, and we are able to act appropriately according to our deepest ethical attitudes.

Self-regulation also means regulating our emotional states. Emotional self-regulation is the complex process of noticing, tolerating, inhibiting and modulating our emotions. This means we need to have access to our emotions, to name and tell the difference between emotions. Therefore, the first step is emotional self-awareness, which is developed by the capacity for self-reflection. The greater our awareness of our own emotions, the greater control we will have over our ethical behaviour. Without such awareness, we will not be able to self-regulate. Therefore, as depth leaders, we need to be consciously aware of our own emotions and make the effort to identify, feel, make sense of and express them appropriately. Emotional regulation is also the capacity to bear or tolerate strong or potentially overwhelming emotions, and not acting on them until the intensity has passed.

Emotional regulation is learnt from caregivers who, over time, intervene to help children to regulate their emotional responses. As children, we will feel and express our emotions without inhibition, and it is the caregiver's role to notice our emotional states and to help us to regulate our strong emotions before we act on them. This means helping us to feel our emotions, to assist us to tolerate the intensity by soothing us, offering a reality check and preventing us from impulsively acting on all our emotions. As children, if well cared for, we eventually learn to how to regulate our own emotions, as the co-regulation offered by caregivers helps to set up internal neurological systems inside us that facilitate emotional functioning. Well-handled emotional regulation supports depth leadership a great deal.

Emotional self-control can be viewed as the subset of emotional regulation where we control our reactions to strong emotional impulses and avoid impulsive behaviour. Emotional self-control is required to achieve goals and direct behaviour. This means that we are able to avoid the spontaneous and/or direct expression of emotions when such expression would be inappropriate or harmful to the self or others. The capacity to control one's emotions implies that one controls whether emotions are expressed in behaviour and whether they are appropriately expressed. As described above, we learn emotional self-control from birth and mostly from our caregivers, but it takes time and experience to develop our capacity for it. Emotional self-control can be problematic depending on how it is exercised. Simply suppressing appropriate emotions could lead someone to behave unethically if faced with breaking social norms. Further, the absence of emotional influence could lead to greater immoral behaviour. Emotional self-control that is helpful to moral behaviour is that which stops inappropriate emotions from driving behaviour.

STEPS FOR EMOTIONAL SELF-REGULATION AND CONTROL

The following self-regulation steps are helpful in a situation that produces strong emotion:

1. If possible, withdraw into a private place where there is safety and disturbance will be unlikely.

2. Allow feelings to surface.

3. Identify and name your feelings, using an emotional wheel (there are many examples available on the internet) as a guide to do so if necessary. Try to be as specific about the nature of the emotion as possible.

4. If the feelings are very strong, consider whether an autonomic complex (an old wound or landmine) has been triggered.

5. Name the wound if possible.

6. Validate your feelings. Accept them and see them as valuable.

7. Consider the purpose of the feelings. What are they trying to tell you? Which of your needs have not been met?

8. Sit with your feelings, allowing them to wash over you, and try to allow the intensity to flow through you. If this is not possible, consider finding a companion who will help you to tolerate the feelings.

9. Use any non-destructive means of expression that help to give voice to the emotions such as crying, sighing, shouting, laughing, moving, drawing, pacing or stomping. Using the defence of sublimation is often useful here, in which we imagine taking strong action to express our feelings, without acting upon it (see page 66).

10. Try to describe to yourself any images that arise as a result of the emotions.

11. Try to continue feeling the emotions until their intensity subsides, which they will once the emotions have served their purpose.

12. Notice if these emotions change, and whether other emotions emerge. If so, return to step 2, and work through the steps with the new feelings.

13. Notice if any ideas emerge for appropriate, non-destructive actions.

14. Once the intensity has completely subsided, implement any appropriate expression or action. Use "I" messages for verbal exchanges.

15. If it is clear that a wound has been triggered, complete the inner work steps offered below.

PSYCHODYNAMIC INNER WORK

Psychodynamic or depth inner work is the process by which we confront our own difficulties, identify and allow our own underlying processes, and realise our own potential. Every time we work with a team or an individual, our psyche will engage with the individual's or team's psyche and new processes will emerge. To maintain our neutrality and thereby be able to truly lead at a depth level, we continually need to do depth inner work. It requires working with our thoughts, feelings, body experiences, symptoms and fantasies. Inner work requires attention, perseverance and a great deal of time for reflection. It also takes practice.

INNER WORK EXERCISE

The following steps for doing inner work in almost any situation combine different psychological theories. The questions are designed to help us think through a particular situation in which we find ourselves. It may be a leadership situation, or it may be a personal relationship situation. It allows us to analyse the psychodynamics of whatever interaction we are in. We can also use these questions to analyse past situations. Although it may be too late now to change their outcomes, it could give us insight into our own psychological make up and potential vulnerabilities as a leader.

Given an interpersonal situation where there is conflict and/or difficulty:

1. What is the situation? Who are the characters (the people involved) and what are the issues?

2. What am I feeling, thinking, experiencing? Try to describe your responses in detail.

3. Have I experienced a heightened emotional, mental or physical reaction? What is it?

4   Is this triggering an old wound for me? (A heightened emotional, mental or physical reaction could indicate the presence of an old wound). What is this wound?

5. What are my edges? What am I anxious about?

6. Am I using any defence mechanisms? What are they?

7. What is happening for the other people in the situation? Try not to interpret, but describe their reactions, behaviours, observable emotions.

8. What could be their edges?

9. Do I notice whether they are using any defence mechanisms?

10. Who has rank in the situation and why?

11. What could have been done or could still be done to make both parties feel safer and less anxious?

12. What could be done to manage the rank differences in the situation?

13. Try to establish the nature of the psychodynamic or pattern of behaviour between the two parties. In other words, what are the two (or more) differing viewpoints in the situation? What are the roles/positions/archetypes that each party is taking? What is the plot, drama, or archetypal story being played out? In Chapter 4, we saw that psychodynamic patterns tend to consist of two polarities that are opposing, but intrinsically linked, such as persecutor – victim; unheard minority – autocratic authority; pursuer – distancer; overfunctioner – underfunctioner; emotional expression – emotional withdrawal. There are many potential patterns, and they function in a self-reinforcing way.

14. Have I seen or experienced this psychodynamic pattern before. Could this be repetition compulsion? This idea refers to the fact that we will continue to recreate psychodynamic patterns that resemble those established in earlier situations where emotional complications occurred, in an attempt to heal the wounds caused by those situations (described on page 70).

15. What do I need to do to address my old wound?

16. What part of myself (archetype) am I maybe not acknowledging or possibly giving to or projecting onto someone else? I explained earlier that these psychodynamic patterns exist intrapsychically, with one part or role of the pattern remaining unconscious, and the other more palatable role existing as a conscious characteristic. For example, I may identify with the unheard minority part but be unconscious of the part of me that is an autocratic authority. The part that remains unconscious and that I do not identify with consciously will usually be projected onto or given to the other.

17. How could the part that I am projecting onto the other person be useful in my own life? For example, the other person may irritate me because he or she is too silly and irresponsible. I may, in fact, be too serious and may need to develop my playful side.

18. How can I integrate that part of myself? In other words, how can I develop the previously unconscious part of myself (which I may have been projecting onto the other) in a healthy and useful way, to achieve more balance in my life?

19. What part of my psychology still needs more work?

20. What could be done now to address the situation?

Inner work is most important when a leader is engaged in depth work. When working with depth processes, we are actively engaging with unconscious dynamics and are, therefore, much more susceptible to being affected by them. The task of the team is not as clear as in surface leadership, and there is no clearly defined process to follow. These factors complicate the work and make it far more demanding. In depth processes, the mechanisms of projection and projective identification (see pages 64-67) are actively employed by team members to manage the challenges of working with potentially threatening unconscious processes. It is highly likely that as leaders we may become a target for these mechanisms and, because they are very powerful, may easily be caught up in them.

GETTING HOOKED

To reiterate, a leader needs to avoid getting caught up in the psychodynamics of the team to remain attentive to the whole of the team psyche. The term getting hooked is one way of describing getting caught in projective processes. Getting hooked means being drawn into an unconscious dynamic through the mechanism of projective identification, and therefore, being drawn into fulfilling a role for the team. The following are signs indicating that you have become hooked:

- experiencing a stronger-than-usual emotion and not being able to move through it
- feelings of protectiveness towards certain members of the team
- a desire to repeat yourself, or actual repetition of a certain point of view

- an inability to observe without intervention
- feelings of dislike towards individual team members or a subgroup
- arguing with the team or certain team members unproductively
- breaking agreements
- justifying behaviours to yourself or the team
- heightened feelings of anxiety when working with the team
- feeling right or being right and
- feelings of unusually strong investment in a particular decision or process

To avoid getting hooked, you as the leader need to go through an inner work process to understand your susceptibility to a particular projection or role.

INNER WORK IN FRONT OF A GROUP

Often, a leader gets hooked without having the benefit of time doing the necessary inner work. To manage this, we have to take action to prevent contaminating the group with their own psychodynamics. Being hooked usually means getting caught in one side of a psychodynamic. We have the following options:

- avoid any further interventions that emphasise our one-sidedness;
- actively take the side opposite to the one with which we over-identified, to provide balance;
- do the necessary inner work in front of the group without involving the group;
- practise self-disclosure and share with the group our awareness of having been hooked.

Which of the options above we choose depends on the group's experience of depth work, the sensitivity and depth of the process, and our capacity to do inner work. A group that is experienced in depth work will be more likely to understand and appreciate self-disclosure and will be able to use it to further the process. A less experienced group may feel anxious with that level of self-disclosure.

ONGOING INNER WORK

It is imperative that a leader who works at a depth level is actively engaged in ongoing inner work. Continual work on our self-awareness is necessary because new situations may produce new blind spots. We need to try to maintain as accurate a picture as possible of:

- our complexes and the roots of these complexes.
- our chosen defence mechanisms.
- our edges.
- our own symptoms of anxiety.
- our role inclinations.
- areas where we hold rank.
- areas where we do not hold rank.
- mechanisms that help us feel safer and reduce our anxiety.
- the developmental processes of our life stage and current situation.

It is useful to have a professional partner for our inner work process. This can be a therapist, a coach, a supervisor or a peer. It is helpful to have a formalised relationship with this partner, in which the boundaries and scope of the work are specified. If we expect groups to commit resources to us as leaders, then we need to be able to commit resources to our own depth process. If we have a particularly traumatic or difficult psychological history, then it is important that we engage in long-term therapy.

MANAGING THE PROJECTIONS OF OTHERS

Regardless of the leader's capacity for neutrality, team members will not necessarily feel neutral about the leader. The leader will be a likely target for team projections. Like any of the other defence mechanisms, projection is a way of coping with the unconscious material or subject matter that feels threatening to us either because it is not in keeping with our self-image or because it is considered a social taboo. With projection, we take an inherent or potential characteristic (or experience, feeling or thought) and to minimise its potential impact on us, we view it as being part of someone else rather than ourselves. We can of course have instances of positive or negative projection.

MANAGING TRANSFERENCE

As we saw in Chapter 3, transference refers to projection that happens over time in a relationship – a transfer of feelings that originally belonged to a parent or other authority figure. Any long-term relationship in which feelings or experiences associated with an earlier relationship are replayed between two people could be considered transference. It has been shown that our unconscious minds will use the mechanism of repetition compulsion to find situations in which those relationships can be replayed to allow for healing of the psyche.

As leaders, we are very likely targets for transference from individual team members or the whole team psyche. We hold positions of authority in organisations and this is one of the key triggers for transference. The likelihood of transference onto us is even higher in depth work because unconscious material is being tapped into and we are playing a containing role. This may lead to a similar transference process as would occur in a therapeutic setting.

Group members may start relating to us as if we are a perfect parent, guru or distant, withholding parents. The difficulty with transference in a relationship is that it distorts individuals' perceptual ability, and they will see only what they want in the leader, which will confirm the transference. This mechanism is useful in a therapeutic process where it can be used to bring understanding. In the psychodynamics of a team, however, transference cannot be used in the same way to serve individual team members and so it is more likely to cause difficulty for the work of the leader.

To avoid unhelpful transference as much as possible, we need to be as authentic as we can be without compromising our neutral attitude. This lessens the potential idealisation of us as leaders. We can practise careful self-disclosure to balance and neutralise the type of transference that has developed. In other words, the more the team members know about who we really are, the less likely it is that they can psychologically view us, on a sustained basis, as representatives of people from their pasts.

Transference tends to consist of either a set of negative projections or a set of positive projections. The one-sidedness is characteristic of projection, as a real relationship will have both negative and positive components. More information is given below about how to deal with both of these options.

MANAGING COUNTERTRANSFERENCE

Counter-transference refers to the leader's psychological response to transference. As we saw in Chapter 3, if someone views us as very nurturing, it is highly likely that we will start feeling the urge to nurture that person. Because transference arises from the unconscious, it triggers very intense feelings in the person who is experiencing it. Similarly, the person who receives the transference may start experiencing an intense response. Invariably, these subtle psychological processes occur between two individuals who each have a need, and because a certain complementarity exists between them. A leader is, therefore, always vulnerable to a strong counter-transference response. We cannot necessarily avoid a counter-transference response, but it is really important to handle it correctly.

The most important thing to do when experiencing counter-transference feelings is to remember the purpose of our role. As leaders, we are there primarily to work with a group to achieve organisational objectives, so any experiences or events need to be used to further that purpose. This means that any feelings of counter-transference should be seen as information about what is happening in the group and used to help the group to achieve its tasks. More detail about how to handle counter-transference is given in the specific situations discussed below.

MANAGING POSITIVE PROJECTIONS

We might imagine that it would be easy to manage positive projections. In many ways, though, a positive projection is much harder to manage than a negative projection. Common language for the psychological phenomenon of positive projection would be terms like 'falling in love', or 'admiration', or 'hero worship'. We all enjoy being viewed positively, and so it is very hard to be neutral when this happens.

If the team member has a very strong, positive transference towards us as leaders, we will be tempted to over identify with the role that is being projected. We will be seen as all-good, all-powerful, completely fair or in some other way as ideal figures. It is important to dispel these one-sided notions. Some of the following guidelines may help.

- Remember that there are aspects of the positive projection that are true and based on reality, and that this may evoke a legitimate and genuine response to positive qualities. However, it is not the full picture; we are human and also possess qualities that are problematic or unedifying.

- Ensure that our self-esteem is intact (or as intact as possible), and do inner work until we can comfortably accept a realistic picture of ourselves.
- Practise careful self-disclosure that offers some reality testing for the unrealistic projections. In other words, carefully reveal our clay feet.
- Actively assist individuals to explore their projected material as aspects of themselves.
- Avoid interpersonal interactions that could fuel the positive projection. Do not treat the person as special in any way.
- Avoid claiming any particular way of being as exclusively our own.
- At all times remember the psychological contract that defines the interaction between us and the team. We have an ethical responsibility to fulfil the contract and avoid interpersonal interactions that could jeopardise it. We need to maintain our professionalism.

Managing negative projections and a strong negative transference also has its challenges. It is very painful when someone is unable to see any of our positive qualities and only focuses on the negative. As a leader, our inner critic may be evoked in such a situation (see page 155), and we could start feeling ashamed and become debilitated by the projections. Some guidelines on how to work with negative projections are given below.

- Ensure that our self-esteem is intact (or as intact as possible) and do inner work until we can comfortably accept a realistic picture of ourselves.
- Check whether there may be truth in the projection and make changes if necessary.
- Do not take the negative projection personally. The individual is caught in a mechanism that most likely has its roots in their childhood, and therefore, the opinion or judgement is not an accurate adult assessment of our qualities as a person.
- Use the feelings that are elicited as information about the team and how it functions.
- Ensure that we treat all team members consistently and with equal care, regardless of their behaviour towards us.
- Avoid any urge to discuss the individual carrying the negative projection with any other members of the team.
- We need to maintain our professionalism.

MANAGING THE DEMANDS OF INDIVIDUAL MEMBERS

Occasionally, individual team members will demand special attention from the leader. This could happen because the individual has a strong transference toward the leader or because the individual is having difficulty with the team and is seeking support. As leaders, we need to engage with the individual in a professional and friendly way, but avoid any special treatment of that person. If an individual comes to us with a particular problem or request that relates to group functioning, always encourage the individual to bring the problem into the group directly.

Sometimes an individual seeks advice on a personal level that is not necessarily directly related to the team. In this instance, we may be able to provide the advice, but always need to check first that it is not a team issue in disguise.

MANAGING YOUR BOUNDARIES

Although playing a leadership role is often rewarding and enriching, it can be dangerous or destructive to the self if not managed carefully. One of the skills of a good leader is the ability to sense underlying processes, but this is only possible through an attitude of openness, which makes us potentially vulnerable. As discussed, a leader is frequently the target of projection for all feelings and ideas relating to authority and therefore parenting. These projections are among the most powerful of all interpersonal processes, and need to be treated with care.

Very strong negative projections have the capacity to produce symptoms in the leader. In other words, without a strong sense of self, someone else's strong negative projection can make us feel or actually become ill. It is therefore vital to do inner work when becoming aware of a negative projection and to consciously avoid falling into a dance that will feed the projection.

The capacity to develop strong personal and psychological boundaries is an important part of protecting ourselves. This involves knowing ourself as well as possible and assertively establishing and protecting our boundaries. If we are leaders who are working at the depth level, we have a responsibility to manage our own psychology and understand it as distinct from the organisation and our staff members. This does not mean that some important relationships will not develop between us and staff members. Such relationships can, in fact, be psychologically helpful in the long term. Nonetheless, it is important to establish psychological boundaries in terms of our expectations of one another.

As leaders, we can be good mentors, but we are not the parents who are going to fix all the problems that staff members might have absorbed from their own parents. Keep the boundaries around the personal/professional relationship clear and ensure that the roles do not become confused. If we help somebody out in a personal capacity, be aware that it may psychologically contaminate the work relationship and, unless we are very good at setting boundaries, it may become increasingly tricky to manage. For instance, if we lend money to an employee, chances are that it will set up psychodynamics that might complicate the whole group's functioning at some point.

Leadership can be a lonely task, in which we have to carry the responsibility of setting direction and managing processes, but we need to be wary of the temptation to assuage our loneliness or have our need for connection met by members in the organisation. If we cross a boundary where we become dependent on the company of certain group members, then we may not be able to retain our integrity as leaders.

In addition, we need to take care not to contaminate the organisation with our own psychological difficulties. To avoid this, it is important for us to have therapists, coaches or mentors we can talk to for support.

Some particular suggestions for protecting ourselves and managing our boundaries are given below:

- We need to make sure that we meet our personal needs outside of the teams we lead.
- We must not mix personal and professional relationships, or be very clear about which hats we are wearing when engaging with group members.
- We must work hard to acknowledge our own needs, so that they do not take us by surprise.
- We need to actively develop interests outside of our roles as leaders, so that our leadership does not become the primary vehicle for establishing our self-esteem.

THE INNER CRITIC

As a leader, one of the most difficult inner voices to manage is that of our inner critics. This constitutes a part of ourselves that manifests as an internal voice that criticises us for not being good enough. A strong inner critic will continually berate us for our poor performance or numerous inadequacies. If we grew up in an environment where our self-esteem was not supported and we were continually criticised, we may have internalised this situation by developing a harsh (and unrealistic) inner critic. This inner critic will often be projected onto the group and we will become defensive about our imagined inability to meet the needs of the team or fulfil our tasks as leaders.

It sometimes happens that the inner critic coincides with an attack from members of the organisation. This situation can only be navigated if we become aware of the projection and introduce a neutralising or transcendent inner voice, such as that of compassion. In other words, we need to try to have a balanced view of ourselves and our abilities. If our inner critic is so severe that it becomes debilitating, then it is usually out of balance and we need to do inner work to correct the balance.

ATTACKS ON THE LEADER

Groups and individuals in organisations will attack leaders in various ways. Leadership, by definition, involves a position of authority in a system, and all positions of authority will create opposition. Attacks from individual members often stem from the projections they hold. It is also important to remember that it is usually the role, rather than us as an individual that is being attacked or demanded of and that if we get hooked and become defensive, the attack or the underlying conflict will be perpetuated. It is also important to resist any pressure to psychologically feed or rescue a team member because this simply encourages the projection. If we choose to fulfil certain roles, we need to do it consciously, openly and with awareness. Without consciousness, there is a great risk, as mentioned before, that we will be treated either as messiahs or scapegoats.

POPULARITY AS A LEADER

As depth leaders, we may need to be unpopular. Since we are taking care of the whole group, and sometimes even the whole system, we will appear to be working against a particular view or sub-group or even person.

It is important to be able to relinquish our need to be liked, approved of and admired in the short term, and sometimes even in the long term. In terms of depth leadership particularly, there may be strong pressure from a subgroup or individual to raise and resolve certain issues, but working with depth processes in teams is only safe if everyone agrees to do so. We may have to hold a team back from entering into a depth process because not everyone is ready. Here, we may need to be unpopular and hold the team at its edge rather than allow a dominant part of the team to push into a process that the rest are not ready for. Pushing a process may lead to unnecessary hurt or damage in the team. As depth leaders, we are responsible for holding the team at its edge tonsure that everyone is ready and thereby eliminate unnecessary pain.

Another scenario in which we may need to be unpopular is if a group cannot reach resolution for one reason or another. If for time reasons we need to move on from a conflict before both sides feel comfortable, it is our responsibility as leaders to ensure that the team moves on. It is also our responsibility to tell them that we are aware that the issue is not resolved and that it will need to be addressed in a different way.

REST AND RECOVERY

We need to ensure that we rest and recover regularly during our leadership role. It can be extremely psychologically burdensome to lead from a depth perspective. We need to be able to contain and simultaneously experience what our team, colleagues, employees and the whole organisation are going through. This means we cannot resort to normal defensive processes that the psyche would use to protect itself. One of the ways we protect ourselves against the pain of others is to use the defence mechanism of isolation, where we separate the feeling from the thinking in a situation. Leaders who practise isolation or other similar defences will not be compassionate enough about what the team or organisation is going through. We need to remain undefended and be able to contain ourselves through potentially strong emotions. We can only do this if we are well rested and well cared for psychologically.

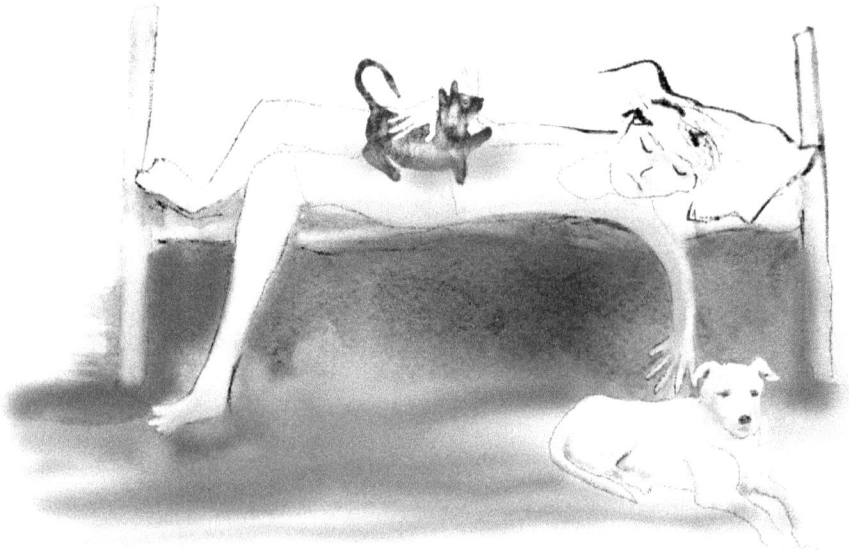

CONCLUSION

Inner work is a critical part of being a good leader. It needs to be an ongoing process. At some times in our work lives, we may need to embark on a more intensive course of inner work and use formal processes such as therapy. The process of inner work and self-reflection is often painful and harrowing, but it can also be delightful and playful. Either way, it needs to become part of our lives as a depth leader.

PERSONAL EXERCISES

1.   Consider your inner critic and document what it might say. Investigate the validity of the inner accusations. Reframe those accusations in a compassionate way.

2.   Consider your need to be liked. How can you manage your potential unpopularity as a leader?

3.   Reflect on the extent to which you do inner work currently. Is it working? Plan an inner work regime for yourself.

4.   Identify a relationship in which you experienced a strong transference with a figure of authority. Consider how you felt in that relationship and how you treated the other person. What were your expectations? What changed the transference? In what way does a real relationship feel different from one based on transference? Identify the signs to look for to identify the presence of transference.

5.   Identify areas of vulnerability that may complicate your work as a leader. Devise an action plan for addressing the vulnerable areas.

CHAPTER
7
DEPTH RELATIONSHIPS

INTRODUCTION

This chapter considers guidelines, tools and techniques to help depth leaders manage relationships with individuals, teams and the organisation as a whole. The key difference from surface leadership is that as depth leaders, we know that there is more going on in a group than is immediately visible, and so we work towards unearthing and resolving unhealthy depth processes, while unleashing potential and creativity that may be lying beneath the surface. This requires us to get to know our organisation and team members as fully as possible, always remembering that there is more to individuals than they may even know themselves. It does, however, require that we know ourselves as well as possible and that we see self-knowledge as an ongoing quest. It also requires that we recognise that people are often anxious and that we use defence mechanisms to cope which obscure the true facts and feelings in a situation. Therefore, we need to create a safe environment to reduce the anxiety that causes defensive behaviour.

ESTABLISHING A HEALTHY GROUP CLIMATE

Psychological climate is an intangible variable that is nevertheless very important to organisational and team functioning. It refers to the general mood and atmosphere of the system and is determined by many things. It is a product of the general emotional experience of individuals and groups, which will be influenced largely by system psychodynamics. Climate will, of course, also be influenced by significant events that affect the system, such as the loss of a group member or the successful completion of a difficult project. As depth leaders, our style and mood are influential in creating a productive and constructive climate. Our use of metaskills will have a significant effect on the system's atmosphere. If we are calm, respectful, and focused but unhurried, then individuals and groups will usually follow suit. Of course, the climate in an organisation will be greatly affected by unresolved depth processes, so if we sense that the climate is tension-laden, it is necessary to keep an eye on depth signals which will be discussed in Chapter 9.

Some of the more important activities that we as depth leaders can do to ensure a positive and functional climate are listed below:

As a depth leader we need to:

- help the organisation to develop healthy psychological group contracts. This involves explicit discussion of group and individual expectations and agreements

- build a safe container (this is considered in detail in the section below on building containment)

- continually do inner work to manage our own mood as a leader

- implement good group practices (discussed in more detail later in the chapter)

- remain aware of the climate and ask for weather reports (discussed in more detail immediately below) and intervene when it appears that there are unresolved depth processes

- make sure that individuals are on the whole as physically and psychologically comfortable as possible, but remain aware that a team that is working on its psychodynamic functioning will experience uncomfortable times while resolving difficulties

- anticipate that events in the organisational environment will have an impact on the organisational climate and provide opportunities to explore this impact openly

We need to develop our skills to read the organisational climate if we are generally oblivious to the atmosphere around us. Often, we do not notice the climate because we are not paying attention, or because we are defending ourselves against the anxiety caused by a problematic climate.

To develop our awareness, it is useful to use the metaphor of the weather in a group or system. For example, a group climate can be described in one of the following ways:

- Sunny
- Overcast
- Misty
- Stormy
- Drizzly
- Partly cloudy
- Drought ridden
- Hot/cold
- Grey
- Calm before the storm
- Sunshine after rain

It is always useful to canvas the opinions of the individuals or the group to build a general awareness of the climate.

The group climate will be significantly improved by the development of containment, the practice of which is discussed in the next section. The work of reading the climate can be extended to making sense of the whole internal landscape of the system. Individuals can be asked to describe the psychological setting in which they find themselves by describing their perception of the landscape as if it were the setting of a film. This can provide significant insights into the nature of the depth processes at work in the organisation or group.

BUILDING CONTAINMENT

Containment of anxiety is an essential component of the depth leader's task when working with groups and organisations. As indicated by Malan's triangle (discussed below), and as understood by individual psychotherapists everywhere, it is only when we contain the individual's anxiety about expressing frightening or undesirable thoughts and feelings that those important underlying or unconscious elements can be expressed. Containment is the process whereby the leader employs a range of metaskills, skills, tools and techniques to create an atmosphere of relative safety, so that defences diminish and the important issues are discussed. Although there are specific proactive steps that can be taken, the process of containment can also be intuitive and subconscious. It requires that we initiate a process of step-by-step exploration, all the time watching for feedback.

Containment strategies can be divided into 'hard' and 'soft'. Hard containment provides practical safety and predictability in form and structure through the use of boundaries, limits, direction, clarity, documentation, routine and information. Soft containment offers emotional safety, predictability and reassurance in the relational atmosphere through listening, non-judgemental relating, trust and empathy. The diagram below indicates the different types of containment that we as depth leaders can offer individuals in a system, distinguishing between soft (internal) containment and hard (external) containment. Some of the hard containment activities, such as setting clear policies and procedures, may sometimes not be in our direct control, but it is important that the aspects that we can control are implemented throughout. We can provide feedback about leadership approaches that are causing a lack of containment in the group and encourage the leaders and members of a group to change these activities to ones that provide greater containment.

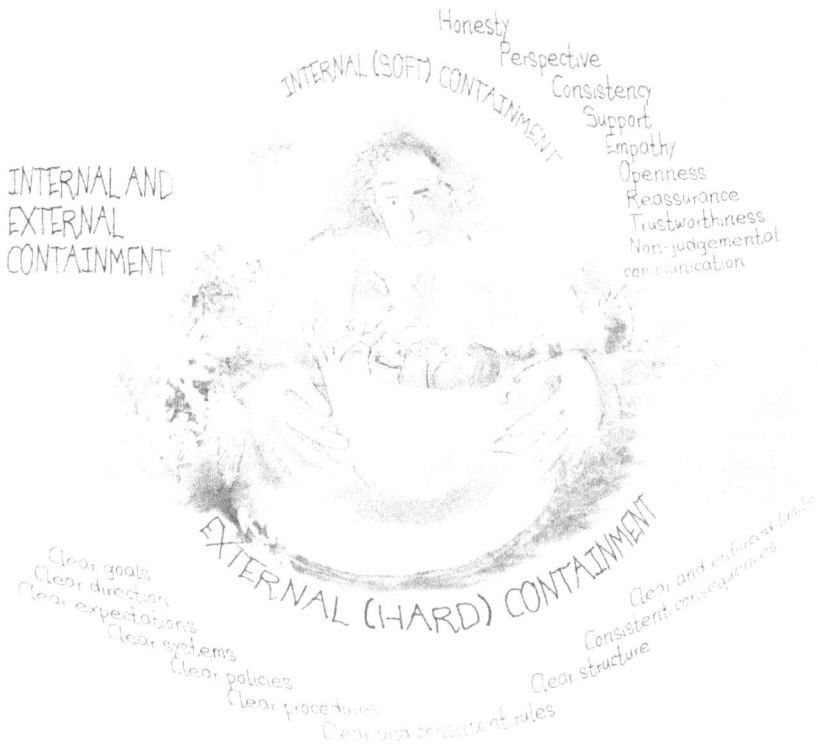

INTERNAL AND EXTERNAL CONTAINMENT

INTERNAL (SOFT) CONTAINMENT

Honesty
Perspective
Consistency
Support
Empathy
Openness
Reassurance
Trustworthiness
Non-judgemental
communication

EXTERNAL (HARD) CONTAINMENT

Clear goals
Clear direction
Clear expectations
Clear systems
Clear policies
Clear procedures
Clear and consistent rules

Clear and enforced limits
Consistent consequences
Clear structure

DAVID MALAN'S TRIANGLE

In his book *Individual Psychotherapy and the Science of Psychodynamics*, David Malan (1979) suggests that when we feel the urge to reveal our true feelings, and they have not been acceptable in the past, we may feel anxious. If our anxiety is not contained, we defend ourselves, thereby reducing our expression of our real thoughts and feelings.

causes a defence mechanism

ANXIETY

DEFENCE MECHANISM

eliminates or buries the anxiety-provoking thoughts and feelings

surface to cause anxiety (frustration, anger or fear) when they are unacceptable

REAL THOUGHTS AND FEELINGS

The triangle indicates the dynamic relationship between potentially dangerous or unacceptable thoughts and feelings, and anxiety and defence mechanisms. As a leader we can work to reduce individual and group anxiety to reverse this dynamic. If individuals become less anxious because they feel contained, their defence mechanisms will diminish and they will become more able to express potentially problematic feelings and thoughts. Without appropriate containment, individuals will not be able to explore depth processes successfully. As a result, containment is in some ways the single most important tool for a depth leader to use.

CONTAINMENT DURING GROUP INTERACTIONS

If team members feel that others are trying to understand their points of view rather than criticise them, they are much more likely to consider the points being made by others. They will try to weigh the ideas and experiences of others as objectively as possible. They may even begin to reconsider their own viewpoints.

If they feel they are being attacked, however, their emotional defences will be activated and they will cut off all further exchange of ideas. For example, this may take the form of resentful withdrawal from the discussion, and a member may suddenly become silent. Alternatively, it may provoke a strong counterattack on the critical person and result in the development of hostility and conflict.

Either way, the effectiveness of a discussion will be damaged as soon as a threatening atmosphere replaces a cooperative atmosphere. To maintain a conducive atmosphere, we need to use a combination of the containment techniques listed below. The list is divided further into hard and soft to distinguish between containment efforts that need to be implemented at the organisational level, and those that can be implemented by the depth leader at the group or interpersonal level.

	Hard containment	**Soft containment**
Organisational level	• Use an inclusive, transparent process to develop a clear organisational vision, strategy and goals • Ensure clear and consistent operational and human resource systems, policies and procedures • Ensure employment equity • Communicate proactively and clearly regarding all organisational changes	• Ensure that leadership is approachable • Make decisions in a transparent way after processes of genuine consultation • Ensure congruent leadership behaviour resulting from leadership integrity
Depth leader level	• Implement clear and consistent leadership practices, including performance management and disciplinary procedures • Establish clear goals and objectives • Be organised and professional • Maintain clear and consistent professional and personal boundaries • Set and stick to clear time limits • Avoid distractions and interruptions during interpersonal interactions • Take responsibility when needed • Be accountable for our actions • Provide information as clearly and often as possible • Enforce limits and consequences consistently • Take corrective action when rules are broken	• Be approachable • Maintain self-awareness • Be non-defensive • Be transparent • Act in trustworthy ways • Be consistent • Don't judge • Be compassionate • Listen without interruption • Practise reflective listening • Empathise • Reassure • Give recognition • Avoid polarising (take a neutral role) • Self-disclose if needed • Provide space if needed

- Comply with agreements and communicate timeously when we are unable to do so

- Comply with procedures

- Make necessary reparation if we have caused harm unintentionally

- Follow through with promises

- Admit mistakes and apologise if necessary

- Pay full attention when communicating

- Give regular and specific feedback

- Give individual attention

- Get to know individual preferences and vulnerabilities

Although a general list of containment actions is provided above, note that not everyone will be contained by the same set of actions. Some individuals need space to calm down, others need gentle attention. The best way to determine what someone needs to feel less anxious and more contained is to ask them. A simple question such as "What do you need right now?" will often provide critical information. Therefore, if we as leaders are unsure of what type of containment is required by an individual or a group, then it is a good idea to ask them.

Another consideration is that we cannot contain others if we cannot contain ourselves as leaders. We need to reflect on what calms us down and makes us feel contained enough to open up and explore difficult experiences, and be sure to put structures and processes in place so that we are contained on a continual basis.

Most leaders are better at one kind of containment than the other. For example, one may be an organised and structured person and so be excellent at providing hard containment. Alternatively, one may be particularly adept at building relationships with people and so be good at soft containment. It is important that we recognise our strengths and develop the areas where we do not have a natural aptitude.

Finally, remember that we are not truly creating safety if our presence is required to prevent a backlash from certain members of a group towards others. In other words, if one participant in a group feels safe enough to give another participant negative feedback in our presence, but will be victimised by the recipient of the feedback when we are not present, then that is false containment and will cause problems later.

BUILDING RAPPORT

Building rapport means establishing a level of intimacy between us, as leaders and group members, so that they feel they have a relationship with us and that they can trust us.

The word 'rapport' refers to the bond, affinity and understanding we have with others. To build rapport, we need to have a genuine interest in the individuals in our system and can build a relationship with others despite the fact that they may be very different from us. It requires that we view others with compassion and are genuinely curious about who they are and what matters to them. Some of the following actions will help with the process of building rapport.

- Use people's names and check the pronunciation and their preferences regarding their names.
- Make relaxed eye contact.

- Match the person's pace and volume of communication.

- Use appropriate and professional language that the other person or the group will be comfortable with. Avoid over-familiarity or excessive formality in our communication. As far as possible (without compromising our own authenticity) match the other person's or the group's style of communication.

- Project friendliness and openness to demonstrate our approachability. In simple terms, smile and be welcoming.

- Remember the content of our conversations with individuals or remember what was said by individuals in the team interactions and refer to it in an inclusive (not a critical way). For example: "As Joe mentioned this morning, we need to ensure everyone is on board."

- Remember any promises made and keep them.

None of these actions will result in genuine rapport if they are simply implemented as techniques and do not reflect an underlying attitude of real interest.

PROVIDING SUPPORT

Individuals need emotional support when addressing psychodynamics because, by their very nature, such discussions cause anxiety. To resolve counterproductive psychodynamics, people will cross edges and it takes courage to do so. The following suggestions are helpful to support people during edge crossing.

- Acknowledge that we are aware that they may be crossing edges.

- Maintain eye contact and gently encourage an individual who seems to be crossing an edge.

- Ensure that the person can do so at their own pace.

- If individuals seem unsure, suggest waiting until they are ready.

- We need to thank individuals for their contributions, without indicating that we feel that certain contributions are more important than others.

- Give all individuals equal support.
- Use reflective listening (see page 129) if needed.

Ideally, we need to try to imagine ourselves in the position of the other person to activate our empathy but remain neutral about the content of contributions.

ENSURING FULL PARTICIPATION

In this section, we consider the extent to which participants engage in group discussions, as well as the extent to which the full potential of each individual and the group as a whole is expressed in the functioning of the group or the system.

We will first consider participation during group conversations. Many factors influence participation in a group and the main ones are listed below.

- The individual comfort level with speaking in front of a group. Many people are not comfortable speaking in front of a group.
- The power dynamics in a room. People with less power will tend to speak less or become disruptive.
- Individual style. Some people prefer to speak only when necessary while others express many of their thoughts.
- Level of comfort with the content. Some individuals may not feel comfortable with the content discussed because they may not have the necessary knowledge.
- A lack of leadership skills or neutrality. If the team members sense that we cannot hold a neutral attitude when listening to their contributions, they will resist the process overtly or covertly.
- Depth processes. An underlying unaddressed issue will affect participation, especially if there is a lack of buy-in into the process.

To encourage individual participation in a group conversation, it helps to centre our attention on the group rather than ourselves during the discussion. It is helpful to maintain eye contact with the whole group, without remaining with one person too long. If we ask open questions in the form of invitations to participate and refer to comments made by the individuals as a way of including everyone in the discussion, participation is easier. It is powerful to use individuals' names and actively invite differing points of view. Without seeming critical, we can signal to dominant individuals to desist for a while by asking if anyone who has not yet had an opportunity to contribute would like to do so. We should avoid putting one individual under the spotlight; rather providing an open invitation to anyone who has not spoken.

MANAGING SILENCE

Sometimes it is important for a whole group to be silent for a while. They may need to process or absorb events that have occurred, or they may need to consider their perspectives. It is useful to build some structured silent times into every conversation. As depth leaders, we need to develop comfort with silence and not feel compelled to fill every silence. Some individuals may be uncomfortable with silence, finding it easier if it is explicitly invited. We can do this by suggesting that the group takes some time to think before further contributions are made.

UNLOCKING INDIVIDUAL POTENTIAL

One of the most important functions of a depth leader is to recognise that some human potential could be locked up by unconscious processes or defence mechanisms and that people may need assistance to develop and express their potential.

As discussed in detail in Chapter 3, all of us have both a conscious and an unconscious part to our psyches. Most of us identify ourselves predominantly with the conscious parts. If we believe we are hardworking and have been explicitly told to be that way, we will not necessarily recognise that we have the potential for playfulness inside us too. If we were raised in a family that did not value creativity and so did not support our creative impulses, our creativity may be locked up inside us. As a depth leader, it is important to remain aware that individuals have more potential than they show or even know about.

Watch for signs that individual potential is trying to emerge. Individuals may tentatively try out a new behaviour and anxiously monitor feedback. For example, someone who never initiates projects may take the initiative when it comes to providing refreshments. As a depth leader, recognise that the impulse for initiative may flourish if actively recognised and encouraged. This can be done through a variety of mechanisms, such as providing training or opportunities for further development.

Recognise that people may operate within false belief structures about their own potential and may have anxiety about developing previously disavowed parts of themselves. In other words, they may need gentle encouragement to cross an edge and significant containment when trying out a new skill.

DEALING WITH STRONG EMOTION AND ANGER

If there is conflict in a group, it invariably produces heightened emotions. Also, if one side becomes emotional it often leads to an emotional response. The following guidelines may be helpful in a situation where everyone is emotionally aroused.

We need to accept that anger is a natural human response, and acknowledge and recognise people's right to feel angry, even if it is directed at us and we regard it as unfair. We need to consider our own feelings and do the necessary inner work to contain ourselves (but also be authentic if necessary).

For example, if we feel unfairly criticised as leaders, we need to acknowledge the value of feedback and calmly state that we will consider the feedback, even if, in our first response, we do not agree with it. We can feed our considered response back to the group.

We need to help participants to make their emotions explicit and acknowledge them as legitimate, allowing both sides to let off steam without becoming abusive to one another and helping them to release their feelings. As leaders, we need to moderate our reaction to emotional outbursts, and acknowledge that the participant has strong feelings about an issue. However, we need to intervene if the angry person becomes abusive and attacking of others, firmly ensuring that they stop such behaviour, and help the person to express their feelings in a non-abusive way. Once the anger has been verbally (and non-abusively) expressed and individuals indicate a capacity to move on, encourage the use of symbolic gestures, e.g., a statement of regret, shaking hands, or an apology.

MANAGING TEAM ENERGY LEVELS

One of the functions of a depth leader is to manage the energy levels of a team as energy is a very important resource when doing depth work. Transformative depth work is energy consuming, but also paradoxically leads to the unlocking of previously blocked energy if successful. To manage the energy levels of a group, it is important first to monitor them. We can ask the group directly how energetic they are feeling. We can also ask what restores their energy and what drains it. The climate or atmosphere in a group will often be the best indication of the energy level.

As depth leaders, we need to be aware that we are not responsible for energising a team; rather, we need to help to remove any energy blockages. A leader may choose to energise or inspire a group, but when doing depth work, the energy for the group needs to come from the unleashing of blocked psychological energy. Many things affect energy levels, but low energy levels are often an indicator of unresolved psychodynamic processes. If we sense that the group energy has changed and that it is not simply a matter of tiredness, then it is an indication that a depth process needs to be addressed.

INTERPERSONAL INTERVENTIONS

To deal with group psychodynamics, we as depth leaders will have to intervene in personal and interpersonal psychodynamics. To intervene meaningfully, we have to apply a range of skills, including reflective listening and specific verbal techniques. These were discussed in Chapter 5. The details of group processes are discussed in detail in Chapter 9, but some general intervention guidelines for depth leaders from a people point of view are given below.

When leading from a depth perspective, we need to practice self-disclosure of our own dynamics that could possibly influence a group unnecessarily. For example, if we are particularly excited or depressed in our personal capacity, it may be important for the group to know the source of our state, especially if they may misinterpret it and take it personally. If we have experienced significant personal events that affect us psychologically, such as losing a loved one or achieving a big goal, we can share this information with a group.

We need to focus on the group as a whole, in addition to the needs of individuals and subgroups. We need to accept all participants equally and to not discriminate negatively in any way; communicating our acceptance through our body language and tone of voice. We need to ensure that any comments we make regarding personal, interpersonal or group dynamics are non-partisan and focused on the achievement of the group's objectives.

We need to create an atmosphere of acceptance and a lack of judgement about the quality of participation in a conversation in which psychodynamics are discussed. This is different to our ordinary performance management tasks as leaders, and the team members should experience this difference in our roles during a depth session.

It is important to remember transference and countertransference phenomena which were discussed in detail in Chapter 6. As a reminder, we should notice when we feel compelled to engage in a particular way with the team or an individual team member. This feeling of compulsion usually indicates that our own unconscious material has been activated, and we need to do the necessary inner work to return to neutrality.

If people dynamics are interrupting the achievement of objectives, we need to bring this to the team's attention. We can ask the team to decide whether they wish to discuss the dynamics, or proceed with the task. If we as leaders become aware that no progress is possible without a detour into a depth process, then we need to work towards getting buy-in from the group for such a process.

ENSURING GOOD GROUP PRACTICES

Many good group practices have been discussed in the techniques covered thus far. To reduce the likelihood that destructive psychodynamics will develop, the leader can encourage a set of generally healthy group practices which encourage constructive participation. If possible, we should try to ensure that the group includes the following aspects in their interactions:

- a clear purpose and vision
- openly discussed, clear values and principles that are respected by everyone
- clearly divided roles, and commitments to those roles
- well-defined projects and goals for those projects
- a well-defined and clearly understood identity as a team if this is necessary
- regular and comprehensive open communication, and communication even when it is difficult
- regular expressions of acknowledgement and appreciation for each other's efforts
- acts of celebration when goals are achieved
- continuous relationship maintenance and feedback activities
- apology and repair activities when needed

If a group is engaged in counterproductive practices, the following guidelines may help us deal with these at a surface level if a depth process is not agreed to or possible.

MANAGING COUNTERPRODUCTIVE PRACTICES

We can manage counterproductive group practices by avoiding them as much as possible through good planning, preparation and preventative action and by being a role model for good practices. Some strategies for avoiding difficulties are given below.

- We need to gather as much information as we can about a group and its members, as early as possible.
- We need to ensure that we implement hard and soft containment tools and techniques on an ongoing basis.
- We can anticipate stereotypical responses and preempt them. For example, if we are female leaders in an all-male group, we can indicate our awareness of this fact and invite suggestions to stop it from being a problem.

When dealing with a challenge or difficulty that has arisen during a group conversation, the following guidelines may be helpful.

- Acknowledge to the team that there appears to be a problem or difficulty.
- Do not assume that we understand the roots of the difficulty or the roots of the behaviour.

- Ask questions and practise reflective listening to gain an understanding of the nature of the difficulty.

- Indicate to the group that we recognise that challenges and difficulties are part of a leader's job and that we will deal with them.

- Ask the team for suggestions to resolve the problem if that seems appropriate.

- Remain neutral and supportive of everyone in the team.

When dealing with difficult people, it is sometimes possible to reframe what they are doing by not viewing their behaviour as difficult, but rather thinking of it as behaviour that is not understood. For example, a great deal of difficult behaviour comprises defence mechanisms that disguise the true feelings of an individual. If we can provide sufficient containment, the anxiety may diminish sufficiently for the individual to forego the need for defensive behaviour and reveal the underlying need or experience. Once someone reveals their true feelings about a situation, it is often possible to solve the difficulty quickly.

CONCLUSION

This chapter considered how a depth leader can manage relationships with group members and the group as a whole. The most important aspect of managing people, however, is managing ourselves and ensuring that we are as congruent as possible in our interactions. We will consider the depth process techniques in detail in Chapter 9.

PERSONAL EXERCISES

1. Consider your feelings about difficult team members. To what do you ascribe their behaviour? Consider the judgements you make about the behaviour of others. Try to develop compassion for those behaviours by understanding the need behind them. Establish the unmet needs that may be motivating your own difficult or problematic behaviours.

2. What makes you feel contained in a group situation? What type of containment do you prefer and practice – hard or soft containment?

3. Consider your own undeveloped potential as a leader. Which parts of yourself have you not developed because you did not have the opportunity to do so, or it was disallowed or disapproved of in some way? How can you develop those parts of yourself now?

4. Choose one case study that you have encountered in the past in which the people dynamics were difficult. How could you handle it differently now?

CHAPTER
8
DEPTH MEANING

INTRODUCTION

Working with meaning is, in some ways, the most difficult for a depth leader because it requires complex conceptual skills. However, learning how to work with meaning is essential to depth leadership because meaning provides the psychological nourishment and inspiration for an organisation or a group to engage and expend effort. The content of a group's life – the nature of their tasks, their opinions, their technologies – will provide a framework for their activities, but the meaning of a group's life – their psychodynamics, their archetypal impulses and the myths being lived out – provides the thread that gives purpose to everything. As Antoine de Saint Exupéry says: "If you want to build a ship, don't drum up people to collect wood and don't assign them tasks and work, but rather teach them to long for the endless immensity of the sea."

Helping a group to understand the underlying stories or myths of their work together will significantly change the quality of their engagement and experience. A depth leader helps to identify the threads of meaning and encourages an organisation or group to change their path if it is destructive, supporting them as they weave a meaningful story together. To identify depth content, the leader needs an understanding of the nature of the content of depth processes. In this chapter we will consider that nature in more detail.

A DEPTH LANGUAGE – SYMBOLS AND MYTHOLOGY

Human beings derive meaning when their personal experiences are connected with deeper archetypal processes. Therefore, to understand how groups derive meaning, we need to investigate the way we make those connections. Human life embraces a fascinating combination of perspectives and levels of functioning and these all contribute to meaning.

We have our concrete, visible and obviously physical world in which we all have to function. We also have the invisible world within our minds, which is neither concrete nor tangible, but nevertheless undeniably real. At the other extreme of the concrete physical world, we have the mythological world, in which human stories through the ages are captured in symbolic form. This is also the world of potential with its archetypes that make up the life force that drives human behaviour.

In depth work, we need to follow and find the connections between the different worlds. We need to move from the concrete, practical and physical world into the mythical realm of the collective unconscious with its archetypes that drive individual and group behaviour, and back to the concrete world again. A depth leader needs to be comfortable with these different worlds and be able to translate meaning from one to the other. Whether we are aware of it or not, all individuals and groups operate on many levels at the same time.

Examples of different levels of individual functioning:

- physical
- practical
- cognitive
- emotional
- psychological
- creative
- ancestral
- spiritual

In addition to the levels described above, individuals also function within multiple groups, and these will add a whole different set of levels to the functioning. Some of these groups are named below:

- a family
- a neighbourhood
- a friendship
- a community
- a culture
- an organisation
- a profession
- a religion
- an ethnicity
- a nationality
- a species

Ihe psyche connects the different worlds by metabolising concrete experience and making sense of it at the other levels. In other words, the psyche translates the concrete experience so that it makes sense at the archetypal level and all the levels in between. It searches for threads of meaning that connect the different levels. The greater the connection between all the levels, the deeper the sense of meaning experienced by individuals and groups will be.

Making the connections requires a language that can capture the full diversity and complexity of human experience, and yet be accessible to all who use it. This language needs to be universal and deeply personal at the same time. The psyche uses the language of symbols to achieve this. To help an organisation to understand the meaning of its depth processes or psychodynamics, we as depth leaders have to help our organisations and groups understand the language of symbolism. This requires a conceptual and communication ability that transcends the use of ordinary language.

The Chambers English Dictionary defines a symbol as an 'emblem': "that which by custom or convention represents something else". It comes from the Greek words 'syn', which means together, and 'ballein', which means to throw. Therefore, a symbol throws things together. A symbol is different from a sign in that a sign stands for something or points to something in a concrete way. A symbol carries greater meaning because it joins things together such that the whole becomes more than the sum of the parts.

Symbolism is a richly textured language in which an object, a picture, a sound, or any other coherent concept that can be perceived is used to represent aspects of our life experience. Multiple meanings can be derived from one symbol, and associated meanings derived from one symbol will differ between individuals and groups. However, there are common meanings based on archetypes that span cultures and generations.

The symbol in itself does not have a complex meaning; it is the human faculty for making meaning that imbues the symbol with meaning. For example, a wheel is a mechanism for movement until we start using it as a symbol. Then it can become a description of our changing fortunes. Although the symbols are not complex in themselves, the psyche uses symbols to express complex experiential states, which can never be described as succinctly and as fully in ordinary language. A symbol is multifaceted in a way that a word is not.

The psyche uses the symbolic world to communicate how it makes meaning out of depth processes. As depth leaders we must recognise that a symbol can contain a range of meanings and possibilities all at once. The following list of possible meanings is applied to the concept of water to illustrate how our symbolic faculty transforms a simple idea into a richly evocative set of meanings.

TYPES OF MEANING

A practical or literal meaning – Water – H2O
A physical meaning – Dehydration
An emotional meaning – 'I feel it in my waters', a wet face
A spiritual meaning – Cleansing, baptism
A psychological meaning – 'Sink or swim'
A cognitive or intellectual meaning – The flow of a conversation, a stream of thought
A course of proposed action – A need to cool down by taking a shower
A creative meaning – Water as the beginning of all creation
A historical meaning – Great floods
An ancestral meaning – Rain dance/Modjadji (An African rain queen)
A transformative capacity – Purification
A transcendent meaning – The parting of the sea

The meanings a symbol can represent are derived from the set of associations that have developed over time – associations that arise from all the varieties of human experience. A symbol only becomes truly meaningful, however, when a person develops a relationship with that symbol. It is only when the symbol refers to a unique experience for the individual that the connection is made between the conscious and unconscious levels in the psyche.

Psychically useful symbols cannot be contrived through rational, logical processes. Rather, they need to emerge through a creative process or dialogue between the conscious and unconscious mind. They can also be produced by the unconscious mind, as we see in dreams. As depth leaders, we cannot, therefore, consciously decide which symbols a group should be using; all we can do is recognise which symbols are emerging from the group itself and help to make connections with myths that will resonate with the group experience.

RECOGNISING THE GROUP'S MYTH OR STORY

Usually, symbols do not appear in isolation in an organisation or a group's depth process. It will usually be part of a myth or story that is playing itself out in a group. When working with a depth process it is useful to try to identify the story or myth (in other words, the psychodynamics) that approximately describes the experience the group is having. Often the narrative will already be present in the way participants speak about the group, and we simply have to attend to the kind of words being used or the kind of metaphors and analogies used to describe the group. By using a story that captures important elements of the group's experience, the group can make sense of, or make meaning of, its experience in a way that enables change and transformation.

It may be useful to draw on any myths or narratives that a group can relate to if this story is not already present in the group conversation. Useful source material includes fairy tales, ancient myths such as tales about the Greek gods, tales from the ancestors, films and books, stories from various religious documents, stories from oral tradition and culture, or any story that spontaneously appears in the mind of the leader. The mythical story should be offered as a tentative possibility that may capture important elements of the group story. By being tentative, we allow the group to modify or alter the myth or story, or generate one that is more appropriate to the group's experience.

Examples of common myths or narratives

- A fight between good and evil
- A love triangle
- Sibling rivalry
- Vengeance
- A power struggle
- Prodigal son/daughter
- A damsel in distress
- Rags to riches
- Abandonment
- Rebellion
- Surviving against the odds
- A fight for justice
- Overthrow of a tyrant

Once a myth or a story that is useful to the group has been identified, the group can use it as a point of reference, and use the symbolism to better understand the situation and the attendant choices it offers. The group now also has the freedom to decide how the story will unfold from that point onwards, and so transformation becomes possible.

For example, a group may experience itself as similar to a group of orphans in an orphanage where there is a cruel housemaster (this example is elaborated on in the next section). Alternatively, a group may experience themselves as similar to a group of brave polar explorers. Whatever the story, a discussion of the story and its alternative story lines could be helpful in suggesting solutions to here-and-now difficulties. It may take a while for the group to identify the most appropriate myth or story, and every member may need to add their personal perspective, but eventually this process results in deeper insight and a constructive shift in the psychodynamics of the group.

MAINTAINING A MULTILEVEL AND DEPTH PERSPECTIVE

It is important for us as depth leaders to be able to maintain a depth perspective when thinking about the content of a group's discussions. A group may be discussing the intricacies of a difficult client relationship, but we need to be thinking about the possible parallels between the client relationship and the internal relationships between members of the organisation. It is also important to remember all aspects of the group context, as discussed in Chapter 4, because these may be playing themselves out in the themes with which the group is preoccupied. It means listening with a metaphorical ear, as well as a practical one, at all times. We need not feed all the perspectives back to the group every time, but occasionally it may be helpful to remind the team of the different perspectives.

As depth leaders we need to help the group decide what a symbol or a collection of symbols in a story means for them. Symbols become meaningful when we investigate the associations that surround them. Human beings create webs of meaning in their minds. Our minds are not neatly organised like filing cabinets in a legal firm. Rather, our minds are organic data storage networks where the main logic is determined by proximity in terms of time and space, and emotional similarity plays a large role.

If we accept the tenets of Carl Jung stating that there is a collective unconscious that we all have access to and that it forms the foundation for our own individual minds, then we can imagine each individual mind as having similar strata of potential concepts and associations. Each individual web of meaning may then start with similar bedrock, but how that develops to furnish the individual mind depends on the particular experiences and idiosyncrasies of the individual.

Meaning is created when a person experiences a particular state and has a feeling response to it. In other words, it is the feeling that provides the meaning. The word feeling here does not denote a sentiment but rather the placing of a personal value on a given experience. Individuals are always asking the question: "How is this important to me?" "Or, how does this affect my life or my development?" "Or my quality of life?" If we can answer those questions in satisfying ways, then we are attaching meaning to our experiences.

When exploring the meaning of symbolism in groups we must remember to investigate associations from multiple perspectives. We cannot assume that our associations are appropriate for the group. We can encourage group members to offer associations from a variety of perspectives, including;

- heir individual, personal perspectives
- the group perspective
- the organisational perspective
- relevant cultural perspectives
- historical perspectives and
- any other relevant perspectives

The group can then derive meaning from a synthesis of all the different points of view. We should not impose meaning on the group, but rather facilitate a conversation in which meaning emerges. Once this happens, it is likely that more symbols will shortly follow, spontaneously arising from the group. These symbols can become very powerful for guiding the group into the future.

For example, one of the teams I worked with was unhappy with the team leader. He was an autocratic and critical man, who often humiliated and belittled staff members. His style led to an added difficulty in that the individual employees were no longer able to be supportive of one another, because the leader attacked any of them who were. One member of the team mentioned that he felt as if he was living in an orphanage run by a cruel housemaster. This myth or story became very useful in understanding the group dynamic that was in operation.

The team started exploring what it meant to be orphans who were victimised when they tried to protect or support one another. They came to understand that they were not only suffering at the hands of the autocratic leader, but that they were also abandoning one another for fear of victimisation. They realised that by supporting one another, they could stop behaving like helpless children with no recourse, and could start taking action that would protect them. The leader was unable to do the inner work that would result in a different dynamic between him and the rest of the group, and ultimately, he left the organisation. However, the group's new awareness meant that they could prevent the perpetuation of the negative dynamic among them.

LINKING SYMBOLISM WITH CONCRETE CONTENT

Once the team has completed a depth process, it is important to move back to the current experience of the team and help to translate the myth or story into its practical meaning for the team as it goes forward. This means discussing in practical terms what the symbolism means for the team's decisions and interactions into the future. It is helpful to identify how relationships need to change, to spell everything out and to document it in the form of specific actions.

EMERGING PSYCHODYNAMIC THEMES

As depth leaders, much of our work is to notice when the underlying psychodynamic processes in a group are preventing or hampering group productivity and creativity. The psychodynamic themes will emerge if we observe the group closely and support them to have reflective conversations. We need to look for emerging themes that will reveal themselves in the way the group interacts and the content of those interactions.

For example, it is also useful to track who occupies which role in the group. As discussed in Chapter 4, individuals will occupy psychological, political and emotional roles in addition to their functional roles. The depth process will start revealing itself through the content of these roles. For example, if the content of the session is concerned with implementing new technology, the psychodynamic of the rank held by more technologically literate members may play itself out. As a depth leader it is useful to keep an eye on the deeper content, without necessarily mentioning it to the group until it is clear. If a clear psychodynamic emerges, we need to create an opportunity to enter into a depth process.

There are some general principles at work when trying to identify the depth content or psychodynamics of a group or an organisation and they are listed below.

- Psychological patterns of behaviour are established in early childhood as a way of ensuring our survival.
- The psychological roles we occupy are designed to lessen our anxiety in some way and so these will provide a clue about what we are trying to avoid.
- Individuals are unconsciously drawn towards organisations and groups when their individual psychodynamic patterns resonate with the collective patterns.
- Psychodynamic patterns tend to operate in pairs of connected roles. If one way of being is apparent, we can look for the presence or absence of the alternative way of being. Psychodynamic patterns tend to present as tensions or dilemmas in the system that are usually not fully discussed.
- Psychodynamic patterns are systemic; in other words, they operate in balancing or self-reinforcing loops, and are often driven by power structures and the context.
- Groups are generally not conscious of their psychodynamic patterns, so may not be able to describe them if asked directly.

There are as many psychodynamic themes in the world as there are groups. However, because of the archetypal nature of the human psyche, certain themes are common and likely to play out in some aspects of the psychodynamics of the group. Some of these are listed below in no particular order.

- The organisation or group's identity
- The group's survival potential
- Threats to membership – belonging or abandonment
- Insider and outsider issues
- Acceptance, tolerance versus criticism and rejection
- Leadership and authority
- Strength and vulnerability
- Birth and death
- Pairing
- Separation
- Age and youth
- Innocence and experience
- Good and evil
- Success and failure
- Individuality and collective behaviour
- Dependence and independence
- Scapegoating
- Death and rebirth

RECOGNISING THE PSYCHODYNAMIC THEME

To help a group move beyond the constraints of its psychodynamic patterns, the leader has to help the group recognise what those patterns are. The following information can help the leader (and the group) identify its psychodynamic pattern:

- the mental, psychological and physical patterns of engagement in the group.

- the areas of conflict.

- the metaphors used by the group.

- mental imagery or physical sensations experienced by the leader or expressed by group members.

- external events that are discussed or paid attention to by the group.

- the content preoccupations of the group.

As leaders, we need to look for recurring patterns and events that seem to capture the interest of the group positively or negatively. We need to try to identify the story that would metaphorically describe how the group is functioning from a psychological perspective. Once you have an idea of a possible story or metaphor that may be appropriate, we can offer it as an interpretation to the group. This interpretation needs to be offered tentatively while inviting the group to comment on whether it feels accurate or not. The group may deny its accuracy, in which case we may need to search for a more appropriate suggestion. Often, the group will suggest modifications to the interpretation, and then begin to elaborate on the story spontaneously. At this point, the leader needs to encourage the group to pursue its own interpretation.

Once the group has agreed that the psychodynamic interpretation feels accurate, we need to encourage the group to examine the meaning of the psychodynamic for the group. This will include considering how to move forward more productively with the new awareness.

MEANING AND NEUTRALITY

We examined the importance of maintaining neutrality in previous chapters. As depth leaders, our greatest challenge will come when working with meaning from a depth perspective. We cannot make meaning; we can only help it to emerge. Therefore, we can only truly lead group depth processes if one part of us as depth leaders remains neutral and we maintain enough awareness to follow the process as it unfolds without any bias. A depth leader who cannot hold a position of neutrality at least some of the time will influence the group negatively in the long run. Practising neutrality does not mean always feeling completely neutral; in fact, it may mean feeling intensely biased for a short time, to relinquish a rigid adherence to a particular point of view. As mentioned before, moving quickly back towards neutrality is an advanced skill that only develops through practice.

To help build our neutrality when it comes to interpreting meaning it is useful to remember that relationships contain conflict as part of their nature. Our conflicts and disagreements are characterised by a variety of different positions and viewpoints that eventually (with appropriate depth leadership) polarise into two opposing voices. By sitting in the eye of the storm or sitting in the fire and remaining neutral, the depth leader helps the process of finding common meaning, as all sides feel supported during the process. To a large extent, this prevents destructive behaviours.

To maintain neutrality, the leader can follow some of the following guidelines.

- Remember that what we see in the overt behaviour of the team is only part of the total group field and that there are always other points of view.

- Remember that a point of view depends on where we are standing.

- Remember that behind every point of view lies an experience.

- Remember that behind every point of view, there is a legitimate human need, although it may be disguised or distorted.
- We can practise moving between points of view by finding the part in ourselves that would agree with a point of view if we were in the same situation.

Sometimes it becomes necessary to break the neutrality rule. Leaders can make contributions under the following conditions.

- We can supply additional information if the team agrees, but we should only do this if we are the only one in the group who has the information, and it is critical to the team's functioning.

- If we really feel a need to get involved, we can ask to join the group and ask someone else to facilitate, or call in a professional facilitator.

AVOIDING POLARITIES

To maintain neutrality, it is useful to recognise that all ways of being human arise from trying to survive particular circumstances. The archetypes offer us blueprints for being human and are not in themselves necessarily good or bad, but rather offer ways of being for surviving in a given context. Each archetypal way of being has its polar opposite as a possibility too, which also has value. It is useful to understand that each behavioural polarity is valuable, but can also be regarded as problematic, depending on our point of view. It is also useful to consider the relationship between different polarities and the essential value behind these polarities. Whether a way of being is regarded as good or bad is simply a matter of perspective. Ideally, we need to adopt an integrated position in which we use the helpful aspect of each way of being when appropriate. To illustrate this, some examples of possible behaviours, their polar positions and the integrated approach are given in the table below.

	Negative view of first polarity	Positive view of first polarity	Positive view of other polarity	Negative view of other polarity	Integrated position
Degree of team cooperation /compliance	Disloyal	Independent mindset	Loyal	Yes-man, conformer	Independent membership
Degree of task focus	Task-master	Driven	Relaxed	Lazy, slack	Optimal use of energy
Degree of playfulness/ seriousness	Stern,boring, miser	Serious, frugal	Playful abundance	Childish gluttony	Sustainable pleasure
Degree of self-confidence	Timid, passive	Humble	Confident	Arrogant	Self-assured awareness
Degree of sociability	Anti-social, shy	Self-contained	Extrovert, gregarious, sociable	Loud, in your face	Self-contained and sociable
Degree of flexibility	No backbone, pushover	Easy-going, flexible	Determined	Inflexible	Focused adaptability

To remain neutral, especially when the team is trying to engage the leader's opinion, the following techniques may be useful.

• Restate the content that has been discussed so far.

• Summarise both sides neutrally if two sides have been offered, distilling the positive essence from each side.

• Hand back strong opinions to the team, in other words, ask the team how they feel about a strong opinion that has been expressed.

• Resist expressing an opinion and tell the team that it would not be helpful to do so at this stage. It is useful to express our opinion only once the group has expressed all their diverse opinions.

BUILDING A DEPTH VISION

To some extent, the depth meaning of a group will play itself out regardless of the explicitly agreed vision of the team. However, if the vision of a team is developed in such a way that it resonates with the deeper processes of the individual members, then it provides a framework of meaning which helps the group a great deal.

As leaders of an organisation or a team it is our responsibility to initiate the creation of a vision in a team, as well as to gain participation and buy-in from team members. If we are part of a larger organisation we have to ensure that the team vision follows from the organisation's vision and is aligned with it. Setting the vision means creating the direction for an organisation or team in a way that enables members to visualise a meaningful outcome for their activities. There are other texts written specifically to help leaders with vision setting processes and there are a variety of methodologies for doing so. What is important here is for the depth leader to recognise that a vision will have very little inspirational power if it does not resonate deeply with the personal goals and individuation imperatives of individual members.

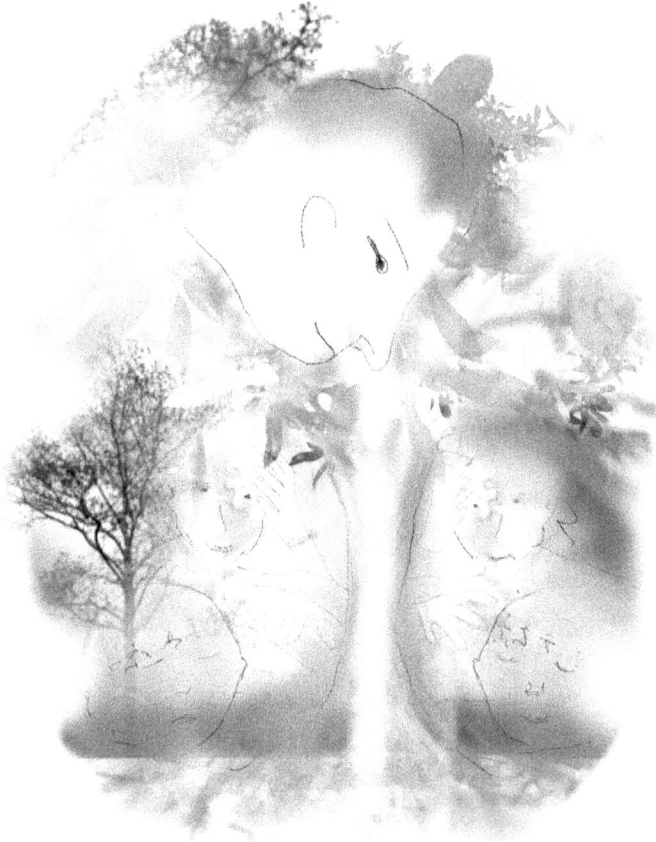

Depth psychology suggests that we all have different layers of motivation, depending on our histories and our talents. Activities are meaningful for us if they ring a personal bell inside us, or more specifically, if they allow us to unleash some of our undeveloped psychological potential. As a depth leader it is important to initiate and manage a process whereby a team can find a vision that resonates for all its members. For example, a vision for an insurance company could be to be the largest insurer in the country. This idea may resonate for some individuals, but probably not deeply with very many. If, however, the vision was restated as creating an environment in which people feel safer because they have a helping hand when things go wrong, it is more likely to resonate with more members of the team because it is an archetypal human need to want support when things go wrong. From a depth perspective, we are living out personal stories and the more closely a team vision aligns or resonates with the values and imperatives in our own stories, the more likely we will be to commit to achieving the vision.

A depth leader will help a group explore their deeper reasons for being part of the organisation or team and see how these reasons resonate with the stated vision. It may even be important to re-phrase the vision to embrace an archetypal motivation.

The first step in developing a depth vision is for the leader to allow and encourage a process whereby all members of the team explore and articulate their personal reasons for being in the organisation or team and for finding meaning in their work. It is important that team members are not interrupted or told what is right and wrong in this exploration.

To tap into less conscious motivations, individuals can follow a process by which they ask themselves why something is important to them each time they identify a particular thing that has meaning for them. For example, if a team member indicates that it is important to her to be of service to others, it is useful for her to investigate further why the idea of service is particularly personally important. This can be done by asking why at least five times. (This process was popularised in terms of under-standing organisational problems by Peter Senge in his book The fifth discipline fieldbook. It has been adapted to investigate deep psychological motivation.) A fictitious worked example is provided in the following diagram:

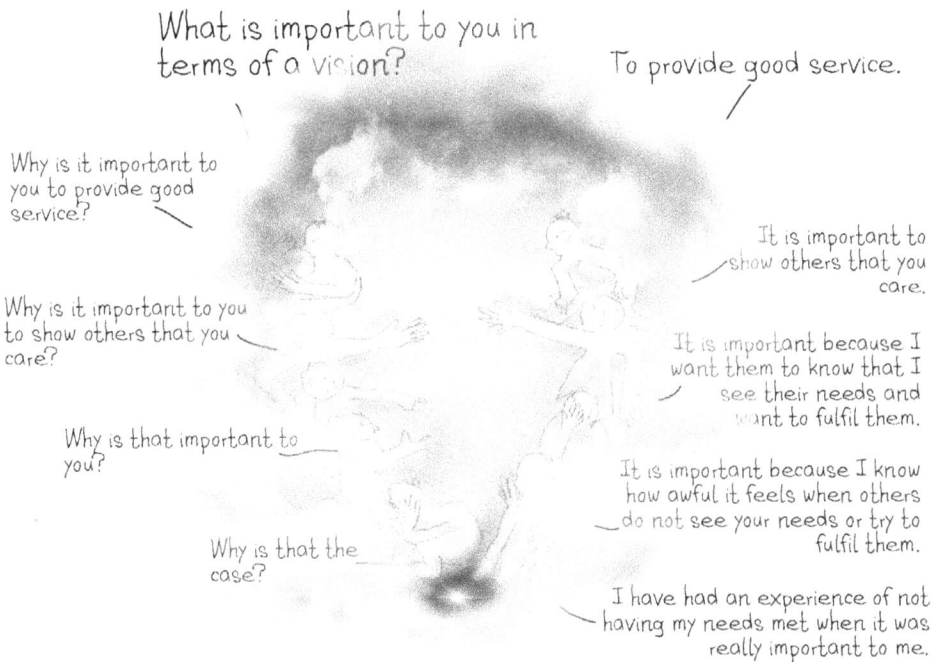

What is important to you in terms of a vision?

To provide good service.

Why is it important to you to provide good service?

It is important to show others that you care.

Why is it important to you to show others that you care?

It is important because I want them to know that I see their needs and want to fulfil them.

Why is that important to you?

It is important because I know how awful it feels when others do not see your needs or try to fulfil them.

Why is that the case?

I have had an experience of not having my needs met when it was really important to me.

This questioning process is potentially very revealing, as the example shows, so it is best if each participant in a team first does this exercise privately. If there is enough trust and containment in the team conversation, participants may be invited to share their answers. If managed with gentleness and respect, this could result in a very deep and meaningful conversation that will strengthen team relationships as a result of the intimacy of such deep sharing of information. Since it potentially exposes individual vulnerability, we should not attempt this process in a team where there is not enough safety and trust.

At the deepest level inside us, we are often motivated by previous wounds. Alternatively, we could be motivated by our essential talents. If we have a significant unresolved deep-seated psychological wound (as is the case with many of us), we may be primarily motivated by the wound rather than our talents. We may need to address and heal the wound psychologically, before we will have full access to inherent talents. As depth leaders, we can help individuals identify when this may be the case, and it may be useful to suggest that the individual receives professional assistance to unleash talents blocked by wounding.

Once individuals have explored their deeper motivations that feed into their vision, the team can embark on a discussion of commonalities between their respective visions. It is interesting that a group often will have been unconsciously drawn together (despite the fact that rational reasons exist for their joining as a group) because they share some deep underlying motivations. This process can then be used to articulate the vision while including as many of the individual perspectives as possible. Of course, the vision needs to be aligned with the overarching organisational vision too, if the group operates within a larger organisation.

CONCLUSION

Working with meaning from a depth perspective requires an added set of skills. We considered the world of symbolism as the language of the unconscious and its relevance to depth leadership. I discussed the emergence of psychodynamic themes, and emphasised the importance of leader neutrality in working with these themes. The chapter also outlined a depth approach to developing a vision, and discussed the basic ideas behind working with the meaning of depth processes, noting that it is a vast and complex field. In some ways, a text of this nature can only scratch the surface of all of the theory associated with depth processes. Leaders are encouraged to develop their knowledge on an ongoing basis.

PERSONAL EXERCISES

1. Consider three areas in which you are currently not neutral, but rather have some strong feelings and opinions. Work to find the validity of the opposing opinion. Spend time convincing someone else of the opposing view to the one you really hold. Check if you are genuinely able to see the validity of both sides.

2. Consider areas in which you will always be unable to be neutral. Decide how you will handle situations in which they arise.

3. Think of three symbols that are important to you. Describe them and their meanings. Trace the origins of those symbols for you. Ask two other people what the symbols mean for them. Compare your view with the views of others.

4. Think of a story or a myth that describes important elements of your life. Decide how you would like the story to unfold.

5. Consider your relationship with your inner world. Spend time getting to know which symbols are important to you and embark on a process of analysing your dreams for a while. If necessary, enlist the help of a professional. Actively develop a familiarity with the symbolic world.

CHAPTER
9
DEPTH PROCESSES

INTRODUCTION

Often, we refer to the term processing or the phrase to process something. These terms are used to denote a set of activities that lead the individual or group towards a planned or emerging goal.

In depth leadership terms, processing something in a team means helping to unfold emerging events or psychodynamics in the most constructive way possible. In this chapter, we consider the leadership tasks, tools and techniques required for managing depth processes.

UNDERSTANDING THE GROUP FIELD

To start working with the depth processes in a group, we need to get to know the group field (described in Chapter 4) so that we can build a picture of the psyche of the group and what it needs. As depth leaders, we may have the opportunity to set up an organisation or a team from scratch. In this case, we can influence and come to understand the group field from the start. Many of us, however, arrive in a ready-made team and have to learn about the group field and its psychodynamic character. It is useful to chat to individual team members and try to determine some of the following information.

- What roles (task, emotional, political and psychological) do the individuals play in the team?

- How do team members view the functioning of the team from a group dynamics (psychodynamic) point of view?

- What works well in the team, and what does not work so well?

- What is the history of the team and the larger system in which it functions?

- In each member's view, is the team performing to its full potential? If not, why is that the case?

- Are there unresolved issues in the team that individuals are aware of? If so, what are the issues?

- Do team members feel that the team needs to spend some time addressing its group dynamics? If so, are there any ideas about which team processes are needed?

Using the information from these questions and other observations, it is useful to build a picture of the group field which includes the group context, the group history and the associated complexes that arise from that history (described in detail in Chapter 4).

ESTABLISHING A GROUP CONTRACT

To create an environment where depth processes can be worked with as they occur, it is important to contract with the team or group explicitly that such depth work will be pursued if necessary. This contract should include agreements between team members about how they will engage with one another. As the leader, you need to explain in general terms what this will mean, as well as reassure the team that nothing will be pursued without their permission. Once this is agreed upon, you can embark on a process. It is helpful to include the following areas in such an agreement.

- The maintenance of privacy and confidentiality. You can suggest that team members may discuss their own experiences outside of the group (as they may want to do), but that they refrain from discussing the comments and experiences of others outside of the group.

- The importance of engaging with an attitude of taking care of themselves emotionally. In other words, team members need to monitor for themselves when they are ready to reveal personal thoughts and feelings, and to protect themselves from intrusion.

- The need to provide time out if the intensity of group discussions becomes overwhelming. It is important, however, to have everyone's agreement to return to the conversation until the completion of the process because failure to have this agreement could result in a half-finished process – and that is often more destructive than not having embarked on a depth process at all.

- Any areas that are important to the team members. You could invite them to suggest possible agreements that are important to them.

Once you, as the leader, have done the preparatory work of analysing the team's requirements and preparing yourself for neutrality, you can work with a depth process. You may believe that a depth process is necessary, but you cannot assume that the whole team is ready to enter into such a process. The group process can only be pursued if the whole team explicitly agrees that it is ready to investigate a certain area – something we will consider in more detail later.

DEPTH PROCESS EDUCATION

Depth processes can happen at any time in an organisation or team's life. It is really useful if the members of a team understand the implications of depth processes, including the possible dangers of these processes. The more knowledge participants have of individual and group psychodynamics (depth psychology), the more constructive it may be for them. Before embarking on the work, it is useful to provide the team with some education about the nature of depth processes and what will be required from them to address such a process. Useful ideas include concepts such as:

- the difference between surface and depth processes (the existence of an unconscious level)
- anxiety (the edge concept)

- defence mechanisms
- rank differences and their impact on a group and
- role dynamics and their impact on a group

It is obviously useful for you as leader to educate yourself as much as possible about these concepts, so that you can explain them as clearly as possible. It is important not to use pointed or specific examples about the team when teaching these concepts, but rather to include generic examples that everyone can relate to safely.

HELPFUL PROCESS MECHANISMS

Fortunately, despite the caution and costs associated with depth work, there are two inherent human mechanisms that, if they can be encouraged, greatly assist the leader in helping the team. These two mechanisms or tendencies are described below.

PHASE LOCKING

Phase locking is the technical term for the tendency of systems to couple into larger wholes, discussed by Bud McClure (2004) in his book Putting a new spin on groups: The science of chaos. In ordinary language, this means that there is a natural tendency for individuals to start functioning synchronistically, or in harmony with one another, if they spend enough time together and they are in the right atmosphere. If you hang two cuckoo clocks together, the swing of their pendulums will eventually become synchronised. Similarly, individuals in a group can become synchronised mentally, emotionally and psychologically.

Once that happens, the individuals will feel themselves to be part of the whole without being constrained by it. This can be a hugely pleasurable experience that leads to great task success. As a depth leader you cannot make phase locking happen, but you can encourage an atmosphere in which individuals become open enough to one another that phase locking can happen by itself.

THE TRANSCENDENT FUNCTION IN GROUPS

The 'transcendent function' – a term coined by Carl Jung – refers to an inherent psychological predisposition for the psyche to move instinctively towards the transcendence of polarities, to a more integrated position, known as a 'transcendent third'. Jung suggested that the psyche does not ultimately like to side with one polarity rather than another and, if possible, will always move towards a more integrated and balanced position. This inherent tendency ensures that a group will have an impulse to do depth work successfully, given the opportunity and a conducive environment.

CREATING A CONDUCIVE ENVIRONMENT

To create a conducive environment for phase locking and the emergence of the transcendent third, apply the following guidelines:

- Use the metaskills described in Chapter 5.
- Encourage full participation and commitment from the group. Commitment is a prerequisite for phase locking to occur.
- Make sufficient space for the minority voices in the group (although they may be unpopular) to speak and be heard.
- Actively resolve conflict when it occurs.
- Use the appropriate containment techniques described in Chapter 7.
- Follow the readiness of the group and do not artificially introduce stimulation of the group.
- Respect the unconscious wisdom of the depth process and allow it to unfold.

IDENTIFYING DEPTH PROCESSES

If the team has difficulties, members will not necessarily openly discuss the nature of those difficulties Psychological difficulties are hard to speak about for anyone, and may need to be brought to the attention of someone else before they can be tackled. Sometimes the problem we tell people about is not necessarily the same as the problem we need to solve. The technical term for this is the 'presenting problem', which is the socially acceptable problem we can talk about. It is important for a depth leader to recognise that there will be a presenting problem when working with a group and that this may be linked to, but different from, the real problem. Therefore, we need to do some detective work to determine what the real problem in a team may be, making it impossible to set an agenda for a depth process. The agenda will often be set for the presenting problem. Also, as leader of the team, we are often part of the problem, and the team may be unable to tell us about this initially (without sufficient containment).

Sometimes, when embarking on a session where depth work may be needed, the leader needs an open agenda because the group wants to explore whatever may emerge. In this case, we may use the approach that Arnold Mindell calls 'sorting the field'. This involves asking the team members to list randomly any issues that they would like to address in a team meeting. We allow the team to decide together which of the topics will take precedence. If a topic emerges that no one in the team wants to work on other than the individual who listed it, this may be an indication that there is a depth process at work.

Ultimately, in depth work, the agenda is set by the group psyche itself. We, as leaders, need to monitor what is happening in the group and use the techniques outlined in this section to address important issues.

Once the team has agreed that it will pursue depth processes, if necessary, we can start working. The first step is to identify that there is a depth process that may need attention, remembering that the team may not know what it is. Once the depth process has been identified, careful work is needed to bring it to the surface. Sometimes the identification and surfacing happen simultaneously. Either way, patience and delicacy are required.

BECOMING ATTENTIVE TO DEPTH PROCESSES

Most of us will pay attention to what is on the surface in a group situation. Obvious events and interactions capture our attention and there is often little room to notice the more subtle events and interactions that occur in a group. Mindell distinguishes between what he calls our 'first attention' and our 'second attention'. To work with depth processes, we need to develop the second or depth attention. To do that it helps to become aware of the following kinds of things:

- body movements while someone is talking;
- the way someone makes eye contact;
- interaction and eye contact patterns between individuals;
- thoughts and feelings that pop unbidden into our minds;
- internal voices (or thoughts) that tell us what to do;
- momentary or chronic physical sensations;
- 'flirts' (a term coined by Mindell) – events from other systems that catch your attention, such as the light falling on water, or a bird moving almost invisibly in a tree, or any of the myriad other things that catch your attention for a moment;
- sudden awareness of certain sounds such as a clock ticking;
- the appearance of a song in our minds;
- the sudden awareness of an object or an image that was present all the time, but was not noticed before.

The list above provides clues about what may be going on unconsciously in the group. Learning to pay attention to these and other examples of signals from the depth takes practice. Asking the following questions in any given situation can actively develop this practice.

- What am I noticing?
- What else is also happening?
- What keeps catching my attention?

Understanding what these clues mean takes practice. Each clue should be noticed and further explored until the story or psychodynamic starts to reveal itself. Techniques to assist in this process are described next.

NOTICING THE POSSIBILITY OF A DEPTH PROCESS

Remember that a depth process should only be worked with if the surface process is being jeopardised in some way or if the team particularly wishes to explore the depth process even if the surface process is going well. The first thing to notice, then, is if the surface process is in some way not proceeding as effectively as it can. Look for signs that the process is getting stuck or taking longer than it should. For example:

- the group is unable to take the next step in a process;
- an activity is unnecessarily repeated;
- there is a lack of energy in the team that cannot be ascribed to other factors, such as it being directly after lunch;
- only a few team members are participating;
- there is criticism of the process;
- there is a continual changing of direction;
- process steps are interrupted regularly;
- agreements are not kept.

Once we have noticed that the surface process is getting stuck, we can start looking for the depth process more specifically. To look for a depth process, it is important to understand where and how to look.

PATHWAYS FROM THE DEPTH TO THE SURFACE

Information from a depth process will invariably find its way to the surface over time. It is useful to understand the ways in which information from the less conscious parts of a system travels to the surface. The possible pathways consist of any methods that human beings use to experience the world or express themselves.

- We experience the world through our senses, so there are pathways relating to touch, hearing, taste, sight and smell.
- We experience the world through other physical sensations such as feeling hot or cold, pain or pleasure.
- We can experience the world through our intuition, in which we know things in a way that has bypassed the physical senses.
- We can express ourselves through physical movement, through words and sounds.
- We can express ourselves through art and through our actions, including the ways in which we relate to people and things.

All these means of expression and experience can be pathways for information about depth processes. The psyche will use different pathways, depending on individual unique talents and preferences and the medium of communication that is appropriate to the cultural and social environments of an individual.

Importantly, the information from a depth process usually will not use the dominant experiential or expression pathway in that system. If the team is communicating through talking, the depth information may travel via the touch or movement pathway.

Mindell refers to these pathways as 'channels', and defines the possible channels as follows:

- The proprioceptive channel: physical sensations i.e., awareness of the state of your own body.
- The auditory channel: refers to external and internal voices and sounds, including music (voices in your head, jingles/tunes that appear spontaneously in your mind).
- The kinaesthetic channel: refers to physical movement or the urge to move.
- The visual channel: external and internal imagery.
- The relationship channel: the way people relate to and interact with one another.
- The world channel: events and trends in the systems surrounding a group.

SIGNALS FROM THE DEEP

A signal is essentially any piece of information that the psyche uses to communicate the nature of a depth process. Therefore, a signal is a message from under the surface. The signal will be noticeable because it communicates information that is different from the dominant message that is being communicated.

A signal should be taken seriously once it has occurred more than two or three times. Until then, it is difficult to know what information the signal is carrying. Also, it is important to understand that the signal is not being given consciously, so it should be treated with great care.

The following list provides some guidelines for using pathways of information to identify a depth process.

- Notice the pathway that the team is using for its ordinary communication.
- Notice any other pathways that may be carrying information.
- Tune into the subtle pathways that the team may be using and pay attention to any signals that occur in this pathway.
- Notice if the team switches pathways. This may be an indication of a depth process.
- Ask the team to comment on any unusual thoughts, feelings or experiences they may be noticing.

Once the overt and subtle pathways that a team uses have been identified, the leader needs to notice and make sense of the signals that come through them.

Signals that indicate depth processes fall into the following categories: signs of anxiety, signs of defence mechanisms, signs of incongruence, and signs of conflict. In Chapter 3, I discussed these signals as being edge symptoms. More information is provided below about each of these areas.

Signs of anxiety

An unaddressed depth process will cause anxiety in the team and its members. It is therefore important to look for any signals that indicate anxiety although some of these may be difficult to observe. Anxiety produces adrenaline in the body, which has the following effects, some of which are directly related to the effects of adrenaline.

- Nervous silence
- Nervous laughter
- Confusion
- Fidgeting
- Losing focus or going blank
- Mental interference – inability to hear or follow current experience
- Dry mouth
- Increased blood pressure
- Sweating
- Loss of energy

Signs of individual and group defence mechanisms

If you observe an intensification of a particular defence mechanism or the arrival of the new defence mechanism, it may be a sign of a depth process. Any other defence mechanisms mentioned in Chapters 3 and 4 may be a sign of the depth process. Some of the more common individual defence mechanisms, as well as some general group ones, are listed below.

- Withdrawal – lack of eye contact, or physical withdrawal
- Aggression
- Searching for an escape
- Chaos – everyone talking all at once
- Discussion of unrepresented third parties
- Sleepiness or boredom
- Continual references to the past or future and an inability to stay in the here and now
- Incomplete acts
- Unfinished sentences
- Switching pathways or channels

Signs of incongruence

Any signs of a lack of congruence in an individual, or a group or a process may indicate the presence of a depth process. The most common example of incongruence is what Arnold Mindell refers to as a 'double signal'. People communicate simultaneously in many different ways. Double signals occur when more than one message is sent out and the messages that are sent are not congruent. They are the result of unconscious processes that contradict the surface one.

For example, while talking, the tone and tempo of someone's voice may be incongruent with the content of what is being said. Another example is where members of a team may send out a message verbally that they are saying yes to a particular request, but through movement or actions they may be shaking their heads to indicate that they are saying no. Those hearing these messages may be consciously or unconsciously aware of the 'no' message and are often confused by it. They may unconsciously realise that regardless of how they respond they will invariably negate one of the two messages and, effectively, one part of the message.

Other signs of incongruence are:

- lack of follow-through – decisions are not implemented
- gossip – communication is not congruent in different settings
- cycling – a group approaches a process but never completes it

Signs of conflict

Many depth processes are partially or completely about conflict. It is therefore useful to look for signs that there is a conflict, such as:

- brief or prolonged verbal disagreements between team members
- a lack of overt communication or team members remaining separated from one another in some way
- individuals or subgroups talking about other group members who are not present
- individuals or subgroups being suspicious or mistrustful of the motivations of other members of the group
- lack of follow-through – decisions are not implemented

Anything indicating that all is not what it seems may be a signal of the presence of a depth process that needs to be tackled. In ordinary language, it is useful for a depth leader to look for three general signs when identifying potential depth processes:

- anything out of the ordinary in the behaviour of an individual member or the team as a whole
- processes that cannot be completed
- mixed messages of any kind

Leaders should, however, take care to wait until these potential signals start coalescing into a clear message before acting on them.

SURFACING DEPTH PROCESSES

Once the leader has identified the existence of a depth process, the decision has to be made about how to bring it to the surface. This task is considered in detail in the following section. However, since the most important part of bringing a depth process to the surface is to gain the permission of the group to do so, this is discussed first.

USING DEEP DEMOCRACY TO GAIN PERMISSION

Once we as leaders have identified a depth process, it is important to gain the permission of the team to pursue it. This permission can be gained in general at the beginning of the meeting, but it is also important to gain permission specifically for the particular process that we are about to pursue. We gain permission by alerting the team to the fact that we are about to explore a deeper issue and asking for its agreement to go ahead. It is useful to practise the process called deep democracy, in which consensus is sought before the leader goes ahead.

Deep democracy is an approach to group decision making that is based on the conclusion that many of our current approaches to groups do not work in the best interests of the group in the long run. The term deep democracy has been used by Mindell to describe a way of working in which the full wisdom of the group is sought regardless of the power divisions in the group.

Approaches to group decision making and the leadership of groups have varied enormously through the ages. There have been numerous attempts throughout time to create political and organisational systems that are both efficient and just. In the Eurocentric cultures, this progression has taken us from monarchy to the present systems of majority democracy. Majority democracy, as it is now widely practised, creates a situation where fifty-one percent of the population can potentially dominate and suppress forty-nine percent. This is certainly an improvement over monarchy, where the king may ignore the wishes of his people, but majority democracy still potentially ignores the wishes of the forty-nine percent. Sabotage – whether politically expressed in random bombings, or represented in the workplace as strikes, slowdowns or absenteeism – is to some extent a symptom of the failures of majority democracy. Deep democracy does not try to get everyone to agree on the same approach or idea. That would be unrealistic and would not value the conflicting opinions.

Instead, the practice of deep democracy is based on the idea that solutions can be sustainable only if they have recognised and incorporated the wisdom of all the conflicting opinions in a given context. The practice of deep democracy requires the leader to create an environment that will allow and offer support for (not necessarily agree with) all sides. The belief is that each side, no matter how apparently bad, has within it a wisdom that is needed by the group before it can move on. Denial of this wisdom and repression of the conflicting opinions will result in sabotage and cycles of ever-increasing hostility.

Deep democracy differs from traditional problem-resolution techniques and majority democracy in that it does not strive for agreement or compromise; it strives for consensus. Gaining consensus means discovering the hidden wisdom in all the sides, and gaining agreement by all sides, to move in a given direction even if the sides still hold conflicting opinions.

Deep democracy is based on the realisation that the full diversity of viewpoints is needed to represent reality and create sustainable solutions. In an organisational setting, this means that the troublesome, annoying or negative people and views are just as important and necessary as the good people and views.

The consensus is achieved by making modifications to the proposed decision or course of action based on the concerns and underlying wisdom of all the opinions of the group. The team needs to be given permission to say no and any individual who exercises this choice needs to be supported and asked what she would need to be able to proceed. As leaders we may need to go through several iterations of this process before the whole team is comfortable to proceed. If we go ahead without gaining everybody's permission, it is not only potentially very damaging to individuals and the team, but we are also unlikely to get enough cooperation from the team to resolve the depth process successfully.

CONTAINMENT DURING DEPTH PROCESSES

Before surfacing any depth processes it is important to remember that helping a team to deal with depth processes requires containment – providing a safe enough space for the team to explore psychologically tricky territory. Containment was discussed in detail in Chapter 7, but a summary of the most important aspects for depth processes is given here. Containment has two broad elements.

- The provision of structural or practical safety in terms of setting and maintaining boundaries related to issues such as time and space, as well as offering a clear structure for the process to be followed. This includes managing the physical environment and ensuring that ethical considerations are in place.

- The provision of an emotional container that holds and soothes the team to counteract anxiety. The leader provides an atmosphere of care, compassion and respect.

Specifically, containment during a depth process needs to have the following elements:

- firm management of time and space boundaries
- clear and detailed information provided about what a depth process may involve
- careful maintenance of a neutral attitude on the part of the leader
- the provision of education and information about psychological processes when necessary
- active application of the metaskill of compassion, which is non-judgemental about ways of being human
- firm implementation of professional boundaries
- the continual practice of deep democracy

SURFACING DEPTH PROCESSES BY NAMING THEM

There are different ways to bring depth processes to the surface. They can be brought to the surface by naming them, or by helping them unfold. Ideally, we should use a mixture of these two approaches. Each approach has its roots in a particular methodology, as is explained in the discussions that follow.

If applying the psychoanalytically-based methodology (or any other similar approach), we may use the intervention of naming or interpretation as a way of bringing a depth process to the surface. By providing a depth interpretation about the dynamics that the leader witnesses in the group, the team members can become aware of their own dynamics and how they are being affected by them. Therefore, in a team that is concerned primarily with the competition between team members, mentioning our observation of such competition may be enough to make team members aware and eliminate the destructive element of competition. The difficulty of making an interpretation is that, as leaders, we are also involved in the psychodynamics of the group, and in this case, we may be unwittingly fuelling or even participating in the competition. If we make an interpretation that shows we feel we are observers rather than a possible participant in the dynamic, then the group may feel that they are being judged. A judgemental comment will almost always produce a response of resistance and may result in greater defensiveness on the part of the team members.

Interpretations need to be selectively given and phrased very carefully. The attitude behind an interpretation is almost more important than the interpretation itself. The most important metaskill when giving an interpretation is that of compassion. This means valuing and respecting the human needs that lie behind any particular behaviour. If the team is caught in a dynamic of competition, needs that lie behind any particular behaviour. If the team is caught in a dynamic of competition, we need to see the requirement to be valued that lies behind competitive behaviour. It is also very important not to make interpretations as absolute statements, but rather as tentative suggestions. It is useful if we indicate that we have a hunch rather than that we are certain about something. We also need to leave open the possibility that we may be involved in the depth process – and this should be spelled out to the rest of the group.

Some examples of appropriate and inappropriate interpretive statements are given below. Remember that tone of voice is almost more telling than the actual words used, and unfortunately this cannot be captured in examples.

Inappropriate interpretation

This team is interested in competition only.

The women are being marginalised in this team.

By interrupting each other you avoid getting any work done.

Appropriate interpretation

The urge to prove your own value seems to be very important in this team. I am wondering about my own contribution to that.

It seems that men's voices carry more weight in this room than women's voices. As a man myself, I am wondering whether I might be adding to that dynamic.

It seems hard for us to allow individuals to take centre stage, even temporarily, and this seems to be preventing the completion of any task.

Other methodologies, such as Mindell's Process Work, are less interested in naming the process than helping it to unfold. By not naming or identifying the underlying dynamic in a group, as mentioned in the previous section, the leader avoids being seen as a judge. However, there are other problems associated with not making explicit what we can see. If we start using a technique such as amplification (which is described below) without explaining to the team what we are doing and why, team members may become confused and lose concentration. However, by not interpreting, we do not prejudice the process with a label that may be inaccurate.

Amplification

Amplification is a technique that helps to bring the depth process to the surface. In this technique, the leader restates a comment made by a team member, emphasising specific aspects. Information regarding a depth process often first appears in the form of subtle signs that need to be made more explicit. Amplification is the process of exaggerating or turning up the volume of a signal. This technique needs to be done with neutrality, without judgement or ridicule. As leaders, we may need to reassure individuals that the amplification is not done to embarrass or mock them.

Amplification is different from interpretation. As leaders, we add nothing but volume to the behaviour and should therefore check continually for feedback from the team member that we are in fact following the behaviour correctly. Amplification works best when it is done respectfully, but playfully. Some examples of verbal amplification are given below.

Original statement	Example of amplification
I suggest you ask the engineers because they have the answers.	What you seem to be saying is: "When I am in the company of engineers from this organisation, I find it hard to feel that my contribution is also legitimate. That makes me feel unsure and unheard." Is that right?
I am not so sure that our new strategy is the correct one.	What you seem to be saying is: "I disagree with the current strategy. It needs more work." Am I capturing it correctly?
I'm not sure there is a point in discussing this further.	What you seem to be saying is: "I disagree with the current strategy. It needs more work." Am I capturing it correctly?
Um, OK, if that is what you want.	What you seem to be saying is: "I do not really feel like doing it but I will go along with you because I do not believe that my opinion will make a difference." Am I hearing you correctly?

The team member can also be asked to amplify a particular signal without the assistance of the leader. A way of doing this is to ask the team member to tell the team more or to give some more information about what they are saying or doing.

General guidelines for amplification

The main consideration when using amplification is to add nothing but volume to the substance of what is being communicated.

- When amplifying, make sure that the person is agreeing with what you are doing. Watch for feedback.
- If the person disagrees with your amplification, ask them to help you.
- When you notice a signal in a particular pathway, it is useful to amplify that signal in its chosen pathway.
- When working with double signals, amplify both signals from a position of neutrality.
- In conflict situations where the opposing parties are attempting a conflict resolution process, amplify the feeling and experiential aspects of the communication and turn down the volume on blaming and accusations if possible.

Stopping

To surface a depth process, we can also use the technique of stopping. This is a technique by which the unfolding process is prevented from happening. Paradoxically, this feeds more energy into it. If we stop something the person (or subgroup) is trying to do, the person (or subgroup) may well become aware of the importance of what she has been prevented from doing. This often makes the person more able to do it.

For example, if a member of the group is using interruption as a way of bringing attention to an issue, stopping the interruptions will force the issue to be brought up more forcefully in a different way. As with amplification, the leader needs to be careful to maintain neutrality.

Meta-communication

One technique for bringing depth processes to the surface that is similar to interpretation, but does not ascribe meaning to the group process, is that of meta-communication, a term from Process Work methodology. Meta-communication is when we as leaders comment about what we are noticing in the team as a whole, without suggesting what it means. Rather, it offers an opportunity for the team to investigate it further and decide what it means. One version of meta-communication is to give weather or climate reports as discussed in Chapter 7.

A climate report is when a leader reports on the atmosphere in the room. The report will neutrally comment on both the surface and depth processes that are taking place. The leader would normally give a climate report when there is a need for clarity and particularly when the team is 'cycling' (going around in circles and not making progress). The climate report enables the team to gain greater awareness. An example would be to say: "It feels like there is a less energy in the room this afternoon. Is that so, what do you think?" Note that the report is not an interpretation, but rather an observation about what is happening in the room. The leader gives no direction. Once we have given a climate report, we can watch for any responses.

Disturbing a group

Sometimes a team is unable to allow a process to surface because their anxiety is too high and their defence mechanisms too strong. In this case the team may need more containment or more time before the depth process can be handled. Sometimes a team is unable to allow the process to surface because they are caught in a habitual pattern of behaviour. Then it may be necessary to facilitate disturbance in a team, so that the team can move through its defensive structures. Most teams will provide the disturbance from inside their ranks. The leader may need to help the team activate a disturbance if the surface process is not flowing and nothing else productive is possible. Disturbing the group will activate potentially difficult projections and transference, which will require additional inner work on the part of the leader.

If we decide that some disturbance is needed because the team is really stuck, the following guidelines may be helpful.

- Switch to a different pathway – for example, if the team has been engaged mainly in talking, suggesting an activity that requires movement may be useful.

- Change the environment in some way. For example, suggest a different seating arrangement.

- Introduce an activity that reorganises the rank distribution. Many team-building approaches do this. For example, completing a physical obstacle course, or going canoeing changes who has rank in the team.

- Work with countertransference by self-disclosing to the team.

- Give the team feedback about your experience without being judgemental.

- Give a break.

- Describe the status quo. For example, you can mention that you notice that the long-standing members of the team make more contributions than the newer members.

- Ask members of the team to share their visions and dreams with one another.

COMPLETING DEPTH PROCESSES

This section considers the leader's activities while completing a depth process in a group. There are certain general interventions that are required no matter what the process is, and there are some specific interventions designed for particular processes.

For the sake of clarity, guidelines are divided into the different categories of process, but in most real-life situations processes do not unfold in neat categories. Rather, each group process is a unique blend of the different categories. Each situation, therefore, requires a blend of the interventions, tools and techniques listed in this section.

MAINTAINING CONTAINMENT

The importance of containment has been mentioned several times throughout this book. It is critical to maintain a strong container while completing depth processes. The following aspects of containment are specifically important while completing depth processes.

- Ensure that the boundaries of time and space are enforced if possible so that team members stay together to complete the process. Often, the process will become very difficult and team members may attempt to leave to avoid the difficulty. However, it will be more destructive for the team if individuals leave in the middle of a process than to manage the stress of staying until completion. This should be explained to team members before a depth process. A metaphor that helps to explain this is that walking out of a depth process is like leaving the operating table in the middle of an operation.

- Attend to individual anxiety levels to ensure that the team members can manage the process, by going slowly and providing emotional support along the way.

- Carefully outline and explain any processes to be followed so that team members know what to expect next.

- Give the team ongoing feedback about the progress that has been made.

- Allow some time for reflection if necessary.

- If we as leaders are so deeply involved in the depth process that we cannot maintain neutrality, then we need to ensure that we bring in an outside facilitator.

ATTENDING TO MULTIPLE LEVELS

As depth leaders, we have a delicate task when we are completing a group process. We are working with the group psyche – a collective entity – and with a collection of individuals, as well as a set of subgroups. Also, collective processes beyond the team will play themselves out in the team, ranging from the archetypal at the broadest level, to processes from all the systems in the group field. Neglecting any of these psychic levels can cause mischief in groups. We need to pay attention to the collective process and be able to view individuals as members of the collective process. However, each individual will be experiencing a process of their own, often feeling bewildered at the power of the group process and the loss of feelings of autonomy.

Our task is to provide containment for the whole team, and to prevent one member of the team from dominating the entire process. Simultaneously, individuals and their personal experiences need to be attended to.

Some guidelines for attending to these multiple levels are given below.

- Regularly move between levels, reminding the team of the collective and personal aspects of the process.

- People cannot process a depth dynamic on an abstract level. Most teams will begin dealing with an issue from an abstract level. Depth work requires moving beyond abstract debate into interpersonal territory. After all, we can only integrate, understand and meaningfully use the archetypes once we have personalised them (made fingerprints from blueprints).

- Once the team has raised an issue at the abstract level, encourage the members to make it more personal and discuss how it has a bearing on the issues and relationships in the team.

- This may take the team into a conflict resolution, cathartic or reconciliation process or a combination of processes, in which it will be required to work at the personal level.

- Once resolution has been reached at the personal level, it is important to move through the levels, eventually getting back to the more general, archetypal level, and then show how these interactions are part of being human. This serves to normalise and legitimise the difficulties experienced, and it also involves other team members in the process. A personal interaction between two team members may well be representative of the larger team process.

- It is also important to keep the context in mind and remind the team of the larger forces at work to balance the role of the individual with the role of the collective.

ROLE MANAGEMENT

In depth processes, there is an ongoing risk that an individual will over-identify with a particular role and potentially be the target of scapegoating. To avoid this, continually take action to prevent over-identification with roles, both on the part of the individual and of the group. Intervention guidelines for preventing role over-identification are given below.

- Remember that individual expression in a group is always an expression of the group psyche too. The individual is greater than the role and the role is greater than the individual.

- Continually distinguish roles from individuals, and remind the team of the universal nature of the roles or archetypes being played out. After a role is identified and acted out, remind the team that the person may be speaking on behalf of others in the team.

- Support all roles that appear in the team, finding and emphasising the wisdom in each one. There is generally some wisdom behind a role, no matter how apparently unacceptable it might be.

- Continually try to spread a given role in a team. This can be done by distilling the essential useful quality of that role, and checking whether anybody else in the team identifies with it. Remember that everyone has the archetypal potential to experience the different roles.

- Assist an individual team member who is caught in a role to move into a different role, by giving the member feedback about what they are doing and alerting them to the danger of role over-identification.

- Remember that a new, unusual or unexpected role is usually a response to one-sidedness in the team.

- Whatever role is being expressed, remember that the opposing role is also a possibility, and may well be needed by the group psyche.

- Where possible, ensure that roles are shared.

- Try to encourage conversations between roles.

- When a role is spoken of as being outside of the group, in other words, occupied by a person or a group not present in the room, ask the group to consider how that role may, in fact, be present in the room.

- As leaders, we need to avoid being caught in a role ourselves.

LEADER ROLE DETACHMENT

As a leader, the most important part of managing collective behaviour is to ensure that you do not start expressing an aspect of the group psyche unconsciously. Obviously, this is very difficult and from certain perspectives, may, in fact, be impossible, but it is important to practise role detachment all the time. Role detachment does not mean not experiencing aspects of the group life. Rather, it means being able to experience what is happening in the group, but not identifying with it.

As a leader, you need to be very fluid, and avoid getting caught or stuck in any particular role. The best way to not get stuck is to be able to experience an impulse as fully as possible, so that it can move on and make space for the next experience. Here are some guidelines to help with role detachment.

- If we notice ourselves repeating a comment or an intervention, it may be an indication that we are being caught in a role.

- If we notice ourselves judging the team, or feeling partial to a particular individual, we may be getting caught.

- If we start feeling passionate or very strongly about something, we may be in a role.

- We need to articulate any of our current life dilemmas clearly to ourselves, and make a note of the roles we are struggling with. This will help us to be alert to areas of vulnerability in terms of role identification.

- If possible, work with a coleader in large groups or particularly adversarial groups.

- We need to continually work on our metaskills, particularly the metaskill of compassion.

THE 'SOFT SHOE SHUFFLE'

In Chapter 4, I discussed the basics of roles. In this section we will investigate in more detail how to work with those roles so as to process and resolve group dynamics. The 'soft shoe shuffle' is a technique from Mindell's Process Work approach to working with roles during a depth process. It is an intervention that uses physical movement to indicate the essential fluidity of roles. It is a conversation on one's feet. Individuals are asked to use their physical presence to indicate agreement with a particular point of view expressed by going to stand next to the person who made the comment. Team members vote with their feet, through clustering or grouping. They are encouraged to move every time someone speaks, even if the next comment comes from an opposing position to the one that they have just supported. Team members are also encouraged to add their own views to anything with which they have agreed.

This technique allows team members to take up opposing views and disagree with what they may have originally expressed. This prevents negative psychodynamics from developing because it helps to prevent over-identification with a particular role, and helps individuals to see the plurality of the psyche in action. The technique also helps to remove hierarchical levels, allowing people to participate in a non-threatening manner. It frees people to make statements but not necessarily to remain attached to the view. Difficult issues can be presented without people being scapegoated for them. The technique encourages low-ranking issues to be voiced and heard.

As leaders, it is important that we can encourage all sides. It is particularly important to support the side of a minority or low-ranking view, which may be very unpopular and possibly expressed by only one person. It is essential to show that the role is greater than the person by standing next to him or her.

This technique should only be used if it has been clearly explained to the team members and some psychoeducation has been offered to explain the distinction between the individual and the role.

RANK MANAGEMENT

As discussed in Chapter 4, rank differences are part of the depth dynamic found in almost all groups. Managing rank differences and minimising the impact that they have on the team is, therefore, an ongoing task for the depth leader. The guidelines below suggest how these rank differences can be handled during the completion of depth processes.

- We need to continually keep our eye on rank differences.
- We need to notice when they are interfering with the process – when minority opinions cannot be openly expressed.

- Offer psychoeducation if necessary. In other words, we can teach the team about the dynamics of rank differences and how these affect relationships and interactions.

- We need to try to bring awareness to those with rank of the impact of their rank on other team members.

- We need to support minority voices to be expressed, but not use our rank as a leader to give them undue power.

- We need to remember to also support those with rank.

- We need to avoid what Mindell calls the 'tyranny of the minority'. The minority opinion should be used to modify and improve the majority opinion, not to hold the majority hostage.

- We need to practise deep democracy whenever possible.

- We need to keep an eye on minority positions that use subtle pathways to express themselves.

- We should always check for minority positions before moving on to a new process or a step in the process.

- Finally, we need to continually remain aware of our own rank as leader in the team and the fact that it may be silencing the team members. We need to work actively to ensure that we are approachable by using all the metaskills discussed.

GUIDELINES FOR DEPTH LEADERSHIP OF SPECIFIC PROCESSES

In Chapter 4, we distinguished between four different types of group processes: relationship-building, polarising , cathartic and reconciliation. These processes often overlap, and so, to some extent, it is artificial to separate them. However, to reduce the complexity of learning how to work with psychodynamics, the strategies and techniques are divided according to the four different processes. The management of these different processes is discussed in detail in the following section.

RELATIONSHIP-BUILDING PROCESSES

Relationship-building processes always run concurrently with all other depth processes, so we have to keep this level of the process in mind all the time. Each team that we work with will be at a different stage. The guidelines below are offered to help with relationship-building processes.

- Determine at what stage the team is
- Ensure that the steps are followed methodically
- Design an intervention appropriate for that stage of the relationship development
- Ensure a comprehensive getting to know each other process right at the start
- Make sure everyone has had an opportunity for each step
- Avoid subgroups dominating
- Ensure that the whole team is part of the relationship-building process
- Notice group collusions and look for signals to indicate that those collusions are a problem
- Remember the overall team goal and keep it in mind in all interventions
- Tap into the visions and the dreams that the team members have for the team

Stage of team development	Purpose of the stage	Healthy characteristics	Symptoms of problems/ Inability to move on/ Inappropriate behaviour	Interventions
Courting	Making initial contact. Establishing commonality. Exploring the possibility of relationship. Forming the team.	Politeness Friendliness Courtesy Information gathering. Openness Receptivity Willingness to make an effort. Shyness	Suppressing feelings of disagreement so that it becomes uncomfortable. Developing groupthink. Not tolerating difference.	Opportunities to share information and get to know each other. Joint activities that build a sense of team. Opportunities to socialise Discussion and establishment of shared values. The allocation of roles and responsibilities. The development of a shared vision.
Asserting	Establishing individual differences. Testing the team acceptance of differences. Testing the team values Exploring conflict.	Disagreement Healthy debate Mutual challenge Listening Tolerance Openness	Offering unsolicited counselling. Attempting to make it better. Rescuing individuals. Excusing individuals from responsibility.	Development of a container. A structured conflict resolution process. Reconsideration of values roles and responsibilities. Allowance of differences.
Revealing	Moving beyond the defences to the expression of real feelings Establishing trust. Establishing shared feeling. Establishing the possibility for team cohesion.	Vulnerability Compassion Openness Respect	Offering unsolicited counselling. Attempting to make it better. Rescuing individuals. Excusing individuals from responsibility.	Establishment of a container. A respectful listening process. Opportunities for repair work. Establishment of ground rules.

Stage of team development	Purpose of the stage	Healthy characteristics	Symptoms of problems/ Inability to move on/ Inappropriate behaviour	Interventions
Fully functioning	Developing robust team cohesion. Using the full intelligence of the system. Rotating roles as needed by task completion. Supporting one another.	Healthy debate. Task completion. Promises kept. Cooperation Teamwork Mutual support and affection. Openness to newcomers.	Stagnation Being closed to newcomers Dwindling membership	Goal-setting Continued feedback and monitoring. Recognition

In terms of depth work, we as leaders have to be aware of how well the members know one another, and what the stage of development is in terms of interpersonal relationships. A more detailed psychodynamic breakdown of the important stages and the required interventions is given in the table below.

Stage of relationship	Characteristics of the stage	Interventions
1. Getting to know one another in terms of personal details	Individuals encounter one another as strangers and get to know demographic and biographic details about one another. They unconsciously get to know and assume psychological information about one another.	It is helpful to engage the group in a storytelling process, whereby individual members provide information about themselves in whatever way they want to. This helps to break down inaccurate stereotyping and dispel wrong assumptions about one another. Team members should not interrupt one another during this process.
2. Activation of projections	They develop their assumptions into opinions of one another and inevitably start projecting onto one another. Projective identification begins. The assumptions about one another are not based on a full picture of one another.	It is helpful to encourage the team to get to know one another even better. More individual information should be given to avoid projection if possible. Sometimes, the unconscious processes are too strong for this to be successful, and a conflict resolution process may be needed.
3. Managing differences	The team develops interpersonal relationships based on the information they have of one an	The leader needs to observe these processes in action and consider moving the team into

Stage of relationship	Characteristics of the stage	Interventions
	other and their projections. The group polarises at this stage. They find ways of managing the differences, usually initially by avoiding them. They may agree to disagree, or less powerful subgroups may choose to become subservient to the more powerful subgroups.	
4. Confronting differences	In this stage, it may no longer be possible for the group to manage differences and pretend that they are not problematic, in which case they may find some way of confronting them. They may choose to have open conflict, or they may try to involve third parties to help them address the conflict.	Here a leader needs to intervene using a depth approach. Usually, a conflict resolution process is required. It may even be necessary to move into a reconciliation process if the group members have harmed one another through their projections and resulting actions.
5. Splitting or transformation (consolidating or withdrawing projections)	In this stage, the team either resolves the differences and a process of transformation happens or it chooses not to or is unable to resolve the differences, and some form of splitting occurs.	A sound depth process in which members are able to drop their defences and show vulnerability will ensure that common ground is established, and that transformation rather than splitting occurs.
6. Task achievement	Team members are able to accept one another and value differences. They are able to work at the tasks they agree to and are able to use their diversity to enhance the task.	At this stage, the leader can usually move back into surface work to ensure task achievement.
7. Ending	In this stage, the team life ends either through circumstance or as the choice of the team members, or both. The team stops existing as an identifiable group in the here and now.	The leader needs to help the team confront the ending process. The team may resist this, but without an ending process in which the group is forced to accept the ending – and use it to honour their experiences with one another – they may end up feeling incomplete. Often the leader has to be firm and containing to avoid the defences caused by the anxiety of impending loss. Here the group needs to move into a cathartic process.

Complications in relationship-building processes

A complication in the development of interpersonal relationships in groups is that different sub-groups in a team will be at different levels. Two members of a team may have worked together for a long time, while others in the team are newer members. This process needs to be addressed until all group members are functioning well from an interpersonal perspective. As leaders, we need to help the group start from the beginning as if it is an entirely new group (which, from a psychological point of view, it is).

A further complication is that as people change over time, so the depth and the nature of interpersonal relationships needs to change too. This means that the process described above is continually evolving.

POLARISING PROCESSES

Polarising processes essentially lead into conflict resolution because the team needs to move past the split caused by the polarities onto common ground. From a depth perspective, it is important to recognise that conflict is an inherent part of depth processes, as a result of the duality in the psyche. It is also important to remember that the psyche has the mechanisms available for transcending that duality given the right environment, and that what causes the splitting in the psyche is anxiety. Conflict is, therefore, resolved and change occurs not as a result of force, but as a result of gentle guidance that contains anxiety.

Different approaches to conflict resolution

There are many different approaches to conflict, and many methodologies for addressing it. It is useful to make the distinction between a legalistic approach to conflict resolution and a depth approach.

Legalistic approach to conflict and conflict resolution

Conflict is caused by a division of resources.

Compromise is regarded as the solution to the conflict.

Resolution involves an attempt to implement fairness.

Involves a third party, such as a judge, who offers a judgement.

Resource division often leaves one party or both parties unhappy.

Very rare that both parties feel it was a fair decision.

Results in either a win/lose or lose/lose scenario.

Usually ends in termination of relationship.

Depth approach to conflict and conflict resolution

Conflict is caused by a psychological dance or pattern stemming from an intrapsychic conflict being played out between two people.

To resolve is not about division of resources or compromise, but about helping the transcendent third position to emerge.

Results in a win/win scenario if it works – integration between different parts rather than division.

Third party does not make decisions – rather, plays a facilitation or mediation role.

Depth leader provides containment.

Ends in a stronger, sustainable relationship.

Root causes of conflict

Most conflict is the result of individuals or groups misunderstanding one another and can be solved easily through communication. Other causes of conflict are less easy to address. The most complicated kind of conflict between individuals is caused by an unresolved intrapsychic conflict in an individual that is played out personally with another individual. In teams, an intrapsychic conflict plays out between the members of the team, and a depth intervention will be needed to resolve it. To ensure that a depth intervention is really needed, first try easier conflict resolution mechanisms, such as communication or attempting to find compromise. The various levels of root causes and proposed interventions are listed below.

Root cause	Conflict resolution mechanism
Miscommunication/misunderstanding	Surface leadership: helping team members to communicate and clear up misunderstandings.
Misperception/stereotyping	Surface leadership: helping team members to get to know one another better, possibly by using storytelling
Differing preferences/needs	Surface leadership: helping team members to alternate in meeting their needs and to compromise
Scarce resources/unshared resources	Surface leadership: helping team members to share resources, exercise fairness by holding a systemic view and emphasising interrelatedness.

Root cause	**Conflict resolution mechanism**
Power imbalance leading to communication breakdown and oppression.	Depth leadership: helping a team to develop consciousness about power and privilege differences, and facilitating conversations that activate empathy.
Projection – present used to address historical conflict	Depth leadership: helping team members to develop psychological self-awareness leading to the integration of the projection by becoming aware of history, accepting the losses of the past, and using the conflict resolution steps discussed in the sections that follow

The process of unmanaged conflict

Intrapsychic conflict that has not been managed tends to unfold in a predictable way. Here is an example of how it might happen.

- A difference in content or expectations occurs. Individuals develop emotional responses to the disagreement. One party or both parties start feeling anxious, but this may be unexpressed and ignored.

- Communication difficulties arise.

- Projection and projective identification mechanisms are used and result in increasing rigidity in roles.

- The team starts repeating actions and communication that entrench the division. Incongruities and mixed messages are communicated. The conversation starts cycling and is unable to move forward. These are signs that the system is trying to balance itself.

- With each cycle the polarities increasingly define themselves in relation to each other.

- At each cycle massive amounts of energy flow into the conflict. The sides begin to switch roles unconsciously.

- The conflict eventually becomes contentless. Once the content is lost attention will focus on the past or the future, but not the present.

- Rigidity in roles becomes complete and communications are severed. Direct communication is replaced with gossip and projection.

- The system now either implodes or explodes and there is a complete breakdown in the relationships.

- At the point of breakdown, there is an opportunity for growth. In many cases, breakdown is a necessary precursor to growth and a prerequisite to openness to the depth process and the healing power of conscious awareness.

Inflammatory behaviour

As depth leaders, it is useful to recognise which behaviours are inflammatory and escalate conflict. If we witness some of these behaviours during a conflict resolution process, it is useful either to amplify an aspect of the communication that is less inflammatory, or to help the speaker to reframe the comment in a less inflammatory way. Many of the behaviours that escalate conflict are unconscious, and so sometimes it is helpful to make the speaker aware of the inflammatory nature of their contribution. We also need to remain aware that we as leaders may use inflammatory behaviour. A list of behaviours that escalate conflict and potential interventions are provided in the table below.

Inflammatory behaviour	Proposed intervention
Double signals (mixed messages) or any examples of incongruence. For example, someone saying she is angry, but doing it with a smile on her face.	Make the speaker aware of both parts of the message by amplifying both sides of the double signal. Suggest that the speaker may be ambivalent or have mixed feelings about the best approach.
Reference to third parties, conscious or unconscious coalitions, references to the past and the future, but all avoiding the here and now. These are all signals of anxiety. Examples are: "Mary said that she also has trouble with your being late." "The rest of the team are also unhappy."	Help speakers to express their own difficulty with the person they are addressing, recognising that they feel their own opinions are insufficiently powerful. Spread the role if possible.
Denying accusations. An accusation is often a statement about an underlying process said in an aggressive way.	Assist the person on the receiving end to acknowledge whether any part of the accusation may be accurate. Encourage the person to pick

Inflammatory behaviour	Proposed intervention
	up the one percent of the accusation that may be true. If the accusation is targeted at us, as leaders, then we can try to acknowledge the part of the accusation that may be true.
Projection. There may be an unacknowledged unconscious part of an individual that the individual is having difficulty recognising or accepting, and hence projecting onto and only seeing in the other.	Encourage a conversation where each party can express what it feels like in his shoes. Amplify the feeling and experience component of the conversation. Play down the accusatory parts of the communication.
Denying or ignoring abuse. Denying that abuse is occurring causes the conflict to escalate because it tells the abusing side that she is not being heard.	Slow the process down and allow the person being abused to react. If the person can express her real feelings of being abused, it may de-escalate conflict.
Continuing the conflict or the attack, even after the other party has stopped attacking.	Bring to the speaker's attention that the other party has stopped attacking. Help the other party to articulate the new role that he is in.
Being condescending, patronising or indirectly hurtful. Those symptoms may indicate a part of the individual or group that does not want to be in relationship.	Alert the speaker to the fact that his comment was hurtful to the listener. Encourage the listener to express his experience of the comment.

Strategies for dealing with conflict

Groups will use many strategies to deal with conflict, and some of the more common ones are described below. Ultimately from a depth perspective, resolution is the only option. Without it, conflict will reappear later.

Avoidance: There are many ways teams can avoid conflict, from running away, to ignoring it or denying that it exists. Quick apologies and breaking off contact also work to avoid exploring the conflict. But avoiding conflict is avoiding the opportunity for the creation of something new.

Acceptance: Knowledge and acceptance of conflict, without doing anything about it, avoids the chance for resolution. "We shall have to agree to disagree" is one well-known way that conflicts are accepted and not dealt with. Acceptance can also be a form of resignation: "OK, so there is a conflict, but I don't want to argue." The effect of such resignation is damaging to all involved; no one is satisfied.

Elimination: The elimination of conflict can happen in two main ways. The first is flight, where one gives up and allows the other to prevail. The second is to fight, where battle takes place and one party is defeated. The conflict has been eliminated, one side has triumphed over the other, but it leaves at least one party dissatisfied and probably resentful. This type of outcome will usually flare up again later.

Resolution: Resolution occurs when all the people involved have explored how the conflict has arisen; how it has affected the parties, what they want to have happen, what is happening, and how everyone involved can achieve a satisfactory outcome. Resolution occurs when the polarities in a conflict are transcended and a transcendent third position emerges that all parties can identify with and feel comfortable with. From this point, it is possible to start working together instead of in opposition, to better reach a new point of agreement. Of course, this form of resolution is difficult to achieve. The depth leader or a professional facilitator who knows how to do depth work with the group may help with the achievement of resolution.

Surfacing the polarities

Polarisation is a necessary group process for resolving conflict. The leader needs to help the polarities emerge. This is different from traditional conflict resolution where we seek compromises. From a Jungian perspective, it is understood that resolution will emerge if the two polarities are held long enough for both sides to see and hear each other clearly. Yet it is important continually to separate the person from the role, because the polarities will tend to constellate between two people in a team. Polarisation involves insisting that each party take its own side as fully as possible. This is often resisted because it feels dangerous, but it is a necessary step for the eventual wisdom that comes through resolution. All members of the team are encouraged to become involved in this process.

Polarities that remain under the surface are damaging to team functioning. It is important to channel the polarities into some form of expression, whether it is language, movement, or some form of art or sound. The vehicle of expression serves as a container for the energy behind the polarity. Also, the vehicle provides the opportunity for conversation, so the group can have what my daughter, Sophia, calls a 'talk fight', rather than one of the more destructive alternatives.

Amplification of the polarities

Sometimes it is important to amplify the polarities to express the two positions more clearly. People may be reluctant to risk distinguishing themselves to that extent from others in the team, and so it is useful to explain the value of polarising to the team. Individual contributions can then be amplified to express all aspects of the position, particularly focusing on the experience and feeling components of the position. The transcendent function can only work its magic once the polar positions are very clearly defined.

Early compromise delays transcendence. Amplification needs to continue until the transcendent third emerges. The depth leader will know when this happens because the atmosphere in a group changes completely. There is a moment in which each party suddenly starts identifying with the polar opposite position. This will be palpable in the atmosphere, and it will be clear to everyone that a de-escalation of conflict is happening. In that moment the projections are withdrawn, and the tension is released.

Conflict resolution steps

The following steps provide guidelines for facilitating a conflict resolution process from a depth perspective that offers the opportunity for a transcendent third position to emerge.

1. **Getting agreement to attempt a conflict resolution process.**
   This step requires that all parties to the conflict agree to attempt a resolution. Parties need to agree to meet for at least an hour or longer to discuss the conflict. They have to commit to the whole process and should not be allowed to leave halfway through because this will cause worse conflict. A neutral time and place should be agreed on. If one or both of the parties do not agree to try to resolve the conflict, they can be worked with individually until they are ready to come together.

2. **Opening and explaining the process.**
   The process should be opened with each side being helped to state its goals and motivations for resolving a conflict. The process should be explained in simple terms. If the parties want to agree on ground rules they can, but it is unlikely that agreement will be reached on more than the most basic rules. Both parties need to agree to stick to the rules of the process described below.

3. **Each party gives its own side.**
   Each party gets a turn and is helped to express their side of the story in as much detail as possible without interruption. A coin can be flipped to decide who goes first. Parties need to be encouraged to take their own side as much as possible and not to try for an early compromise.

4. **Each party plays back the other side.**
   Each party is then asked to play back what they heard or take the side of the other party. Invariably, they will not be able to do this for long, and will quickly revert to responding from their own side. At this point, the leader needs to interrupt and ask the parties to repeat step 3. The process moves between step 3 and step 4 as many times as needed until the parties start being able to see the point of view of the other. The more heard they feel, the more likely they will be to hear and withdraw their projections.

5. **Each party restates its original position with new awareness.**
   If step 4 has been successful, parties will automatically move into this step. At this stage, each party needs to include in its side the acknowledgement of the truth of the other side. At this stage, it may be appropriate for parties to apologise to one another, which they will do spontaneously or with a little assistance if necessary.

In healthy groups, the above steps are followed naturally. The more complex and multilayered the group, the more complex the above process becomes. The most important element to remember is that all parties need to commit to talking about their feelings and needs and attuning to the other to hear their feelings and needs, until all aspects of their stories, including the vulnerable parts are expressed, from which a creative win/win solution can emerge in which everyone feels heard and seen.

CATHARTIC PROCESSES

Cathartic processes are those in which team members are encouraged to express their true feelings about a situation. This can only happen if the leader creates an environment in which the team members feel safe enough to explore and express their feelings. As leaders, we may need to alert a team to their underlying feelings by amplifying signals that indicate those feelings. The following set of guidelines will help when the depth process requires catharsis.

- We need to provide a strong container and ensure that the team will not be interrupted during this process.

- We should prepare the team for the possible discomfort that may occur in such a session.

- We must remember that team members are often ashamed of expressing emotion, and that it causes them great anxiety to do so.

- We need to create an atmosphere in the team that is accepting of the expression of emotion through appropriate self-disclosure and discussion of behaviours and ways of being that would be considered appropriate.

- We need to provide ample time for this kind of depth process because catharsis cannot happen under pressure.

- Once team members start expressing emotions or sharing their experiences, we need to hold off with new interventions and just be quietly and patiently present and attentive.

- We should not intervene to make individuals or groups feel better; the expression of emotion will achieve that.

- We need to remember that catharsis is a process and individuals may need to go through several different emotions before the process is complete. Sometimes anger is a precursor to grief or hurt. We need to allow the process to unfold while providing sufficient containment.

RECONCILIATION PROCESSES

Reconciliation processes are notoriously difficult. Both parties need to be available for the complex emotions that will arise in such a process. In a sense, a reconciliation process is a combination of a polarising process, conflict resolution and catharsis, and so all the guidelines mentioned above apply. It is important that all parties state their objectives about entering into such a process, and commit explicitly to the full duration of the session. As leader, keep the following guidelines in mind.

- We need to remain aware that most perpetrators have been victims in the past, and so we need to resist over-identifying with the parties in the victim role.

- The perpetrator needs support because she is in the minority position and does not hold rank morally.

- The perpetrator may be suffering from shame, which is one of the most debilitating emotions. Treating all parties concerned with equal respect and compassion can help to counteract this.

- We need to ensure that a new role and rank division does not emerge in terms of moral righteousness.

- We need to ensure that the victim is fully heard for their experience.

- We can encourage the use of symbolic gestures, e.g., a statement of regret, shaking hands or an apology. These symbolic gestures should not be prescribed, but rather chosen by the participants.

A reconciliation process has additional stages to polarising and cathartic processes and these are outlined below. The terms victim and perpetrator are used to discuss the steps. These terms do not refer to one specific individual in each case, but rather to the roles in such a situation, and more than one person may occupy these roles. Also, a person or subgroup may be both a perpetrator and a victim. In this case, there will be several iterations by different parties of the steps listed in the table below.

Stages in a reconciliation process	Characteristics of that stage
1. Gaining agreement to attempt reconciliation	Here both parties have to agree to enter into a reconciliation process. Often the party who has been aggrieved will refuse to enter into such a process because they do not believe that the damage can be repaired or at least forgiven. The party who is viewed as the perpetrator may also refuse to enter into a process, either not believing that he is a perpetrator or that reconciliation is possible.
2. Victim's expression of the experience of harm	At this stage, the individual perceives themself to be a victim and needs to express their experience of the hurt. The victim may not be fully aware of the levels of hurt, or may be unable to express them. Also, victims often need to express their outrage at the hurt that was caused to them before they can articulate the suffering. Victims need to articulate their experience as fully as possible for

	this stage to be successful. This may also be traumatic for the victim to do and, therefore, the leader needs to be as supportive as possible.
3. The perpetrator's acknowledgement of the harm that he caused	The perpetrator needs to be able to hear and absorb what the victim say they have experienced. This is an exceptionally painful and anxiety-provoking stage for the perpetrator, as it may evoke guilt and shame and requires the ability to integrate a negative view of the self. The perpetrator risks being annihilated psychologically and needs support for the healthy part of the self to survive it. Once the perpetrator has heard the victim's experience, they now needs to be able to acknowledge the harm that has been done. The perpetrator will need a great deal of support and containment from the leader during this process.
4. Perpetrator's apology for harm done, and commitment to efforts to repair the damage	The perpetrator needs to apologise for the harm caused, and needs to take steps to repair the harm. The victim can help the perpetrator to identify suitable reparation activities.
5. If necessary, the victim's acknowledgement of his role in the situation	Very few situations are as one-sided as having a clear perpetrator and clear victim. Often victims did not take enough steps to protect themselves, or in fact may have provoked the perpetrator. It is important that the victim acknowledges their own role. In many aggressive interactions, the harm done is reciprocal, and unless this is acknowledged, it is likely to be repeated.
6. Forgiveness and reconciliation	Both parties have a better understanding of why the hurt occurred, and the victim can forgive the perpetrator. This effectively means that the victim pardons the perpetrator and no longer feels angry about the situation. This does not mean that the victim will forget, but will be able to resume a relationship with the perpetrator.

Reconciliation processes are difficult, and should only be attempted with full agreement of the parties. They are psychologically harrowing and the leader needs to build a very strong container, particularly ensuring that parties do not leave halfway through the process. However, although they are difficult, reconciliation processes can be enormously rewarding to facilitate and to witness.

INTEGRATING DEPTH PROCESSES

To complete a depth process, it is always necessary to ensure that integration has occurred and that it is possible to return to the surface processes with enthusiasm. The depth process is only complete once the group or team has indicated a willingness to return to the surface process. It is useful for the team to have a discussion about how the depth process and its outcomes can be integrated back into future team interactions.

If the depth process was successful, there will be several signs that the leader can watch out for to confirm it. Some of these signs are listed below.

- The group atmosphere will feel calm, and the body language will indicate relief and a sense of ease.

- The team may articulate the presence of a transcendent third position, which unites the polarities previously explored. They will be in agreement about how to proceed. There will be both a feeling and concrete examples that common ground has been reached.

- The team may spontaneously start talking in symbolic language. They may use metaphors or images to describe the current psychological state. These symbols will resonate with everyone else in the team, and other team members may elaborate and build on the symbols used. This happens because deep meaning has emerged which connects the surface level to the deepest archetypal level.

- The group will more openly discuss issues that were previously undiscussable. For example, different subgroups may reveal what they have been saying behind each other's backs.

- The team will indicate their readiness to move back to the surface process or close the session.

- They may well have a feeling of exhaustion, but also have the energy to embark on a new process after appropriate rest.

ALLOWING THE MAGIC

Depth work requires great caution, skill and attention, but there is also a magical aspect to the process. Groups doing depth work often encounter their archetypal roots. Carl Jung said when we come into contact with our archetypal roots, we may have what he referred to as a 'numinous' experience. The word numinous was first used by a theologian called Rudolf Otto (1958) to describe a sense of awe-inspiring wonder, which may feel like being in the presence of something divine (in whatever way one understands the notion of the divine).

A numinous experience is most likely to occur when someone encounters an archetype that was lodged in the unconscious. When in a state of numinosity, the individual experiences feelings that are similar to an altered state. The individual will feel as if they are in the grip of something bigger than themselves, and this can be either pleasant or unpleasant, but either way may feel overwhelming to them.

When you allow unconscious contents to emerge in a group and there is a successful integration into the conscious world, the connection between the two worlds produces great psychic activity and gives the individual or group a numinous experience. When in the grip of such an experience, the individual or group will feel a powerful sense of awe, as well as a sense of goodwill and belonging to the collective of which they are part.

Positive numinous experiences can result from depth processes where the unconscious encounters the conscious in a sufficiently constructive and creative way to achieve a new integrated state. In some ways, this is the ultimate work that a depth leader can aim for. It can be enormously rewarding for the leader and life-changing for everyone who participates in such a process.

In all the depth processes discussed in this book – including relationship-building, polarising, cathartic and reconciliation processes – numinous experiences are possible. However, encountering the numinous in an uncontrolled and uncontained way can be dangerous and too overwhelming for the psyche. It will be psychologically too burdensome if the individual is over-identified with the archetype. All the cautionary notes and injunctions about appropriate containment, role management and strong ethical boundaries are in part to ensure that numinous experiences are psychologically constructive.

Here are some guidelines for ensuring that depth interventions allow constructive encounters with the numinous.

- We need to be faithful to the natural pace of the team.

- We should work hard to prevent role over-identification.

- We need to identify and work with transference, and prevent the team from attributing a fixed role or archetype to us as leaders or to a member of the team.

- We need to remember that a numinous experience is a gift from the unconscious and cannot be manufactured by us as leaders.

- We need to remain connected to the concrete rational world and the primary team task.

- We need to avoid providing the team with spiritual guidance that may not resonate with or be appropriate from everyone.

- We should not impose symbols on the team, but work with emerging symbols that arise spontaneously from the individuals themselves.

- We need to remember that we are human and offer but one limited perspective.

- We need to practise the metaskills of reverence, compassion and humility.

CONCLUSION

Depth processes are complex and difficult to work with, and should only be approached by a depth leader who feels equipped to manage the difficulties they represent. However, if we work carefully, depth processes are truly transformative to groups. Fundamental problems are solved and great potential is unleashed. Working as a depth facilitator for the past thirty-five years has enriched my life enormously, and while my work has enabled transformation for some groups (success is never guaranteed), it has also resulted in continuous learning and transformation for me as a person.

PERSONAL EXERCISES

1. Choose a group of which you are a member. Describe the processes that you have witnessed in the group that relate to the depth perspective. Which process needs attention? Is the group mainly concerned with defensive processes or developmental processes? What could you do to help the group now?

2. Make a list of all the potentially difficult roles that you have encountered in groups. Decide how you, as leader, will manage these roles from a depth perspective.

3. Consider any experiences that you have had of depth processes. Remember how you felt after the process. Decide what helped you survive the process and what made it more difficult for you to complete the process. How could these ideas improve your depth leadership?

4. Consider your experience of processes that have been successfully completed. What factors helped with the successful completion, and what factors or interventions hampered the process? Identify critical success factors for completing depth processes.

5. Start developing your own toolkit of depth interventions.

CHAPTER
10
SPECIAL CASES AND SITUATIONS

INTRODUCTION

In this chapter, we will consider special individual and group cases and situations, giving indications of how they should be addressed from a depth leadership point of view. It is not intended to be an exhaustive list and is a selection of particular challenges that we may encounter as a depth leader. Also, in some senses, every group interaction is special in its own way, so it would be impossible to cover all the special situations. The following categories will be covered:

- General guidelines for managing special cases and situations
- Managing special behaviour and roles in groups
- Managing special group situations or phases
- Managing special leadership situations
- Using alternative methodologies
- Rule breaking as a depth leader

Let us start with a summary of the general depth leadership guidelines that have been offered so far in the rest of the book.

SUMMARY OF DEPTH LEADERSHIP GUIDELINES

The summary given here does not constitute an exhaustive list of every single depth leadership guideline, but is designed to serve as a reminder of the important areas. It is divided into the two broad areas of managing ourselves and managing the group.

MANAGING OURSELVES

On an ongoing basis, we need to:

- Pay attention to our metaskills, including compassion, empathy, discipline, detachment, humility and others.

- Maintain a neutral position when necessary, so as to encourage the expression of all points of view. This may mean keeping our opinions to ourselves until everyone has had an opportunity to express theirs. It does not mean that we become inauthentic, but it does mean that we need to control our impulses to express our opinions.

- Continually develop our self-awareness and engage with others from a position of awareness about our own psychological profile and the impact it has on others, including the rank we hold in the world. Self-awareness is developed through the inner work of observing ourselves and our responses. The more work we do on our ourselves, the less vulnerable we will be to getting caught in projections from others. The group psyche is powerful and it is important to distinguish between 'what's me?' and 'what's them?'.

- Maintain what Arnold Mindell refers to as a beginner's mind, which is characterised by true curiosity and no judgement. We do not know how a group process will unfold until it does.

- Always maintain appropriate confidentiality about the processes we lead.

- Establish and assert our authority when needed. It is our task as leaders to set the boundaries and parameters for group sessions. Our authority comes from the knowledge and skills we have, as well as our psychological rank. If we are unsure of our authority, we need to do the appropriate inner work to develop it.

- Remember that occasionally a group will challenge us in a variety of ways. If we are challenged about the content of a discussion, we need to listen to and consider the merits of the challenge as neutrally as possible. If we are challenged on the process we have chosen for the group, consider the merits, but resist changing the process unless the whole group agrees. A process challenge is often a challenge for leadership, and we may need to assert our authority to maintain our leadership role.

- As a depth leader we are there to serve the group's needs, not our own social needs (e.g., for recognition). Leadership is, in some ways, a suppression of our own needs. We need to ensure that we have a plan to meet our own needs and have a place where our own opinions can be heard. We need to look after ourselves physically.

MANAGING THE GROUP

We need to:

- Remember that much difficult behaviour is caused by anxiety and, therefore, the behaviour only changes when people feel safer. One of our main roles as depth leader is to provide containment in the form of hard containment (structure, information, direction, clarity) and soft containment (trustworthiness, empathy, listening, understanding) to reduce individual anxiety. Anxiety is caused by the existence of issues that are often undiscussable. If we can help people feel safer, undiscussable issues can be discussed and resolved.

- Make sure that we contract carefully and clearly about any processes we would like the group to follow. We need to set goals and ensure that everyone agrees with them. We need to explicitly outline the goals in the form of an agenda and ensure that we work consistently towards reaching those goals.

- Remember that there are at least two levels of processes going on in a group – surface and depth processes. An unresolved depth process will eventually hijack a surface process. To address the group's depth process, we need to get the group's permission to pursue a discussion about it. The motto is: "Decide, don't slide into a depth process." Always fall back on the original agreement if full consensus to proceed cannot be reached.

- Pay attention to the group's stage of development and customise our interventions to accommodate that stage.

- Remember that there is a group psyche – a group-as-a-whole – and that there are also distinct individual psyches in the group. We need to keep our eyes on both levels.

- As depth leaders, we do have the responsibility to act as a traffic controller in discussions to make sure everyone gets an opportunity to speak. This occasionally means interrupting someone while they are speaking. We need to interrupt the individual politely, but firmly, acknowledging that we know it is an interruption.

- Not push people over edges. In other words, we need to make sure that individuals can choose what and how they contribute to a group process in terms of a depth engagement. We should not put individuals on the spot. We can rather invite members to comment by saying: "Would someone who has not yet said something like to contribute to this conversation?"

- Not use humour at someone else's expense. When in doubt, we should not use humour. If we do use it, we need to be self-deprecating and genuine.

- Remember that a large part of the depth leadership role is to garner the full intelligence of the group and, therefore, make sure that all opinions are heard. It is not helpful to serve the needs of one part of the group and not take the other parts into account. In other words, search for and support the wisdom that is present in all the roles. We need to practise deep democracy when there is no consensus.

- Keep in mind that the psychodynamics of a group will emerge over time, so we can take our time to observe before acting. Psychodynamics are cyclical patterns and will therefore, repeat themselves and provide us with an opportunity to observe them before you need to intervene.

- We need to pay attention to the group context. In other words, we should try to gather as much information of the larger context as possible and remember that the psychological pressures and patterns of the larger context will affect the psychodynamics of the group.

- Understand that certain themes will play themselves out in the group psychodynamics and that the group history will have an impact on those themes. We need to help the group to determine the myth or story that symbolises their psychodynamic process, but remember that psychodynamic processes of groups or individuals change over time. Myths, metaphors and stories will, in some way, capture the human story that is playing itself out beneath the surface process.

- Maintain an attitude of humility and keep in mind that groups are generally more powerful than a leader. Ultimately, we cannot take full responsibility or control for exactly what group members or the group-as-a-whole does.

- To provide some psychoeducation to a group if they are embarking on a depth process, to build their psychological knowledge. The contents of Chapters 3 and 4 will be useful here.

- Support all sides, including those with less and more power. However, we should be aware that group members or subgroups with less power may be vulnerable if we artificially inflate their rank with our support. They are likely to be victimised when we are not present. We need to rather ensure that individuals and subgroups build the strength to assert themselves over time when they are ready.

- Remember that sometimes comments or events in groups are emotionally explosive or pro-vocative in some way. Mindell refers to these events as 'hotspots'. Examples are someone criticising another person in the group, or someone making a politically incorrect comment. As depth leaders we cannot ignore these; it is important to address them and to allow affected parties to comment. We could say something like: "I'm aware your name was just mentioned. Would you like to respond?" Anything that could be perceived as embarrassing or offensive is a potential hotspot.

- Be aware that depth work in itself is potentially threatening to a group because it results in the exposure of conscious or unconscious group collusions. If we are not very careful, the group may close ranks and try to scapegoat us as leaders. We need to avoid being judgemental or explicitly critical and maintain our metaskill of compassion, which helps us understand that groups collude for important psychological reasons that have to be carefully addressed to help the group interact more authentically.

- Strike a balance between being tentative in our interpretations and suggestions about possi-ble group psychodynamics, and being authoritative when containing the group and working towards agreed outcomes. We need to be explicit if we are uncertain.

- Work at creating rapport with group members, but avoid creating unrealistic pictures of ourselves which feeds positive transference unnecessarily. We need to reveal our humanity and flaws and do not try to be the perfect leader who solves everyone's problems. We are not gurus – even if group members are caught in a transference relationship with us and try to treat us as if we are.

- Remember that most groups will tend to polarise or develop a duality in their interactions because of the conscious/unconscious duality in all of us. A group will manage this normal human dynamic by splitting into an us versus them arrangement. We as depth leaders can help the group transcend the polarities by enabling a meaningful conversation that helps the group to reach a transcendent third position. We do this by encouraging the expression of the full thinking and meaning behind each of the two sides.

- Remember that there are different pathways or channels between the surface and the depth levels and they may not all be verbal. We need to pay attention to other pathways, such as body language and symbolic interactions.

- Keep in mind that a variety of techniques can help bring a depth process to the surface. These include amplification (turning up the volume on the thing that is happening), symbol analysis and stopping.

- Ensure that surface and depth processes are properly completed and closed and always allow an opportunity for reflection about the process before we close a session. Surface processes need to end with a tangible accomplishment and depth processes may need to end with some kind of ritual. However, as leaders we cannot impose the nature of the ritual. It is important to see if suggestions for an appropriate ritual arise spontaneously from the group and then to help the group to follow through.

GUIDELINES FOR SPECIAL CASES

In addition to everything that has been said so far, it is important in all unusual situations to follow some basic rules. We need to:

- Behave ethically and professionally at all times and remember our metaskills.
- Gain agreement from the group for the process we are embarking on.
- Articulate the areas in which we do not have the necessary competence. In other words, practise self-disclosure.
- If necessary, seek out help in the form of mentoring, coaching, therapy or leadership supervision.
- Check whether we are hooked, and do inner work if necessary until we feel that we can be neutral. We need to take a break if necessary and refrain from further intervention until we feel clearer.
- If possible, work with our dreams (ask our unconscious mind to help).

Finally, we need to remember that as long as we maintain ethical and personal boundaries and ensure that our metaskills are in place, we cannot do harm to the group. There are some groups that we cannot help, and it is important to accept this with grace. It may be necessary to call in a skilled professional facilitator. For example, if part of the depth process seems to be because of our own difficulties and projections and we cannot do the appropriate inner work, then we may need an outside expert to help us.

SPECIAL BEHAVIOUR AND ROLES IN GROUPS

In this section let us consider specific instances that could arise during group processes. Of course there are myriad possibilities, so only the more common ones are discussed here.

RESISTANCE

When there is resistance in a group or an individual, this is a sign that an anxiety is present. In other words, the individual or the group is using defence mechanisms to deal with anxiety. Either an un-addressed depth process is interfering with the surface process, or someone is being taken into a depth process against their will – for instance, being asked to reveal something which they cannot or will not. In the case of an unaddressed depth process, it is important to gain the team's permission to work with the depth process or simply make them aware that there may be something that needs to be addressed. In the second case, it is important to slow down and hold the team at the edge. In this way, the edge can be negotiated until everyone is ready.

RAGE

If someone is very angry in a team, that person will almost certainly be in a role for the whole team. In this case, the person may be terrified by their rage. The leader needs to contain the strong feeling by showing calm acceptance, no judgement, and a willingness to hear. If possible, slow the process down and allow the person to speak. Also, separate the person from the role as far as possible. Try to spread the role. If an individual is being abusive, firmly ask that person to refrain from such abuse, but encourage them to express underlying feelings. Remember, though, to give other participants an opportunity to express their feelings at being the recipients of such strong feeling. They may need to express hurt if they felt abused.

SABOTAGE

Sabotage happens in a situation where someone with less rank is trying to communicate with an in-dividual or subgroup with more rank, but cannot do so directly. The person with less rank will attack the power and privilege of the individual or subgroup with rank in an attempt to force that individual or subgroup to become aware of their rank. The saboteur needs to be assisted in finding support and other ways to communicate. The individual or group under attack needs to become aware of the power of their rank and be assisted in listening to the person with less rank. This is often a long, delicate and complicated process.

CRYING

Crying is not unusual during depth processes. Tears are an expression of a variety of emotions and so they are part and parcel of the exploration of deep feelings. As a depth leader, it is important that we do not react with alarm when someone starts crying. We need to stay calm and not rush into making it all better, but also to not ignore the crying. We need to make eye contact with the person if possible, to indicate that we are aware that they are experiencing strong emotion, and we are compassionate in the moment. Provide tissues if necessary, or ask others in the group whether they have some if we do not have any. Allow the individual to make the choice about how they want to manage the tears. We can check if the individual wishes to say something, and if not, we can simply allow the person time and space to self-contain.

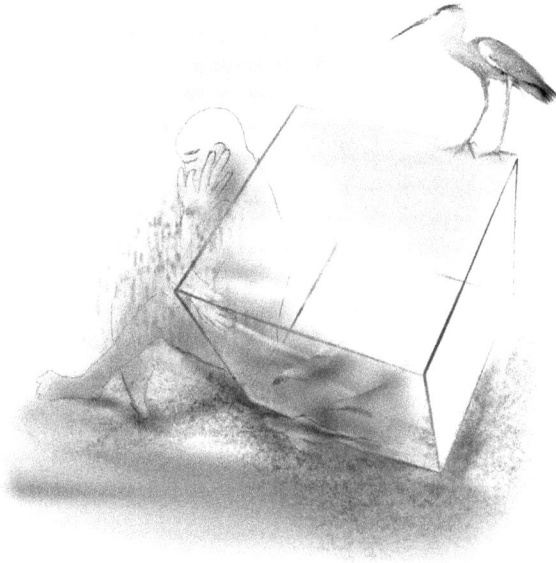

We need to remember that most of us may feel embarrassed if we cry as adults in the workplace or in a public setting, and it is important not to exacerbate the embarrassment. Crying also affects others in the group and usually evokes a complex range of emotions, from a desire to rescue the person, to anger at the expression of emotion. We can normalise the idea of crying during a depth process. Once everyone is calmer, we can check in with the person again to determine whether they are ready to talk about it.

GHOSTS

A ghost role (another term coined by Mindell) is an absent role that the group is talking about; it is not present or not being owned in the room. The term ghost is of course being used metaphorically to refer to a person, thing or group that is experienced as being emotionally present in the psyches of the group members, but not physically present in the session. In the case of employees talking about management, the ghost role of management is clear. Often the role is not clear, for example, when people are talking about being criticised but are not acknowledging who the critic is; the critic is the ghost role.

Another example is when people are talking from the victim position (they regard themselves as being hurt by something or somebody) and no one is prepared to step into the role of the abuser or perpetrator (understandably so). The abuser is the ghost role.

Role theory indicates that all roles are in fact psychologically present in the room, but they are not consciously being recognised. The task of the leader is actively to bring the ghost role into the room – if not in reality, at least symbolically – so that the dynamic with that ghost role can be addressed. The ghost role is often representative of an unconscious or unacknowledged part of the team – it is difficult to acknowledge. We need to practise strong containment during this process.

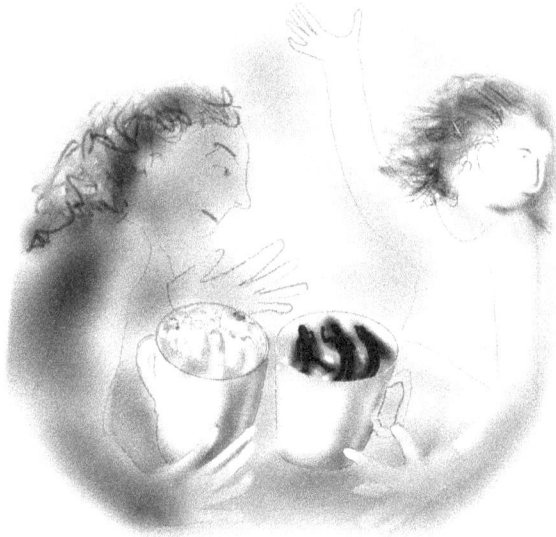

Ideally, we as leaders should encourage the team members to see if they can take the position of the ghost and so bring it into the conversation more directly. If that is not possible, we can introduce the ghost role by taking up the role and speaking from it. It is important that we are neutral in relation to the role before adopting it. If there is a lack of neutrality the team will very quickly attack us as leaders.

We can amplify the role of the ghost to make it more real for the team. The exaggeration of the role makes the ghost visible and real; it gives permission for people to disagree with the role. In so doing, they will actually begin to identify the true nature of the ghost role. We can also encourage people to adopt the ghost role in a playful and non-threatening manner. The participants may move in and out of the ghost role as they wish.

For example, if a group from a regional office of an organisation keeps referring to head office as problematic, but no one from head office is physically present, it is useful to ask someone in the group to speak from the position of head office, or to do it ourselves (but we need to explain that that is what we are doing).

SILENCE

There are, of course, many reasons that cause people to be silent in a team. Whatever the reason, a silent participant is treated differently in depth work from how they are treated in on-the-surface work. Unlike in the more rational modes of group work, the silent person is not always perceived as a shy person who needs to be encouraged to talk.

Silence occurs in two broad ways in groups. One or more individuals could be silent, which will be discussed in the next paragraph. Alternatively, the whole group could be silent. Silences may be productive in that they give people a chance to think. The silence may be an expectant silence or an emotional silence. A silence within the group may mean that the group is at an edge. If we as leaders fill the silence too quickly, it may prevent the group from using the silence to think, to process emotion or to move over the edge. As depth leaders, we need to develop our comfort with silence so that we can wait and observe the silence to sense what it may be signifying. We can also carefully break the silence by asking a group what may be making it difficult to speak up.

If one or more individuals in the group are silent, rather than the group as a whole, it could mean a range of different things. Someone may be silent because they are afraid to speak. Or someone may be silent because they can see the process that is unfolding and feel that they have nothing to add. Silent people can be invited to comment, but not by naming them directly or putting them on the spot. Sometimes, if someone is silent, it is because she is not ready to speak, and will speak when ready.

DISTURBERS

The disturber role refers to the role that continually works against the prevailing process in the team. The disturber may be critical of team members, the process, or even the leader. This role is disruptive throughout the process. In depth work, the disturber is seen as the source of information about the underlying issues in a team. The disturber is often the messenger for the depth process.

A leader needs to help the disturber express their views in such a way that other team members can hear them. It helps to search for the wisdom in the disturber's contribution because it will invariably be designed to balance a one-sided surface process. The disturber needs to be helped not to over identify with the role, as there is a very high chance that the team will scapegoat this individual. This means that the depth leader needs to rephrase the disturber's contribution in a more palatable form to see if the meaning of it resonates with others if it is expressed less confrontationally.

Often the disturber will unconsciously be carrying the voice of an unheard part of the group, who are not able to express their dissatisfaction with something because they lack confidence or fear reprisal. For example, there may be several people in a group who are unhappy with an issue (such as their performance appraisals), but only one person speaks up about it and questions the validity of having a performance appraisal. However, the truth may be that they are not the only one who is unhappy, but is the only one to risk crossing the edge and speaking up. Often the very fact that the disturber is carrying the unconscious or unexpressed energy of the rest of the group makes the individual more vehement than they otherwise would be. It is important that the disturber is not left to carry the voice of others alone.

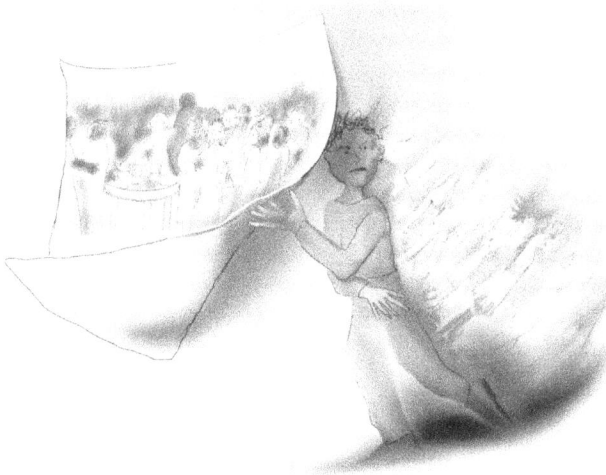

FATIGUE

Sometimes a group is tired. Fatigue can happen for a number of reasons and it is important to determine the exact reason if we are working from a depth perspective. A group can be tired simply because they have not rested enough or are under pressure, or they have a poor physical environment. In this case, the group simply needs to be given a break. If this is not possible, it can be helpful to allow the group to verbally express their tiredness, or simply take a few minutes to feel as tired as they wish. Sometimes the expression of the experience re-energises the group.

Alternatively, tiredness could be caused by the chronic presence of energy-draining psychodynamics. Groups who are sitting at an edge for a long time – in other words, groups who need to address an issue, but find it undiscussable for some reason – will become tired because of the anxiety and frustration generated by the situation. If we observe fatigue in a group and suspect it is because there is an unresolved depth process, we need to look for signals that will help us bring it to the surface carefully and with the group's permission.

SCAPEGOATS

Often depth processes play themselves out in teams by targeting one individual or a subgroup as the scapegoat or the problem. The team believes that its problems will be solved if that individual or subgroup is no longer part of the team. In this case, it is likely that the team is projecting its unconscious roles onto the scapegoated individual or subgroup. The targeted individual or subgroup is often lower in rank and unconsciously volunteers for this position, and may entrench the team's view by becoming a disturber or disturbing element in the team. Alternatively, the targeted individual or subgroup becomes marginalised and may choose to actively or passively withdraw from the team. As leaders, we need to help the team become aware of the scapegoating element of their interactions. We need to help the projecting group to consider how the projected quality may be a shared, albeit unpopular role (or experience) in the team, and may in fact need to be consciously integrated by the team as a whole to transform the group dynamics into a healthier pattern. For example, a very hardworking, driven group may be projecting its need for rest onto the least hardworking member of the team.

The group needs to understand how embracing the need to rest in a constructive way may be more sustainable for the team in the longer term. Often when the projection is withdrawn, the scapegoated individual or subgroup can become a productive participant in the team. As leaders, we will also need to be a role model for a more integrated way of being.

THE MESSIAH SYNDROME

The messiah role is an alternative to the scapegoat role; it uses the same mechanism but is the result of positive rather than negative projection. Often one individual or subgroup is seen as the potential saviour of the team in some way. This is unrealistic because no one individual or subgroup can transform a group's difficulty without the involvement of the whole team. The problem with this mechanism is that it is seductive for the individual or subgroup to be given this role and they often willingly take it on. As leaders, we are particularly vulnerable to this role.

As leaders, our role is to help the team in the same way as when scapegoating occurs, but in this case, particularly to help the targeted individual or subgroup to disidentify with the role. The team as a whole needs to understand that they all have to be involved in resolving their difficulties. If we are the targeted messiah in the group, we need to refuse to identify with the role. We need to ensure that we are not seduced into believing that we can solve all the problems of the team – and communicate this fact to the group.

SPECIAL GROUP SITUATIONS OR PHASES

In this section, we consider group situations that are challenging as a whole, rather than being challenging in the moment, as is the case with the situations described above. Each group leadership situation is special in its own way, but particular group situations place extraordinary demands on a leader. Four of these situations are discussed in the sections that follow: large groups, groups in crisis, individuation in groups, endings, and loss.

LARGE GROUPS

Large groups are groups of more than twenty-five people. We need to work with large groups with great care and only once we have a lot of experience. The power of the roles in large groups or teams is equal to the combined power of all the individual psyches, as well the collective power of the whole group.

These groups have special characteristics that make them difficult to lead in a depth process.

- There is a loss of personal identity in a large group. Individuals become relatively anonymous.
- Individuals do not have face-to-face and eye contact.
- The group more easily divides into subgroups.
- Individuals spend much more time in particular roles. For example, an observer may remain an observer for the entire duration of a session. This is more likely to lead to role over-identification.
- The psychological energy is greatly increased in a large group, which results in much more energy in each role. Individuals who carry the roles for the group are, therefore, much more at risk psychologically.
- Stereotyping and labelling are far more likely in a large group.
- The psychodynamics of a large group are more like those of a herd or a pack than those of a family.
- Crowds instil fear or additional anxiety in many members, so a large group is more naturally anxious than a small group.

Leading large groups

To manage the characteristics of large groups already listed, it is important for the leader to follow the guidelines below.

1. We need to work with co-leaders until we are more experienced. In a situation where we are addressing depth process issues, we need to have more than one leader if possible. We should not attempt conflict resolution in a large group without at least two leaders, or professional facilitators if needed.

2. We need to ensure that we have a variety of hard containment techniques in place, such as those listed below.

   - Plan and prepare for a session in detail. Specify times and activities in advance, and inform the group of the agenda and the objectives of the session as formally as possible.
   - Set a clear structure for the discussion.
   - Ensure that the room is spacious and comfortable enough.
   - Ensure that the room is private and has doors that can close.
   - Use very strict traffic control to manage participation.
   - Enforce group maintenance rules such as turning off cell phones.

3. We need to use any techniques that reduce the depersonalisation of individuals. For example:

   - Have name cards or badges available.
   - Seat participants in smaller groups, such as around tables.
   - Ask that participants identify themselves when they make contributions.
   - Use participant names whenever possible.
   - Continuously spread the roles that are taken up.
   - Remind the group that you are aware there is a variety of perspectives.

4. We need to be on the alert for scapegoating processes, and work to prevent them.

5. We need to remember that there are many observers in the group and include them in your summaries and reflections on the group process.

6. We can use small group sessions in between plenary sessions. We need to structure the small group sessions carefully, outline the roles required in the small groups and give the groups guidance on how to manage them. Ideally, small group sessions should also be actively led by a nominated (or group-selected) leader. We can change the group composition for the small group if more than one session is held.

GROUPS IN CRISIS

Groups in crisis are groups that find themselves in an unusual, intense or dangerous situation. A group that has been exposed to an event such as an accident or a significant loss will be in crisis.

Some specific examples of situations that would lead to a crisis in a group are listed below.

- A sudden loss of one or more group members
- Trauma suffered by group members or the group as a whole
- The discovery of theft, fraud or other illegal activity
- Financial difficulties possibly leading to retrenchment
- Organisational changes such as mergers or takeovers
- Leadership changes
- System failure of any kind
- A group that deals with clients who are in crisis

Guidelines for leading groups in crisis

The following guidelines will assist in managing a group in crisis.

- Groups must be allowed to address pressing practical issues if necessary, but the group process must be resumed once the practical issues are dealt with.
- Groups in crisis have heightened anxiety so we must provide more stringent hard containment. Instructions need to be clear, firm, and consistently enforced.

- Understand that catharsis (emotional expression) is necessary at some point during and after the crisis. Schedule time for them and provide additional soft containment for these processes.

- Understand that catharsis will take different forms and that the group will need to express a range of emotions at different times and in different ways. Help the group to manage the different stages of the catharsis without judgement. Understand that the process will seem chaotic at times, and that participants may need to express unpleasant emotions.

- Understand that crises have an impact on all group members, even those who are not directly affected. For example, in a retrenchment situation, members who are not retrenched may suffer from survivor's guilt and therefore also require a cathartic process.

- Accept that the group may resort to a variety of defensive behaviours. Keep reminding the group of the unusual nature of the situation and normalise their unusual reactions.

INDIVIDUATION IN GROUPS

In some ways, everything discussed about group work thus far in this book is aimed at helping groups individuate. In this section, we focus specifically on what this means and what is required if we as depth leaders want to work towards it. Individuation in its strict technical sense, however, is a term that applies to an individual, not a group. It is defined by the Cambridge Companion to Jung as: "The process leading to a more conscious awareness of one's specific individuality, including a recognition of both one's strengths and one's weaknesses."

It refers essentially to self-realisation – becoming as fully oneself as possible. This means encountering all aspects of the self, even those that are unpleasant and limiting, and those that frighten us. It means allowing all the voices inside us to speak. Individuation is a journey rather than a destination. It is an approach where we continually broaden our experience by attending to the quieter parts in ourselves. It means encountering the unconscious and listening to all the pathways through which the unconscious can speak.

The concept of group individuation is not a Jungian one because Jung did not really concern himself with the psychology of groups. However, a group can develop a more conscious awareness of its specific individuality, just as an individual can. Also, a group can move towards self-realisation or expressing itself as fully as possible. However, the group psyche is far more complex than the individual psyche, and has a different relationship to time. A group lifespan is different to an individual lifespan in that the group lifespan varies enormously – from five minutes in a lift to 150 years of an organisation. As a result, group individuation has many more possibilities in shape and form than the individual individuation process. It operates at a different level of complexity because the conscious and unconscious divisions in the group psyche cut across a number of individual psyches and subgroups in an infinitely varied set of combinations.

Leading group individuation

The depth leadership of group individuation is a complex and ever-developing task. As a result, some general principles will be discussed below, but true leadership skill in this area will be developed through experience.

- We cannot lead individuation in groups if we are not exploring our own individuation. This means actively working with our own unconscious material.

- To fully unleash creativity and transcendence in groups, we have to assist the group in removing blockages to expression and diversity.

- Individuation means embracing the full diversity of human experience and then distilling the essence and allowing the full potential of the group to become manifest. As a result, we as leaders need to be comfortable with as much diversity in ourselves as possible, so as to create an enabling environment for diversity to emerge in the group.

- Removing blockages means paying close attention to the possibility of depth processes in a group, and facilitating the emergence of such depth processes and completing them.

- As depth leaders, we have to be comfortable with apparent chaos for certain periods of time and trust that the psyche will return to order if a containing, yet open environment is created.

- We must alternate between providing strong containment and allowing disturbing factors to emerge.

- We need to provide an environment in which the group's potential is allowed to unfold without pre-determining the nature of the end result.

- Group individuation happens when everyone in the group can contribute as fully as possible to the group life and the group thereby achieves meaningful and significant goals or outcomes.

ENDINGS AND LOSS (INCLUDING RETRENCHMENT)

All groups have to end or face some kind of loss at some point in time. This does not mean that a group cannot continue over generations, but members will change and so a specific composition will always end. As discussed earlier, the duration of a group lifespan is much more variable than the lifespan of individuals. Generally, people will belong to many different groups during their lifespan. Also, the experience of belonging to a group will resonate at an archetypal level for most people. If anything disturbs our feeling of belonging, it generally causes an emotional response because it will remind us of all our other similar experiences, many of which happened when we were young and vulnerable and relied on belonging to survive.

As a result of the inbuilt human capacity for attachment, when human beings join together in groups – for whatever reason, for even a short time – they may, and generally do, develop attachments to one another. This means that they will have to face separation when the group life ends. Separation is painful, even when one has an ambivalent attachment to a group. The separation process is complicated further if a group continues, but loses one member or subgroup, especially if it is against the will of the individuals, as is the case in retrenchment. In such a case, there is loss and separation, but also other complicated feelings such as guilt, envy or resentment between those who are staying and those who are going. In summary, groups and their members will sometimes have to face difficult feelings as a result of endings. Many people are not prepared to face this fact and groups will engage in a variety of defensive processes to avoid facing or dealing with ending and loss.

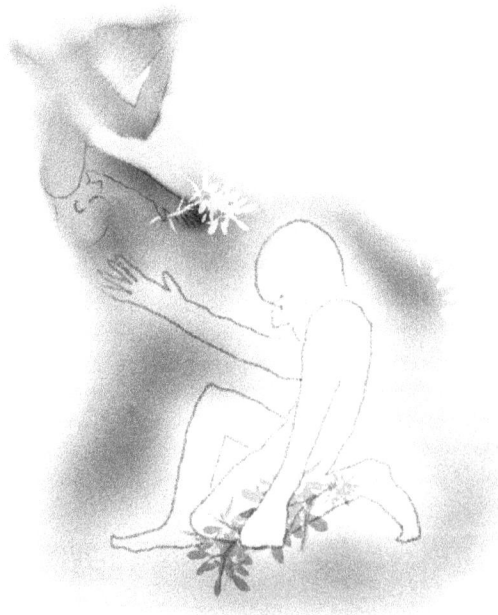

From a depth leadership point of view, it is important to help groups experience difficult or complicated feelings, so that these feelings do not lodge at the depth level where they can cause blockages. This sometimes means gently insisting that the group talks about the impact that any ending or loss had on them. The work of psychiatrist Elizabeth Kübler-Ross (1997) is particularly useful here. Kübler-Ross spent her professional life studying human responses to endings and loss, particularly with reference to terminally ill people. She demonstrated in her work that humans have an inbuilt capacity to come to terms with endings and loss (even the prospect of losing life) if they are able and allowed to feel and express a range of emotions, including anger and grief.

Many of us, however, avoid the discomfort of these types of feelings and so we deny our very human response to loss. To manage the pain of separation or other difficult emotions, many group members or the group as a whole will develop extensive defence mechanisms against facing reality. The depth leader has to do the opposite: help the group to break through denial by not colluding with it, and provide an environment where a cathartic process is possible. Some specific guidelines are provided below.

- Create a safe and contained environment in which the group has privacy.

- Name the impending loss or ending to the group if it has not yet occurred but it is clear that it is going to.

- If it is a loss or ending that has already happened, ask the group whether they wish to discuss their responses and legitimise such a discussion as psychologically healthy or useful. If necessary, become acquainted with and teach Kübler-Ross's five stages of grief: denial, anger, bargaining, depression and acceptance.

- Implement all the guidelines given in Chapter 9 for managing a cathartic process.

- Firmly, but gently insist (or remind the group) that the ending cannot be changed or postponed. Keep repeating this until the group hears it. Keep in mind that emotions may be confused and complex – do not simply expect sadness. Encourage the group to explore all their responses without being deterministic about them.

MANAGING COMPLEX LEADERSHIP ROLES

In the previous nine chapters of this book, I discussed leadership as if it is usually possible to perform a pure leadership role in the world. This would mean:

- The leader has designated authority in the group
- The leader has a vested interest in the outcome of the group
- The leader can explain their role to the group and explicitly contract for that role
- The individual has full responsibility for executing the role effectively

Sometimes individuals do not have the luxury of such a pure leadership role. In many instances, the individual will be in a complex role, and have to juggle the different aspects of the role. For example, we may not be the designated leaders in groups, but we still end up with the psychological leadership. We may have to share leadership with another person. We may be the expert in a technical field as well as the leader of the team. Each role in a group has a different task and objective, so the foundation or philosophy behind the execution of the role will be different. The individual effectively has to switch between different paradigms within the same interaction. This requires a great deal of mental agility and presence of mind.

Key principles of managing complex leadership

The following key principles will help you to manage the various roles.

- We need to articulate our main objectives in each role to ourselves.

- We need to remain conscious of which aspect of the role we are in at any particular time.

- If possible, we need to tell the group which role we are occupying.

- Anticipate the possible group response to the role. For example, a leadership role will always be open to challenge at some level.

- Do not assume a complex role if you cannot separate the different components in your mind successfully.

- Be transparent about the difficulties of juggling different aspects of the role.

CO-LEADERSHIP

Co-leadership is sometimes necessary when working with groups. Co-leadership involves sharing the leadership role with one or more people. It adds a great deal of complexity to the leadership task because it requires managing an additional psychodynamic on a continual basis. The relationship between ourselves and our co-leaders will influence the group directly or indirectly, and the chances of psychologically contaminating a group are much higher as a result. Nonetheless, co-leadership is necessary and appropriate under certain circumstances so it is useful to develop your skills in this area.

When is co-leadership appropriate?

- In a large group, where the psychological weight of the group process is too much for one person
- In distinctly polarised group situations, where two different depth leaders are needed to support different sides adequately
- In groups that have a great deal of psychodynamic complexity or intensity
- In a situation where someone is learning to lead and needs to work with a more experienced co-leader

Advantages of co-leadership

- Sharing of the psychological and energetic load
- Greater flexibility in role identification – different co-leaders will pick up different roles or different aspects of the psychodynamic
- Access to more channels or pathways – each leader will have their own special channels for accessing depth information, so a greater variety will be possible
- Greater potential neutrality and detachment; while one leader is hooked by the group, the other can maintain neutrality
- Each partner can have more time for inner work in front of the group because the other partner can carry the group for a while
- Ability to truly reflect the duality of conflict; each leader can take up one side of the conflict and so more fully support either side.

Possible co-leadership problems

As much as there are advantages to co-leadership, the co-leadership pair itself will set up its own psychodynamics which may negatively affect the group. The following issues and situations can cause difficulties in co-leadership partnerships.

- Style and pace differences
- Problematic psychodynamic patterns could emerge between the co-leaders (these may be immediate or constellate over time), for example.
  - sibling rivalry
  - critic – victim
  - leader – follower
  - majority – minority
  - scholar – fool
- Collusion with group projection and loss of neutrality
- Gender or race difficulties
- Differing approaches to conflict resolution
- Romantic attraction

Criteria for a co-leadership partnership

A co-leadership partnership is almost as demanding as a romantic partnership, without the romance. The two (or more) individuals have to be sufficiently in tune with one another so that they can contain their differences within the partnership itself.

The following criteria are useful for a successful co-leadership partnership.

- The leaders have a similar philosophy and methodology
- They have equality in rank or consciousness of rank issues
- They have an ability to communicate and process difficulties
- They have similar levels of professionalism and ethics
- They have a common motivation for co-leadership
- They have similar experience levels or they are comfortable with the power differential in the relationship
- They have similar ability to do inner work
- They have an established relationship in which they have developed trust in one another over time

Necessary co-leadership activities

The following co-leadership activities can be before, during and after engagements with a team or group:

- careful planning and preparation
- continual sharing of observations and conclusions
- explicit role allocations
- role switching and sharing
- playing out of roles to test group process
- detailed feedback and debriefing
- ongoing inner work
- ongoing joint checking and processing of psychodynamic patterns

WHEN TO BRING IN AN EXTERNAL FACILITATOR/CONSULTANT

Sometimes as a depth leader it is advisable to use an external facilitator. This is necessary under the following conditions:

- when we do not have sufficient formal or informal rank to manage powerful individuals in a given session
- when we cannot maintain a position of neutrality with regard to the key issues; and
- when our interventions are not yielding results and a fresh perspective is required.

USING ALTERNATIVE METHODOLOGIES

Most group leadership in organisations use the verbal channel and the methodology of a discussion in which issues are raised. In other words, the group process is essentially managed by talking about it in a literal and rational way. However, there are many other modes of expression in the world. There are also many different methodologies for accessing depth processes in groups.

A list of examples of alternative methodologies is given below.

- Individual or group drawing or painting
- Meditation
- Nature activities such as forest or bush walks
- Adventure processes such as abseiling or river rafting
- Sand play
- Movement or dance
- Making music with or without instruments
- Games such as ball or board games
- Storytelling
- Theatre sports – skits and plays
- Pottery or sculpture
- Labyrinth design
- Mime
- Working with found objects
- Puzzles and riddles
- Scenarios (such as Survivor)

ADVANTAGES OF USING ALTERNATIVE METHODOLOGIES

The advantages of alternative methodologies are as follows:

- Alternative methodologies may tap into depth process in a way that verbal processes cannot.
- They allow for direct symbolic expression, which is the language of the unconscious.
- They sometimes allow for a greater inclusion of diversity.
- They take people over edges and into unfamiliar territory, which sometimes reduces the functioning of unhelpful defence mechanisms.
- They add an element of fun to group processing.

PITFALLS OF USING ALTERNATIVE METHODOLOGIES

The pitfalls of using alternative methodologies are:

- The group members may be out of their comfort zone and may become anxious and more defensive as result.
- Alternative methodologies often change the rank dynamics of the group in unanticipated ways. For example, in a river rafting trip, the more senior members of the organisation may be less physically competent than some junior members.
- Group members may be suspicious of the methodology and resist our leadership unnecessarily as a result.

PRINCIPLES OF USING ALTERNATIVE METHODOLOGIES

The following principles are useful to consider when one uses alternative depth process methodologies:

- Group members have to give explicit permission for the approach to be used. As leaders, we may have to provide detailed information about what will be expected from participants.
- If anyone in the group resists, we cannot proceed with the approach.
- A range of firm containment techniques may be required even though the group has provided their explicit permission. For example, instructions need to be very clear and boundaries need to be carefully managed.
- The purpose of the use of an alternative methodology needs to be clearly articulated.
- As leaders, we should always assume that there will be a greater level of discomfort than can be spoken about.
- We need to notice when an alternative method of expression emerges spontaneously in the group. Unplanned processes can be very successful if we faithfully follow what the group is naturally trying to do.
- The group should always be given the opportunity to return to the verbal channel for a debriefing process. As leaders, we have to contract explicitly with the group members for such a debriefing process and should never force participants to self-disclose.

RULE BREAKING AS A DEPTH LEADER

Throughout this book we have given many guidelines and rules that describe the role of depth leadership. Many of these rules are particularly useful if we are learning how to be a depth leader. As our experience builds, however, we may find that sticking to the rules is not always the best thing to do. Some specific situations in which it is probably a good idea to break some of the rules are listed below.

Situation	Rule to break
The group is actively destructive towards itself or other groups.	Forgo our neutrality and feed our observation back to the group.
The depth process is so overwhelming that the group cannot stop it, even though not everyone in the group is ready and has given permission for it.	Allow the group to slide into the depth process and provide firm containment. Bring them back to the surface process after the depth process has resolved itself.
The group does not respect our authority.	We need to tell them so and remove ourselves if possible, or refuse to work until they listen to us.
Nothing else seems to be working and the group is stuck.	Forgo our neutrality and tell them what we really think.
An individual is so over-identified with a role that they are not allowing us to spread the role.	We can see the person individually and advise that they are hurting themself.

FINDING OUR ALLY

Sometimes, we will encounter a situation that is so different or odd, that none of the normal depth leadership rules seem to apply. At that point it is sometimes helpful to try to engage with the deeper parts of ourselves, and come into contact with what Mindell refers to as our allies. These are symbolic or mythical figures that represent our deepest selves as leader. One way of meeting our ally is to ask ourself for such a meeting, then close our eyes and wait for an answer. Invariably, the unconscious will provide an answer in the form of a symbol. We can use the essence of this symbol to guide our activities with the group.

WHEN TO STOP LEADING

As depth leaders, we may find ourselves considering every group situation that we encounter from a depth leadership point of view. This will make social situations more interesting, but possibly less comfortable.

One of the difficulties of being leaders is that we do not always express our real thoughts and feelings in a leadership setting. It is important to have an outlet where we can clearly express ourselves without reserve. Therefore, we should ensure that we completely abandon our leadership roles in certain settings where we are not required to lead. If we do not do this consciously, the chances are that we will do it unconsciously in ways that are not helpful. We may find ourselves expressing opinions when it is not appropriate.

Finally, leadership should be interesting and ultimately enjoyable. If we are not enjoying it, it may be time to stop doing it altogether.

PERSONAL EXERCISES

1. Document the group situations that you find most difficult to manage. Investigate why they are so difficult for you. Draw up an action plan for managing such situations in future.

2. Over time, build a case file of group psychodynamic processes. Describe each situation in as much detail as possible. Consider your own work as a leader in these cases. Identify areas in the leadership of group individuation processes where you would like to develop your competence.

3. Think about your own approach to endings and loss. Do you avoid expressing the associated emotions, or can you respond appropriately?

4. Consider the complex roles that you occupy in your profession. Consider in which roles you are most comfortable, and why. Practise role-switching in informal situations and document your experience.

5. Consider your experiences of partnerships in general. Document difficulties you have experienced in the past and which are likely to occur in co-leadership.

6. Consider any alternative methodologies you have used or been exposed to as a participant. List any leadership errors that you have witnessed in the implementation of such methodologies. Consider the benefits you have experienced in participating in an alternative process.

CHAPTER

11

A DEPTH WORLD

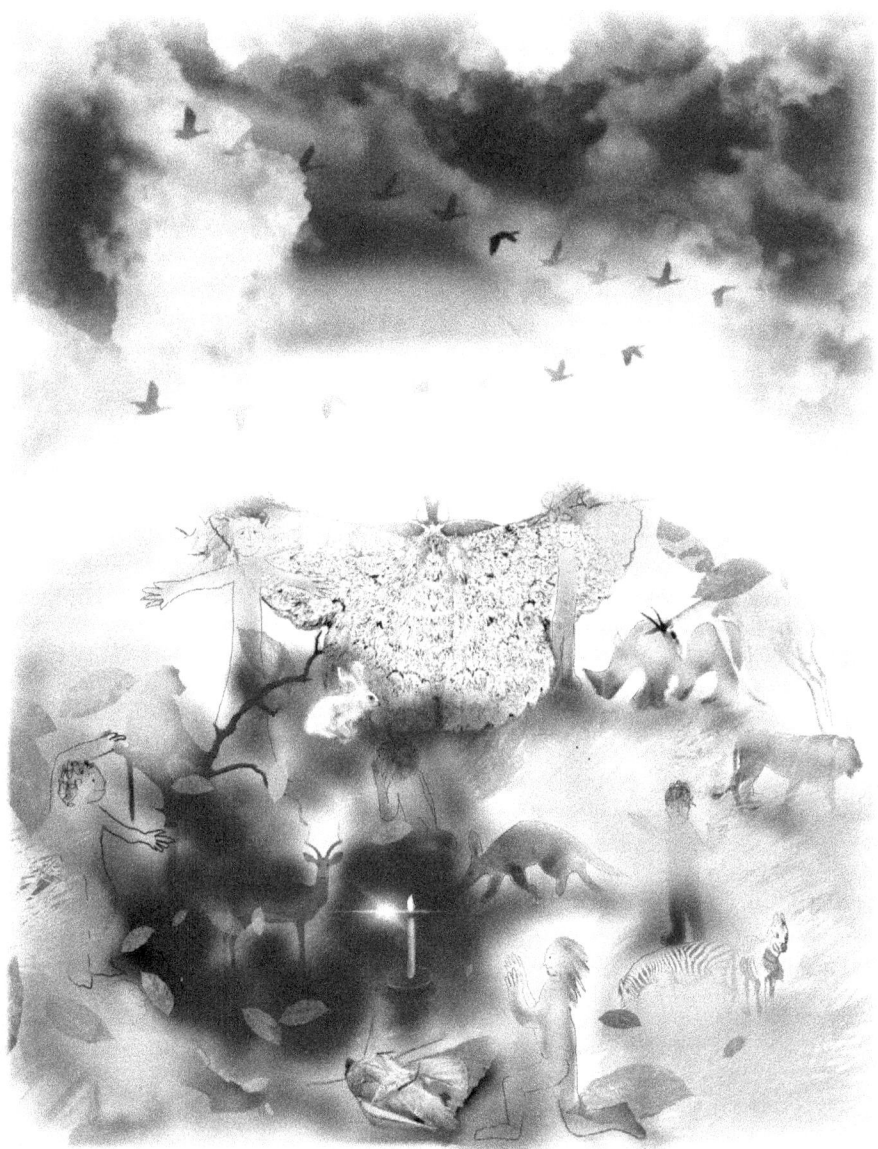

INTRODUCTION

In Chapter 1, I offered a definition for depth leadership as leadership in which leaders are: "Working beneath, between and beyond for a thriving psyche, community and planet." Three aspects were highlighted:

Beneath: the leader actively pursues integration of the whole self or psyche, both the conscious (on the surface) self and the unconscious (under the surface) self, which includes the body and the imagination, to help the individual psyche to thrive.

Between: the leader pursues integration between people to help groups and communities to thrive.

Beyond: the leader considers factors beyond the entity of concern, using an integrative approach towards larger systems, including governance systems and the natural environment, to ensure a thriving planet.

Much of this book has focused on the first two aspects, and extensive detail has been given about how to work **Beneath** and **Between**. This chapter is devoted to discussing the importance of working **Beyond** – ensuring that we care for our communities, and if not more importantly, protect, sustain and restore our natural environment to ensure that biodiversity thrives on the planet.

This book has said much about relationships, but has not talked about communities as a whole. Here, we look at the necessity to ensure the wellbeing of all communities on the planet, as we are all interconnected and consuming resources as a collective. A lack of equity and inclusion causes profound suffering and dysfunction in many people, some of whom live down the road. It is beyond the scope of this book to describe the statistics of the socioeconomic devastation faced by many communities in our world, but we will consider some theory and practice of caring for communities.

Also, one of the tenets of depth psychology is the importance of 'psychodiversity' and the necessity to include all the existing voices to access the full intelligence of the system. Similarly, biodiversity is essential for the well-being of the planet as a whole. We know what humans have and are having extensive negative impacts on the natural environment and those will not be discussed further here, but we will look at the theory and practice of caring for the ecosystems around us.

THE IMPORTANCE OF COMMUNITY AWARENESS AND CARE

Although this book has talked at length about managing interpersonal relationships in the workplace, it has not talked much about how we as depth leaders need to care for the communities in which we live and around us in our larger environment. At macro level, as depth leaders, to pursue wholeness means that we need to consider and be involved in the larger systems around us, starting with the human systems. As leadership scholar Sandra Waddock compellingly says:

> A major challenge of integrity, of which one framing might be wholeness for the world – and a challenge that must increasingly be faced by business leaders and managers – is how to contend with the dissonance, cracks, and other signs of significant social and ecological problems that increasingly make clear that the globalized knowledge economy is only part of the picture. (Waddock, 2007, p. 546)

At micro level, to have integrity in a modern world, it is necessary to have an attitude of integrated engagement with ourselves and the people around us, and a capacity for dialogue that allows cooperative problem solving. Such an approach can be described by the notion of 'ubuntu'. The notion of ubuntu exists in many sub-Saharan cultures and is referred to by a variety of names. Ubuntu implies that the values of caring for others are essential to one's own humanity and are therefore fundamentally part of our identity. Mnyaka and Mothlabi (2005, p. 218) describe how much ubuntu becomes part of one's identity:

> [I]t is a spiritual foundation, an inner state, an orientation, and a good disposition that motivates, challenges and makes one perceive, feel and act in a humane way towards others. It is a way of life that seeks to promote and manifest itself and is best realized or evident in harmonious relations in society.

Ubuntu implies that we hold an identity in which our well-being is inextricably linked to the well-being of the people and communities around us. Letseka (2013) argues that we need to view the needs and interests of the members of our community as at the same level of our own, and that freedom and comfort are essentially reciprocal in nature. Our concern for others needs to be an inherent part of our identity. According to Ben Ze'ev (1997, p. 205), there are Western ideas that concur with the notion of ubuntu and the view that our identity should include others and they say the following:

> Martha Nussbaum describes the following Stoic metaphor of moral development. Imagine that each of us lives in a set of concentric circles, the nearest being our own body, the furthest being the entire universe of human beings. The task of moral development is to move the circles progressively closer to the center, so that our parents become like ourselves, our other relatives like our parents, and strangers like relatives.

Therefore, we need to develop our communal selves to fully function as depth leaders. It is beyond the scope of this book to delve into all the ways in which we can care for the well-being of the communities in which we live and those around us, but some high-level principles and activities are offered below.

PRINCIPLES OF COMMUNITY ENGAGEMENT

The following principles can guide us when considering our role as depth leaders in our own and surrounding communities:

- Our increasingly interconnected world means that humans no longer live in isolated separate communities. Rather, we affect one another and need to take our impacts on each other into account in our decision-making and activities.
- As depth leaders, we and the members of our organisations are linked to communities that may not be close in physical proximity.
- Our decisions as leaders also affects future generations, and we have an ethical responsibility to do everything in our power to preserve and ensure hopeful futures for them.
- We need to actively pursue understanding and awareness of the state of well-being of the communities around us or connected to us.
- We need to use resources at our disposal in a fair and equitable way.
- We need to ensure that we use at least a portion of our resources to empower those who have access to fewer resources.

- We need to establish the true needs of any communities we are part of or engage with, by ensuring equal participation in conversations, the practice of deep democracy (discussed in Chapter 9) and a deep awareness of rank differences (Chapter 4) to reduce their impact.

- When there are value and cultural differences, we need to engage in depth conversations that allow the emergence of a transcendent third position (Chapter 9).

- Endeavour to design activities that both serve the needs of the community and contribute to the care, protection and restoration of the natural environment.

- Design community engagement activities that have a high-leverage character (as discussed in Chapter 1, page 16) and a multiplier effect, such as education.

POSSIBLE COMMUNITY ENGAGEMENT ACTIVITIES

The following activities could be considered by depth leaders and their organisations:

- Develop a vision that embraces the role of the organisation as custodian of shared resources and the environment, and as a global citizen with commensurate responsibilities.

- Develop a spatial map of all the communities connected to and affected by the organisation.

- Explicitly investigate and articulate the direct and indirect organisational impacts on the ecology of each community. This includes psychological, social, economic, spatial / infrastructural and environmental impacts on the community.

- Engage in facilitated conversations with the communities, ensuring that there is full representation of the majority and minority views, to discuss the actual and perceived impacts.

- Actively and collaboratively work with the communities to ensure optimisation of the positive impacts and mitigation of the negative impacts.

- Share a portion of the essential skills and resources of the organisation with members of stakeholder communities who would otherwise not have access to them.

THE IMPORTANCE OF ECO-AWARENESS AND ECOLOGICAL CARE

As depth leaders who value integrity, we need to pursue the notion of wholeness by attending not only to social problems, but also to ecological problems, in addition to our more immediate personal and interpersonal challenges. This means using systems thinking, in which we take the whole system into consideration in an ethical decision-making process.

Systems thinking (which was introduced in Chapter 1) has been referred to by other terms or names, including 'eco-intelligence', which is described as "the capacity to recognize the hidden web of connections between human activity and nature's systems, and the subtle complexities of their intersections" (Goleman, 2010, p. 1). The prefix 'eco-' comes from Latin 'oeco', which means household, and from Greek 'oikos', which means house (Merriam-Webster Online Dictionary, 2021). In the terms 'eco-awareness' or 'eco-intelligence' the prefix 'eco-' is used in the metaphorical sense of the "whole house" (Fleming & Olivier, 2015, p. 4). We need to speak of "eco-system awareness", which rises above "ego-system awareness" (Scharmer & Yukelson, 2015, p. 34), in which the awareness is extended beyond the ego to include the "whole house" or the whole system.

'Holism' is another word that was coined by Jan Smuts in 1925, which is used in a similar way, and refers to: "…an attitude, a perspective; a statement of the relationship between parts of a system that makes the whole more than the sum of the parts, and of the interdependence of the parts in determining the well-being of the whole" (Swayne, 2015, p. 38). All the above terms – 'systems thinking', 'eco-intelligence' or 'holism' – imply that as depth leaders, we need to see and engage with the world as a complex system.

Finally, there is a difference between "anthropocentrism" and "ecocentrism" (Kortenkamp & Moore, 2001, p. 261), as each offers a way of engaging ethically with nature. In an anthropocentric ethic, nature is treated morally because nature affects humans, and in an ecocentric ethic nature is treated morally because of its intrinsic value.

Our planetary house is changing in disruptive, damaging and unpredictable ways because of the way humans live, use and consume resources. In addition to accelerated climate change, there is significant evidence of mass extinction all around us. Many of us live in denial, partly driven by feelings of despair and helplessness, but also because we are confronted with trade-offs that require the sacrifice of our needs, comforts and privileges. As depth leaders, we need to interrogate our denial, and live as role models in our organisations. One of the ways to do this is described in the following section.

AN ECO-SELF

The idea of an eco-self, or an 'ecological self', was first described in the work of Arne Næss (2005) and was part of the philosophical approach known as 'deep ecology'. He proposes that one of the approaches to ensure environmental ethics is for individuals to cultivate what he calls an "ecological self". He does not give a definition of what he means but he gives a lengthy but evocative example to explain his opinion:

> I was looking through an old-fashioned microscope at the dramatic meeting of two drops of different chemicals. At that moment, a flea jumped from a lemming which was strolling along the table and landed in the middle of the acid chemicals. To save it was impossible. It took many minutes for the flea to die. Its movements were dreadfully expressive. Naturally, what I felt was a painful sense of compassion and empathy. But the empathy was not basic, rather it was a process of identification, that "I saw myself in the flea". If I had been alienated from the flea, not seeing intuitively anything even resembling myself, the death struggle would have left me feeling indifferent. So there must be identification in order for there to be compassion and, among humans, solidarity. (Næss, 2005, p. 227)

Næss argues that humans will only treat the environment ethically if an individual extends their identity, in other words, the answer to the question, "who am I?" to include the natural environment in all its forms. If we do not identify with the natural environment as part of ourselves, then we will see any care for the environment as a sacrifice, and this may feel too burdensome. If we feel that we are part of the natural environment, then our self-care extends into protecting, caring for and sustaining nature.

This means that we, as depth leaders, need to develop eco-selves, and infuse our teams and organisations with a similar ethos. We need to engage in intimate relationships with the natural world, in which we experience and honour our interdependencies. Although this may require deliberate efforts, there are many benefits to such an approach.

There is an abundance of literature that describes the benefits of a relationship with nature. In one article, Sandifer et al. (2015) and numerous other studies found significant benefits to humans as a result of a relationship with nature in all of the following categories: psychological, cognitive, physiological, disease exposure and regulation, social, aesthetic, cultural, recreational, spiritual, tangible materials and increased resiliency. Other research found that a relationship with nature leads to increased happiness and results in what they call a "happy path to sustainability" (Zelenski & Nisbet, 2014, p. 6).

PRINCIPLES OF ENVIRONMENTAL CARE, PROTECTION AND RESTORATION

Environmental care, protection and restoration is an extensive discipline in its own right and this book cannot begin to do justice to it. However, some general principles are offered based on those of the United Nations, the European Union and the African Union:

- As depth leaders, we need to integrate environmental awareness and action into all our strategic and operational goals, policies and activities.
- We need to remember that our psychic landscape is only as well as our external landscapes.
- It is our responsibility to preserve ecological processes and use our access to environmental resources in a sustainable way.
- We need to primarily aim for the prevention of environmental damage, anticipating and avoiding any negative environmental impacts, preserving biodiversity and natural habitats.
- We need to take a precautionary approach so that we do not take action that may result in environmental damage, even though there may be scientific uncertainty about the nature and extent of the potential damage.
- We need to be effective and efficient in all our use of natural resources.
- If environmental damage is caused by our pollution (including air, water, radioactive contamination, soil, litter, plastic, sound, visual, light, and thermal), we need to remedy such pollution and proactively bear any short and long-term costs for any that we cause knowingly or inadvertently.
- We need to ensure that as users of resources we carry the full costs associated with such resources.
- We should ensure that there is intergenerational equity in our use of and impact on ecosystems.
- We should prioritise the prevention of impacts to biodiversity and if that is not possible, then we need to minimise impacts, and restore adverse effects. Any residual negative impact should be offset through environmental restoration to ensure a net positive impact on the environment.
- We should ensure the full participation of all affected communities in environmental decision-making, using a deep democracy approach.
- We should actively encourage our organisational and team members to develop their awareness of and involvement in environmental care, protection and restoration. This can be partially achieved through exposure to and integration of the natural environment in daily activities, and through environmental education.
- Even if we are not directly impacting the natural environment, we should launch and support initiatives that preserve and restore biodiversity and habitat.

POSSIBLE ENVIRONMENTAL ACTIVITIES

The following activities should be considered by depth leaders and their organisations:

- Reduce waste, compost, recycle, repair and re-use equipment and materials.
- Eliminate plastics and choose sustainable materials.
- Go paperless and switch to digital.

- Avoid toxic chemicals.

- Use biodegradable cleaning products.

- Implement sustainable food policies and processes.

- Support and encourage vegetarianism and veganism.

- Choose locally sourced resources.

- Choose suppliers who practice environmental care.

- Implement sustainable manufacturing and packaging policies and processes.

- Conserve water.

- Build energy efficient buildings from renewable materials.

- Select and generate renewable energy.

- Reduce energy usage.

- Sequester carbon and implement carbon offsetting.

- Implement mechanisms that reduce our carbon footprint, including supporting and using environmentally friendly public transportation and promoting remote working.

- Become involved in the restoration and rehabilitation of forests, rivers, wetlands and corals.

- Create green spaces wherever possible.

- Plant indigenous vegetation with the guidance of local botanists and remove alien vegetation.

- Design projects and initiatives that are high leverage and so have a range of positive environmental ripple effects.

- Be aware of and identify unintended negative environmental consequences

There are many initiatives worldwide that can be joined and supported if we as depth leaders are unable to launch initiatives in our own capacity. As a start, much can be achieved through simple awareness of the need to care for the environment.

CONCLUSION

This book offered theory and practice for the approach that I have called Depth Leadership, to help all of us as leaders to work beneath, between and beyond for a thriving psyche, community and planet. I have spent the last thirty-six years working with this approach, studying and developing theory, trying out methods and tools, learning what works and what doesn't. This endeavour is always work in progress, and both the theory and practice are evolving, and I would enjoy hearing from others who are developing their own bodies of knowledge and experience.

After a lifetime of focus, I am still fascinated on a daily basis by the endless intelligence, creativity and resilience of the psyche and the complex interdependent relationship between our internal and external landscapes. I am blessed with an active psyche that produces dreams prolifically, which keeps me on my toes in all aspects of my life. I believe depth work is essential to our well-being and that of our planet and all life on it, and it has been an enormous privilege to be allowed to apply this approach to my work with clients, creative partners, other practitioners and the teachers and students in the small school that I founded – The Prince Albert Skills School in the Karoo in South Africa.

PERSONAL EXERCISES

1. Review your involvement with the larger systems around you, including the communities that you are in (and those that you are connected to that may be farther away) to develop your awareness of your impact.

2. Engage with the communities to establish their perception of your impact.

3. Investigate ways in which you can reduce your negative impact and enhance your positive impact.

4. Consider your environmental footprint and develop your awareness of your impact.

5. As an individual, and with your organisation, engage in conversations to determine and understand the needs of the communities that you are connected with.

6. Consider your resources and skills and determine if you are able to collaborate with the community to meet their expressed needs.

7. Learn about the environmental situation around you and consult with knowledgeable others to determine how you and your organisation can use your resources and skills to care for, protect and restore the natural environment.

ABOUT THE AUTHOR

DR HÉLÈNE SMIT
B.A. (HDE), MBA, PHD.

Hélène Smit is a specialist in the process of relationship building in organisations. She uses depth psychology theory in facilitation, conflict resolution and leadership development, building psychological and systemic literacy and integrity in individuals and groups in a variety of settings. Specifically, she is skilled in helping small and large groups deal with seemingly intractable and chronic conflicts and dilemmas.

Hélène originally trained and worked as an English and Mathematics high school teacher but left teaching to start her own firm called Feather Learning (Pty) Ltd. For the past 30 years, Feather Learning has offered a variety of services and courses including facilitation, coaching, psychological literacy training, and leadership development.

Through Feather Associates, Hélène facilitates a variety of processes, including team building, strategic planning, stakeholder involvement and conflict resolution in a range of contexts and sectors. She has worked with NGO's, local, provincial and national government, and many large and small business organisations. She has spent many years coaching and facilitating processes for academics in universities. One of the highlights of her work is her facilitation of the leadership development of Southern African Development Community (SADC) Chief Justices and other senior judges in the three-year leadership course offered by the Judicial Institute for Africa at UCT (JIFA).

Hélène is a trained executive coach and holds a Certificate in Executive Coaching from the Tavistock Institute. She uses a variety of coaching methodologies, depending on client needs. However, she specialises in what she calls "depth" coaching, in which she considers the deep underlying patterns for individual functioning and performance. She has coached senior executives and academics from a range of institutions.

In addition to running Feather, Hélène was a Visiting Senior Lecturer at the UCT Graduate School of Business in the areas of psychological literacy, systems thinking, people skills, change management, diversity management and facilitation for 17 years. She lectured on the MBA, Executive MBA, AIM and other executive programmes. Hélène now teaches at Henley Business School, looking after the MBA groups, and occasionally teaches at the Gordon Institute of Business Science and Duke Executive Education. Together with the South African College of Applied Psychology, Hélène launched the (first of its kind) National Diploma in Facilitation and was the Programme Director for five years. Hélène was included in the book "50 Faces of Wits Business School" which profiles 50 exceptional alumni who have graduated from Wits Business School over the past 50 years.

In 2013, Hélène established The Depth Leadership Trust, a non-profit organisation that aims to develop and promote understanding of depth psychology amongst leaders, organisations and civil society. The Trust is also involved in a variety of small community projects that help people find their voices and develop their leadership capacity. As part of the Trust, in 2017, she started and still runs the Prince Albert Skills School, a small school for marginalised teenagers who have dropped out of the formal schooling system.

Hélène's main interest is the application of depth psychology principles to group contexts. This involves working with unconscious processes in organisations and general society, in order both to unleash greater creativity and to minimise the negative organisational impact of under-the-surface conflict. Hélène has published three books, the first called *The Depth Facilitator's Handbook* which describes facilitation skills in detail. The second one is called *Beneath – Exploring the Unconscious in*

Individuals, a book for a general audience that explores the functioning of the unconscious mind in order to unleash potential. Her third book, called *Depth Leadership*, was published in December 2013 and teaches the theory and practice of depth psychology to leaders. In 2016, Hélène completed the making of a feature film called *Eerstewater* (First Water) which tells the true stories of some remarkable Prince Albert residents, and which illustrates the ideas in Beneath. The film was selected for and screened at the 2018 Encounters International Documentary Film Festival.

For the past nine years, Hélène has run the Every Voice Matters collaborative art installation project which explores various themes that emerge from the nexus of art, science, psychology and social activism. Her work in this project included working with farmers who are struggling with the impact of climate change.

Hélène holds a PhD from Stellenbosch University where she formulated a model for the development of leadership integrity. She designed a business school curriculum which builds integrity in students of leadership, so that, over time, they develop an internal moral ecology that addresses the complex and conflicting demands of individual, collective and systemic well-being.

helene@depthleadership.co.za
www.depthleadership.co.za

ABOUT THE ILLUSTRATIONS

The illustrations for *Depth Leadership* stem from my long friendship with Hélène Smit and my deep admiration for her work.

Like depth workers, artists tend to look for the many interconnections in life, and although my training has not been in the field of psychotherapy, the impulse to look and to listen deeply has been developed and extended by my own depth work as well as my formal art training and ensuing creative practice.

Drawing digitally enabled a new layering and merging of material and ephemeral realities. Photographs and images have been reworked together. Different visual relationships became possible, invoking a greater sense of the ever-mingling hybridity of contemporary perception and communication. I made as many references as I could to the natural world in these drawings, trying to keep in mind the interconnectedness of all realms of life. Animals appear frequently, drawing attention to the natural world as much as to their strong symbolic role in the human psyche. I often chose birds and fish for their fluidity of movement and their ubiquitous symbolic presence in all human cultures and religions. Depth work requires fluidity.

The immense privilege of being able to recalibrate in the African wilds is a rare gift which Hélène and I both share. Many of the animals which appear were photographed by one or other of us during enlivening encounters in the wild.

The human figures which I draw arrive as they have always done since I was a child. They seem to belong to a world where the internal "one who watches" appears to be somewhat androgynous and lives within the playground of the archetypal child. I hope that stylistically, the drawings work to help and not hinder understanding. This is never a given. One cannot choose what one is born to, but one has every option to work with the raw material and transform it.

ABOUT THE ILLUSTRATOR

Katherine Glenday

Katherine is a professional artist working in various media. She has explored porcelain extensively and creates vessels which function as translucent canvases in the round.

Over the years, her exploration of symbolism, the human predicament, qualities of the natural world and the dance between nature and humanity have led to many different types of work, culminating most notably in the creation of vessels which have the qualities of serenity and peace. Her porcelain works have become distinctively essential in nature and form.

She also participates in collaborative processes, exploring new insights which emerge between artists, writers, musicians and dancers. She is interested in many elements of material culture, sifting to find expressive forms which are inclusive, collaborative and open. She sees conversations with sand, rocks, mud and clay and with other living creatures and fellow humans as being mutually calibrating. Katherine has exhibited extensively in South Africa and abroad, and her work is held in many private and public collections in her own country and abroad.

She lives and works in Cape Town.
www.katherineglenday.com.

REFERENCES

Ackoff, R. L. (1974). *Redesigning the future: A systems approach to societal problems.* Wiley.

Adler, A. (2005). *The collected clinical works of Alfred Adler, Volume 1: The neurotic character.* Alfred Adler Institute.

Allen, S. J., Shankman, M. L., & Miguel, R. F. (2012). Emotionally intelligent leadership: An integrative, process-oriented theory of student leadership. *Journal of Leadership Education,* 11(1), 177–203.

Bass, B. M. (1990). *Bass and Stogdill's handbook of leadership: Theory, research, and managerial applications.* Free Press.

Ben-Ze'Ev, A. (1997). Emotions and morality. *The Journal of Value Inquiry,* 31, 195–212.

Bion, W. R. (1961). *Experiences in groups and other papers.* Brunner-Routledge.

Blake, R. R., Mouton, J. S., & Bidwell, A. C. (1962). Managerial grid. *Advanced Management - Office Executive,* 1(9), 12–15.

Bleuler, E. (2013). *Textbook of psychiatry.* Literary Licensing LLC.

Bowlby, J. (1982). *Attachment and loss, Volume 1: Attachment.* Basic Books.

Breitenfeld, T., Jurasic, M. J., & Breitenfeld, D. (2014). Hippocrates: The forefather of neurology. *Neurological Sciences,* 35(9), 1349–1352.

Brown, M. E., Treviño, L. K., & Harrison, D. A. (2005). Ethical leadership: A social learning perspective for construct development and testing. *Organizational Behavior and Human Decision Processes,* 97, 117–134.

Burns, J. M. (1978). *Leadership.* HarperCollins.

Capra, F. (1997). *The web of life: A new scientific understanding of living systems.* Knopf Doubleday.

Claxton, G. (2005). *The wayward mind: An intimate history of the unconscious.* Little, Brown.

Collinson, D., & Tourish, D. (2015). Teaching leadership critically: New directions for leadership pedagogy. *Academy of Management Learning and Education,* 14(4), 576–594.

Cowen, A. S., & Keltner, D. (2017). Self-report captures 27 distinct categories of emotion bridged by continuous gradients. *Proceedings of the National Academy of Sciences of the United States of America,* 114(38), E7900–E7909.

Craig, E. (2008). *The human and the hidden: Existential wonderings about depth, soul, and the unconscious. The Humanistic Psychologist,* 36, 227–282.

Darwin, C. (1998). *Expressions of the emotions in man and animals.* Oxford University Press.

Erikson, E. H. (1963). *Childhood and society.* Penguin.

Fleming, K., & Olivier, S. (2015). Developing leadership capabilities: Transitioning from ego to eco intelligence. *In Developing Leadership Capacity Conference* (pp. 1–6). Henley Business school.

Forrester, J. W. (1991). System dynamics and the lessons of 35 years. In K. B. de Greene (Ed.), *A systems-based approach to policymaking* (pp. 199–240). Springer.

Freud, S. (2017). *The collected works of Sigmund Freud.* Delphi Classics.

Fry, L. W. (2003). *Toward a theory of spiritual leadership. The Leadership Quarterly*, 14, 693–727.

Gabriel, Y., & Carr, A. (2002). Organizations, management and psychoanalysis: An overview. *Journal of Managerial Psychology*, 17(5), 348–365.

Goleman, D. (1996). *Emotional intelligence: Why it can matter more than IQ.* Bantam Books.

Goleman, D. (1998). *What makes a leader? Harvard Business Review*, 76(6), 93–102.

Goleman, D. (2010). *Ecological intelligence. Psychotherapy Networker*, 34(1), 1–6.

James, W. (1890). *The principles of psychology.* Henry Holt.

Janet, P. (1925). *Psychological healing: A historical and clinical study.* Macmillan.

Jung, C. G. (1968). C. G. Jung: The collected works. Volume 9i: *The archetypes and the collective unconscious* (H. Read, M. Fordham, & G. Adler, Eds.; R. F. C. Hull, Trans.). Routledge and Kegan Paul.

Jung, C. G. (1969). C. G. Jung: *The collected works. Volume 8: The structure and dynamics of the psyche* (2nd ed.; H. Read, M. Fordham, & G. Adler, Eds.; R. F. C. Hull, Trans.). Routledge and Kegan Paul.

Jung, C. G. (1970). C. G. Jung: T*he collected works. Volume 10: Civilization in transition* (2nd ed.; H. *Read,* M. Fordham, & G. Adler, Eds.; R. F. C. Hull, Trans.). Routledge and Kegan Paul.

Jung, C.G. (1971). C. G. Jung: *The collected works. Volume 6: Psychological types* (H. Read, M. Fordham, & G. Adler, Eds.; R. F. C. Hull, Trans.). Routledge and Kegan Paul.

Jung, C. G. (2012). *Collected works of CG Jung.* Princeton University Press.

Kets de Vries, M. F. R., & Cheak-Baillargeon, A. (2015). *Psychodynamic approach.* In P. Northouse (Ed.), Leadership: Theory and practice (7th ed., pp. 295–397). Sage.

Klein, M. (2017). *The collected works of Melanie Klein.* Karnac Books.

Kohlberg, L. (1969). Stage and sequence: The cognitive-developmental approach to socialization. In D. A. Goslin (Ed.), *Handbook of socialization theory and research* (pp. 347–480). Rand McNally.

Kohut, H. (2009). The restoration of the self. University of Chicago Press.

Kortenkamp, K. V., & Moore, C. F. (2001). Ecocentrism and anthropocentrism: Moral reasoning about ecological commons dilemmas. *Journal of Environmental Psychology*, 21, 261–272.

Kubler-Ross, E. (1997). *On death and dying.* Scribner.

Lerner, H. (2014). *The dance of anger.* William Morrow Paperbacks.

Letseka, M. (2013). Anchoring ubuntu morality. *Mediterranean Journal of Social Sciences*, 4(3), 351–359.

Lewin, K. (1935). *A dynamic theory of personality: Selected papers.* McGraw-Hill.

Lewin, K. (1939). Field theory and experiment in social psychology: Concepts and methods. *American Journal of Sociology*, 44(6), 868–896.

Malan, D. (1979). *Individual psychotherapy and the science of psychodynamics*. Butterworth.

Maslow, A. (1943). A theory of human motivation. *Psychological Review*, 50(4), 370–396.

Mate, G. (2018). *In the realm of hungry ghosts: Close encounters with addiction*. Vermilion.

McCallum, I. (2005). *Ecological intelligence: Rediscovering ourselves in nature*. Africa Geographic.

McClure, B. (2004). *Putting a new spin on groups: The science of chaos*. Psychology Press.

McFarland Solomon, H. M. (2001). Origins of the ethical attitude. *The Journal of Analytical Psychology*, 46, 443–454.

McFarland Solomon, H. M. (2007). *The self in transformation*. Karnac Books.

Mead, G. (1934). *Mind, self and society from the standpoint of a social behaviorist*. University of Chicago Press.

Meadows, D. (1999). *Leverage points: Places to intervene in a system*. http://drbalcom.pbworks.com/w/file/fetch/35173014/Leverage_Points.pdf

Merriam-Webster Online Dictionary. (2021). https://www.merriam-webster.com/

Mindell, A. (2001). *Metaskills: The spiritual art of therapy*. Lao Tse Press.

Mnyaka, M., & Mothlabi, M. (2005). The African concept of ubuntu/botho and its socio-moral significance. *Black Theology: An International Journal*, 3(2), 215–237.

Næss, A. (2005). Self-realization: An ecological approach to being in the world. In H. Glasser & A. Drengson (Eds.), *The selected works of Arne Næss* (Volume X, pp. 515–530). Springer.

Neisser, U. (2014). *Cognitive psychology: Classic edition*. Psychology Press.

Otto, R. (1958). *The idea of the holy*. Oxford University Press.

Pavlov, I. P. (2020). *Psychopathology and psychiatry*. Routledge.

Petriglieri, G., & Petriglieri, J. L. (2020). The return of the oppressed: A systems psychodynamic approach to organization studies. *Academy of Management Annals*, 14(1), 411–449.

Peus, C., Wesche, J. S., Streicher, B., Braun, S., & Frey, D. (2012). Authentic leadership: An empirical test of its antecedents, consequences, and mediating mechanisms. *Journal of Business Ethics*, 107(3), 331–348.

Piaget, J. (1997). *Jean Piaget: Selected works*. Psychology Press.

Plutchik, R. (1982). A psychoevolutionary theory of emotions. *Social Science Information*, 21(4/5), 529–553.

Rank, O. (1971). *The double: A psychoanalytic study*. The University of North Carolina Press.

Reynolds, F. C., & Piirto, J. (2009). Depth psychology and integrity. In T. Cross & D. Ambrose (Eds.), *Morality, ethics, and gifted minds* (pp. 195–206). Springer.

Rogers, C. R. (1961). *On becoming a person: A therapist's view of psychotherapy*. Houghton Mifflin.

Rogers, C. R. (1975). Empathic: An unappreciated way of being. *The Counseling Psychologist,* 5(2), 1–10.

Scharmer, O., & Yukelson, A. (2015). Theory U: From ego-system to eco-system economies. *Journal of Corporate Citizenship,* (58), 35–39.

Senge, P. (1990). *The fifth discipline: The art and practice of the learning organization.* Doubleday/Currency.

Sharp, D. (1998). *Jungian psychology unplugged: My life as an elephant.* Inner City Books.

Skinner, B. F. (1985). Cognitive science and behaviourism. *British Journal of Psychology,* 76, 291–301.

Stogdill, R. (1948). Personal factors associated with leadership: A survey of the literature. *Journal of Psychology,* 25, 35–71.

Swayne, J. (2015). The concept of healing and integrative care. *Journal of Medicine and the Person,* 13(1), 36–44.

Van der Kolk, B. (2014). The body keeps the score: *Mind, brain and body in the transformation of trauma.* Penguin Random House.

Von Bertalanffy, L. (1969). *General system theory: Foundations, development, applications.* Braziller.

Vygotsky, L. S. (1987). *The collected works of L. S. Vygotsky* (R. W. Rieber & A. S. Carton, Eds.). Springer.

Waddock, S. (2007). Leadership integrity in a fractured knowledge world. *Academy of Management Learning & Education,* 6(4), 543–557.

Weiner, N. (2019). *Cybernetics or control and communication in the animal and the machine: Reissue of the 1961 second edition.* The MIT Press.

Wilber, K. (1999). *The collected works of Ken Wilber.* Shambhala.

Winnicott, D. W. (1992). *The child, the family, and the outside world.* Da Capo Press.

Zelenski, J. M., & Nisbet, E. K. (2014). Happiness and feeling connected: The distinct role of nature. *Environment and Behavior,* 46(3), 3–23.

INDEX

ghost, 90–91
identification and scapegoating, 88–90
suction, 88
theory, 87
types, 86

S

scapegoating, 89
school
cognitive-behavioural school, 10
of thoughts, 14
schools of psychology, 9–14
behavioural, 9
cognitive, 10
critical leadership, 24
development, 11–12
self-awareness, 142–143
self-reflection, 143
self-regulation, 144–147
emotional regulation, 145
integrated regulation, 145
steps, 146
Senge, Peter, 15
signal, 201
skills
awareness and observation, 131–134
communication, 122–131
face-to-face, 127
medium of, 125–127
group facilitation, 134–138
Skinner, 9
Smuts, Jan, 265
soft shoe shuffle, 215, 216
Solomon, Hester McFarland, 112, 113
Stogdill, Ralph, 19
stopping, 209
strong emotion and anger, 169–170
support, 167
emotional, 167
survival and individuation, 50–51
survival, 51
symbol, 178
symbolism, 178, 183–185
sympathy, 130
system, 15
mechanistic, 15

T

technology and intelligent machines, 7
teleological, 45
theme(s)
psychodynamic, 183
theory(ies), 41
attachment, 14
behavioural, 19

contingency, 20
great man, 19
human behavior, 9
psychodynamic, 23, 92
style, 20
trait, 19
thinking
mechanistically, 15
systems, 14–17, 264
Machine Age, 15
threats, 53
external, 54
internal, 54
survival, 54
Tiefenpsychologie; see depth, psychology
Tourish, 24
transcendent function, 196–197
transcendent third, 196
transference and countertransference, 67–68
transference, 67, 151–152
trauma, 68–70
traumatic, 68
traumatised world, 6–7

U

unconscious, 23
mind, 28

V

victim, 101
voices, 56
de Vries, Manfred Kets, 23
Vygotsky, 11

W

Weiner, Norbert, 15
Wilber, Ken, 12, 25
Winnicott, 11

Z

Zaleznik, Abraham, 23

www.ingramcontent.com/pod-product-compliance
Lightning Source LLC
Chambersburg PA
CBHW080130270326
41926CB00021B/4420